All Things New

Princeton Theological Monograph Series

K. C. Hanson, Charles M. Collier, D. Christopher Spinks,
and Robin A. Parry, Series Editors

Recent volumes in the series:

Melanie L. Dobson
Health as a Virtue: Thomas Aquinas and the Practice of Habits of Health

Alfred H. Yuen
Barth's Theological Ontology of Holy Scripture

Bernadette McNary-Zak
Seeking in Solitude: A Study of Select Forms of Eremitic Life and Practice

Andrew Shepherd
The Gift of the Other: Levinas Derrida and a Theology of Hospitality

Brendan Thomas Sammon
*The God Who Is Beauty: Beauty as a Divine Name in Thomas Aquinas
and Dionysius the Areopagite*

Dick O. Eugenio
*Communion with the Triune God:
The Trinitarian Soteriology of T. F. Torrance*

Mark R. Lindsay
*Reading Auschwitz with Barth:
The Holocaust as Problem and Promise for Barthian Theology*

Kin Yip Louie
*The Beauty of the Triune God:
The Theological Aesthetics of Jonathan Edwards*

Anthony G. Siegrist
*Participating Witness:
An Anabaptist Theology of Baptism and the Sacramental Character
of the Church*

All Things New

*The Trinitarian Nature of the Human Calling
in Maximus the Confessor and Jürgen Moltmann*

BROCK BINGAMAN

Foreword by
JÜRGEN MOLTMANN

☙PICKWICK *Publications* • Eugene, Oregon

ALL THINGS NEW
The Trinitarian Nature of the Human Calling in Maximus the Confessor and Jürgen Moltmann

Princeton Theological Monograph Series 213

Copyright © 2014 Brock Bingaman. All rights reserved. Except for brief quotations in critical publications or reviews, no part of this book may be reproduced in any manner without prior written permission from the publisher. Write: Permissions, Wipf and Stock Publishers, 199 W. 8th Ave., Suite 3, Eugene, OR 97401.

Pickwick Publications
An Imprint of Wipf and Stock Publishers
199 W. 8th Ave., Suite 3
Eugene, OR 97401

www.wipfandstock.com

ISBN 13: 978-1-61097-420-2

Cataloging-in-Publication data:

Bingaman, Brock.

All things new : The trinitarian nature of the human calling in Maximus the Confessor and Jürgen Moltmann / Brock Bingaman ; foreword by Jürgen Moltmann.

xvi + 196 p. ; 23 cm. —Includes bibliographical references and index(es).

ISBN 13: 978-1-61097-420-2

Princeton Theological Monograph Series 213

1. Theological anthropology—Christianity. 2. Trinity. 3. Maximus, Confessor, Saint, approximately 580–662. 4. Moltmann, Jürgen. I. Moltmann, Jürgen. II. Title. II. Series.

BT111.3 .B45 2014

Manufactured in the U.S.A.

For my parents, John and Jan Bingaman

Καὶ εἶπεν ὁ θεός Ποιήσωμεν ἄνθρωπον κατ' εἰκόνα ἡμετέραν καὶ καθ' ὁμοίωσιν . . . καὶ ἐποίησεν ὁ θεὸς τὸν ἄνθρωπον, κατ' εἰκόνα θεοῦ ἐποίησεν αὐτόν, ἄρσεν καὶ θῆλυ ἐποίησεν αὐτούς.
   Γένεσις 1.26–27

Καὶ εἶπεν ὁ καθήμενος ἐπὶ τῷ θρόνῳ, Ἰδοὺ καινὰ ποιῶ πάντα. καὶ λέγει, Γράψον, ὅτι οὗτοι οἱ λόγοι πιστοὶ καὶ ἀληθινοί εἰσιν.
   Αποκάλυψις 21.5

Contents

Foreword by Jürgen Moltmann   ix

Preface   xi

List of Abbreviations   xiv

1. Introduction   1
2. The Trinitarian Matrix of the Human Calling   13
3. The Christological Basis of the Human Calling   30
4. The Redemptive Goal of the Human Calling   63
5. The Trinitarian-Christocentric Practice of the Human Calling   118
6. Conclusion: The Human Calling in Creation—Rooted in God   166

Bibliography   173

Index   187

Foreword

I AM VERY GRATEFUL FOR THIS EXCELLENT BOOK BASED ON BROCK Bingaman's dissertation. It is a model for logic in thinking and clarity in style. But what impressed me most was what I learned not only about Maximus the Confessor but also about my own theology. This type of comparative theology between premodern and postmodern theologies is most fruitful.

There is a *communio theologorum*, not always a *communio sanctorum*, for an understanding across time and space. The contexts are different, but the text is the same. The cultures and ages are separated, but what matters in the theological community is always and everywhere the same: the Logos of God.

With regard to the theologians of the ancient church we have to take into account that they lived in premodern times. The theology of modern times was different. Today we are attempting to develop a postmodern, ecological theology because our world needs an ecological future if we want to survive. We therefore return to premodern concepts to translate them into the postmodern mind. The new trinitarian thinking in western theology, replacing the simple monotheism or Unitarianism of modern theology, shows this clearly. This can also be observed in the new doctrines of creation: Modern theology had taken up only the fundamental distinction between God and world from the biblical creation narratives. Transcendence and immanence were separated so that at the end there is a worldless God and a godless world. With this distinction, theology wanted to serve the modern disenchantment and the secularization of the world. The "world" is humanity's world. From the biblical creation stories, only Genesis 1 and 2 were relevant. The new ecological theology, as demonstrated in this book, understands creation as a trinitarian process and therefore a cosmos filled with the energies of the divine Spirit. A Christian interpretation of creation must begin with the reconciliation of the cosmos in Christ according to the letters of Ephesians and Colossians, as orthodox theologians always did.

Foreword

With this worldview, the position of humans also changes. We are no longer "lords and owners of nature," as Descartes stated, but co-creatures among all living things and members of the greater creation-community. Instead of the "arrogance of power" of modern human beings, we learn a kind of cosmic humility. Anthropology in the work of Maximus is important in this respect, because it is part of his "Christocentrism." At the center of his christology are the two movements of God: incarnation and resurrection. God became human, as Athanasius asserted, so that human beings might become God. This is the theology and eschatology of *theosis*. From the Reformation in modern times we may add another perspective: The humanization of inhuman beings. God became man to make human beings from "proud and unhappy gods," as Luther maintained. This is not directed against the *theosis*-expectation, but is the necessary presupposition. Without dismantling the "God complex" of modern men and women, there can be no reconciliation between human culture and the nature of the earth. Ancient church incarnation-theology and the theology of the cross of the Reformers complement one another and form a common theology of resurrection for the salvation of humans and the salvation of nature.

I want to show with these few remarks on pre- and postmodern theology and on trinitarian and ecological thinking how promising the comparisons are that Brock Bingaman has started with this remarkable study.

Jürgen Moltmann
Tübingen, March 15, 2014

Preface

Motivation for the Study

THIS STUDY CENTERS ON THE THEOLOGICAL ANTHROPOLOGY OF TWO theologians from markedly different worlds, Maximus the Confessor (580–662) and Jürgen Moltmann (b. 1926).[1] Its central thesis is that both Maximus and Moltmann root their understanding of the human calling (or vocation) within their trinitarian-christocentric visions. The motivating factors behind this investigation into Maximus and Moltmann are threefold. The first is *ecumenical*. By collating Maximus and Moltmann, I seek to demonstrate remarkable points of convergence between two theologians from such disparate contexts. In doing so, my aim is to offer a critical example of constructive dialogue across traditions, one that furthers knowledge of the other and fosters mutual understanding and respect.

A second motivating factor is *historical*. By this, I mean that through juxtaposing Maximus and Moltmann, I intend to show the historical importance of a proper understanding of the human vocation, a theme that spans the history of Christian thought.

The third factor is *practical*. That is, I propose that reading Maximus and Moltmann together sheds mutual, supplementary, and increased light on the important theme of the human calling in creation. Two theological perspectives, with all their overlapping and distinctive ideas, offer more insight into this intriguing subject of the human calling in creation. These three motivating factors, therefore, suggest some of the impulses that led me to probe Maximus and Moltmann's trinitarian and christologically based theological anthropology.

---

1. Excellent background information on Maximus is found in Nichols, *Byzantine Gospel*, 1–23; Louth, *MC*, 3–18; Blowers, *CMJC*, 13–43; and on Moltmann in Bauckham, *TJM*, 1–27; Moltmann, *Broad Place*, 3–94; Moltmann, *How I Have Changed*, 13–21; Prooijen, *Limping but Blessed*, 1–117.

Preface

Background of the Project

The background of this research project entails, basically, three experiences. First, in a remarkable doctoral seminar at Loyola on creation theologies, I was immersed in Moltmann's *God in Creation*, studying his creation theology alongside other fertile thinkers like Irenaeus, Athanasius, Origen, Augustine, Aquinas, Bonaventure, and Barth. I was struck by the way Moltmann integrates a panoramic vision of the triune God who is revealed in Christ, with a sweeping perspective on the cosmos, in terms of his panentheistic understanding of creation and its consummation through the indwelling of God's glory. Moreover, the way Moltmann works out his trinitarian structured theological anthropology in critical conversation with Orthodox creation wisdom, piqued my interest. To counter modern tendencies that understand human beings distinct from or against creation, Moltmann develops a theological anthropology with humanity living in communion with creation.

A second experience was another doctoral seminar, one that focused on Orthodox theology and spirituality. This provided the opportunity to study Maximus in-depth. His all-embracing vision of the Holy Trinity, "the Holy Trinity's creation" (as he puts it), the cosmic links between Christ's incarnation, crucifixion, and resurrection and the transfiguration of all things, and humanity's calling in creation, seemed to fit so beautifully with Moltmann's theology.

Thirdly, in preparation for presenting a paper on Christian spirituality and ecology at the American Academy of Religion, I had the opportunity to search out my initial hunches regarding Maximus and Moltmann. Through developing my argument in the paper for the AAR, I began comparing, contrasting, and coalescing some of the elements in their theological anthropology. And in the course of the various paper presentations, our lively panel discussion, and the constructive feedback given by colleagues, I was on my way to developing this current research project. Since its completion as a dissertation at Loyola in 2009, I have continued to rework it in several places based on discoveries emerging from further research, including a new final chapter.

Preface

Scope of the Research

While both Maximus and Moltmann offer extensive theological visions[2]—analogous to sprawling mosaics made up of numerous, interlocking tiles—it is necessary (in a study like this) to pick one central motif on which to focus. Thus, I have selected the theme of theological anthropology, which I argue springs out of their trinitarian and christological reflection, as a way to define the scope of the study. Selecting this theme of trinitarian and christologically grounded anthropology will allow me to focus on a number of salient features within this area of their theological "mosaics."

Purpose of the Study

In light of the above motivating factors, background, and scope, my overall purpose in this study is to explore Maximus and Moltmann's theological anthropologies[3] and demonstrate how they spring out of their trinitarian-christocentric visions. That is, I propose that their conception of what it means to be human is based on and formed by reflection on the Trinity and the revelation of God in Christ. Moreover, as I develop my argument, I highlight correlations between Maximus and Moltmann. I also point out key distinctive features, in order to recognize their differences and avoid homogenizing their theological visions and portrayals of the human vocation.

---

2. Please note that I am using the term "vision" with reference to both Maximus and Moltmann's theology. Maximus' theology, as Florovsky and Blowers assert, is not a thoroughly condensed system. It is an organic collection, a series of "sketches" that portray the ascetic life. As Florovsky argues, "It is the rhythm of spiritual life rather than a logical connection of ideas which defines the architechtonics of [Maximus'] vision of the world, and one could say that his system has more of a musical structure than an architectural one. This is more like a symphony—a symphony of spiritual experience—than a system" (*Byzantine Fathers*, 213). See also Allchin's introduction to Thunberg, *MM*, xvi, where he reflects on Maximus' system of theology as a spiritual vision. Moltmann's theology is characterized by its resistance to creating a complete "theological system." As Bauckham says, Moltmann's theology is known for its openness to dialogue, its ongoing, partial, and unfinished nature (*TJM*, 7). This is one of the reasons Moltmann calls his works of systematic theology "contributions." Moreover, like Maximus, Moltmann's theological vision is marked by its biblical basis, christological center, trinitarian dimension, and eschatological orientation (*TJM*, 8, 26).

3. Metropolitan Kallistos (Ware) suggests that theological anthropology will be a primary focus for theological reflection in the twenty-first century ("La théologie orthodoxe," 219–38).

Abbreviations

Works of Maximus the Confessor

AL	*The Ascetic Life*
Amb.	*Ambigua* [*Books of Difficulties*], ed. Oehler; in *Patrologia Graeca* 91
CC	*Capita de caritate* [*Centuries on Love*; or, *Chapters on Charity*]
Ep.	*Epistula*
QT	*Quaestiones ad Thalassium*
VT	*Various Texts.* A "Maximian anthology," included in the *Philokalia*, vol. 2, trans. and ed. Palmer, Sherrard, and Ware.

Works of Jürgen Moltmann

BP	*A Broad Place*
CoG	*The Coming of God*
CG	*The Crucified God*
CPS	*The Church in the Power of the Spirit*
ET	*Experiences in Theology*
GC	*God in Creation*
SL	*The Spirit of Life*
TK	*The Trinity and the Kingdom*
WJC	*The Way of Jesus Christ*

Works by Other Authors

BT	*Byzantine Theology*, Aidan Nichols
CL	*Cosmic Liturgy*, Hans Urs von Balthasar

Abbreviations

CMJC	*On the Cosmic Mystery of Jesus Christ*, Paul Blowers
CWS	*Selected Writings*, Maximus Confessor, trans. George Berthold
DaT	*Discernment and Truth*, Mark McIntosh
DivT	*Divine Teaching*, Mark McIntosh
KP	*The Kingdom and the Power*, Geiko Müller-Fahrenholz
MaC	*Man and the Cosmos*, Lars Thunberg
MC	*Maximus the Confessor*, Andrew Louth
ME	*Man and the Environment*, Anestis Keselopoulos
MM	*Microcosm and Mediator*, Lars Thunberg
MT	*Mystical Theology*, Mark McIntosh
OT	*Orthodox Theology*, Vladimir Lossky
PL	*Pilgrimage of Love*, Joy Ann McDougall
PG	*Patrologia Graeca*, ed. J. P. Migne
SMC	*St. Maximus the Confessor: The Ascetic Life; The Four Centuries of Love*, trans. Polycarp Sherwood
TJM	*The Theology of Jürgen Moltmann*, Richard Bauckham

1

Introduction

And the One who was seated on the throne said, "See, I am making all things new."[1]
　Rev 21:5

The doctrine of the Trinity ... summarizes what it means to participate in the life of God through Jesus Christ in the Spirit. ... [It] is a way of contemplating the mystery of God and of ourselves, a heuristic framework for thinking correctly about God and about ourselves in relation to God.
　—Catherine Mowry LaCugna[2]

Human beings are created in the image and likeness of the Creator. This means that Christian anthropology must be both christological and relational in nature. "In the image of God" means firstly "in the image of Christ the Creator Logos," and secondly, "in the image of God the Holy Trinity."
　—Kallistos Ware[3]

---

　1. See Moltmann's exegetical comments on Rev 21:5, where he discusses this passage in light of Gen 1:1; 2:2 (the Hebrew terms *asa* and *bara*); and Isa 65:17 (the creation of a new heaven and a new earth). Moltmann's concluding point is that in the eschatological new creation "it is not something different which replaces creation; it is *this* creation which will be made new" (Moltmann, "Bible, the Exegete and the Theologian," ch. 5 in Bauckham, *God Will Be All in All*, 231).

　2. LaCugna, *God for Us*, 379.

　3. Ware, "La théologie orthodoxe," 238.

The Argument

IN THE FOLLOWING STUDY, I EXAMINE THE THEOLOGICAL ANTHROPOLOGY of Maximus the Confessor and Jürgen Moltmann, arguing that they root their understanding of the human calling in creation[4] within their Trinitarian and christological visions. Though coming from distinct theological traditions, I analyze the ways that both Maximus and Moltmann's theological anthropology springs to life from Trinitarian and christological grounds.[5] Therefore, as I will demonstrate in Maximus and Moltmann, we realize the human vocation, what it means to be fully and authentically human, as we contemplate the Trinity,[6] pattern our lives after Jesus Christ, and serve within the church. As we will see throughout this study, human beings, created in the image of the triune God, are called and graced to cooperate with God in the restoration of all things,[7] a renewal initiated and guaranteed by the life, death, and resurrection of Jesus Christ.

---

4. Mark McIntosh's work on the "human calling in creation" is especially helpful. See his *Divine Teaching*, where he elucidates: what it means for the whole creation to have humans in its midst; how humans are graced to draw elements of creation up into language, conversation, and communion; developing a peaceful and holistic vision of the human calling that corrects humanity's misuse of creation; how humans are saved so that they might share and draw the rest of creation into the communion of the Trinitarian life; how humanity is called to serve and facilitate the creation's consummation in glory. McIntosh's discussion on Trinitarian Illumination and the Human Calling in Creation has also been helpful, from the chapter, "Trinitarian Perspectives on Christian Spirituality," in *Blackwell Companion to Christian Spirituality*, 177–89.

5. Moltmann speaks in these terms when he explains that the "nature of human beings springs from their relationship to God," that humans are defined and understood as the image or appearance of God on earth, so that there is a reciprocal reflection that takes place between theological and anthropological thinking (*GC*, 220ff.). As I will show, for both Maximus and Moltmann, their reflections on the Trinity and Christ profoundly shape and structure their understanding of the human vocation.

6. Regarding the contemplative life expounded by Maximus (and others featured in the *Philokalia*), Philip Sherrard says that it is "only through the contemplative life in all its aspects—ascetic watchfulness, prayer, meditation, the whole uninterrupted practice of the presence of God to which the *Philokalia* is the guide—that humans can actualize in themselves the personal love and knowledge of God on which depend not only their own *authentic existence as human beings* but also their capacity to *cooperate with God in fulfilling the innermost purposes of creation*" (*Christian Spirituality*, 428, italics mine). Throughout the study, I will illustrate how the contemplation of the Trinity and the Person of Christ, for both Maximus and Moltmann, illuminates the meaning and purpose of human existence.

7. Miroslav Volf provides an informative analysis of Moltmann's discussion on "the restoration of all things," particularly in relation to the soteriological concepts of

Introduction

A Preliminary Portrait and Contrast

In analyzing the theology of Maximus and Moltmann, we are presented with remarkable visions of the human calling in creation. According to Maximus, who draws from the rich traditions of Origen, Gregory of Nyssa, Evagrius, and Pseudo-Dionysis, the human vocation is rooted deeply in the life of the Trinitarian God—the Father, Son, and Spirit who together are the source and goal of creation. As an icon of the Holy Trinity, a living image of God revealed in Christ, the human being is called to reflect the divine glory and function as God's microcosm and mediator within God's creation. Though humanity's fall into the sin of self-love interrupted this primordial vocation, Maximus details how women and men are restored by the coming of the Word, through intimate fellowship with Christ and his Body, so that through the deifying energies of the Spirit, they are made new, unified with God, and enabled to fulfill their divine calling in the cosmos.

While in different terms, colors, and shades, Moltmann's portrait of the human calling shares some interesting, convergent elements with Maximus, in the midst of all the distinct features. According to Moltmann's theological vision, Trinitarian thinking provides the matrix for a genuine and fertile understanding of the human calling in creation. Inspired by concepts employed by early Christian theologians, such as *perichoresis* in John of Damascus and divine Eros in Maximus, Moltmann also roots his portrayal of the human vocation within the Trinity, the community of overflowing divine love. Furthermore, Moltmann's vision of the human vocation is constructed on a christological basis, with special attention to the reality of Christ as the enfleshed Word, the one in whom the divine glory dwells, and the one who paves the way for the eternal Sabbath rest of all creation in God's presence. While Moltmann does explore the notion of human being as a microcosm, he elaborates on God's image in creation along different lines, discussing the *imago Dei*, *imago Christi*, and *gloria Dei*.

In contrast to Maximus and Moltmann, many modern theologies, influenced by the turn to the human subject, tend to devise an account of human being first, then attempt to find ways in which the Trinity and Christ are somehow relevant to the notion of human being. As opposed to the Trinitarian and christocentric anthropologies of Maximus and Moltmann,

---

reconciliation, completion, and redemption ("After Moltmann," 250ff.); cf. Müller-Fahrenholz's discussion on this theme in Moltmann (in relation to Barth and others), in *KP*, 213ff. Regarding Maximus's perspective on this, see Daley, "*Apokatastasis* and Apocalyptic," 201–2; and Balthasar, *CL*, 354–58.

modern theologians often start with the human person, then attempt to account for elements of our human existence that we think we already know about.

What makes the theological anthropologies of Maximus and Moltmann so intriguing is the way that they begin in the opposite order from many modern, anthropocentric theologies. That is, Maximus and Moltmann start by turning their gaze to contemplate Christ and the Trinity, then proceed to explicate how the human being comes to exist and is called and drawn into the ever increasing fullness of life in God.

My goal, therefore, is to demonstrate how Maximus and Moltmann construct their theological anthropologies, to show how they shift from contemplation of the Trinity and Christ to a concrete vision of what it means to be human. In other words, we can only really understand and properly interpret the human calling in Maximus and Moltmann when we have seen how it emerges from their thinking on the Trinity and Christology.

Consequently, this insight into the theological anthropologies of Maximus and Moltmann has important implications for contemporary theology. We live in an era in which the turn to the subject has influenced our thinking, so that many scholars assume that if we can know anything at all, it is ourselves and our human existence. According to this kind of thinking, theological reflection properly begins from anthropology, then considers how the doctrines of the Trinity and Christ may (or may not!) have something to say about human being. This study strongly suggests that, paradoxically, the opposite might be the case. That is, the richest and deepest understanding of human existence and our calling in creation emerges out of reflection on the Trinity and Christ, not by beginning with ourselves. This means that the doctrine of the Trinity, and its emergence from reflection on the paschal mystery of Christ, turns out to be far more intrinsic and basic to theological reflection, and more fruitful for theological construction, than some tendencies in modern theology might suggest.

Structure of the Argument

In the development of my argument, the book is structured in the following way. After the introduction, chapter 2 focuses on the Trinitarian matrix of the human calling. First, I look at the Trinitarian matrix in Maximus, including his teaching on the Trinity as source and goal of creation, the divine ideas tradition, adumbrations of the Trinity within creation, and the

Introduction

Trinitarian features of *The Church's Mystagogy* (his mystical ecclesiology). I then examine the Trinitarian matrix in Moltmann, including the perichoretic dimension within the Trinity and in creation (a concept he adopts from John of Damascus), and the missional feature that entails the notion of the Trinity as a community of seeking love and a Trinitarian theology of the cross.

In the third chapter, I elucidate the christological basis of the human calling in creation, looking at how Maximus grounds his vision for humanity's vocation upon the christological formulations of Chalcedon, with an emphasis on the incarnational context, while Moltmann establishes his vision based on a messianic Christology, underscoring the need for holistic and developmental thinking.

The fourth chapter centers on the redemptive goal of the human calling, demonstrating how each theologian describes the graced role that humanity plays in the restoration of creation. I examine *theosis* in Maximus, its biblical and patristic background, Maximus's appropriation of the concept, various agents of *theosis*, the fruits of deification, and an illustrative text in which Maximus shows the deep connections between *theosis*, Trinitarian and christological thinking, and the human vocation. Then I consider Moltmann's portrayal of the redemptive goal as the Sabbath rest of all creation, looking at the biblical background, the completion of creation, the mystery of God's presence in the Sabbath (in Maximus and Moltmann's meditations on 1 Kings 19), human rest in God's rest, Trinitarian and christological patterns, and the implications for the human calling.

The fifth chapter looks at the Trinitarian-christocentric praxis of the human calling. I demonstrate the Trinitarian and christological aspects of Maximus's reflection on the human being as ordered microcosm, the disintegration of the microcosm through the passions, its reintegration through the virtues, and the ongoing incarnation of Christ in the virtues. Additionally, I consider Maximus's understanding of the human being as universal mediator, including his appropriation of the Evagrian threefold schema of the spiritual life, further threefold patterns of spiritual development that he restructures in Trinitarian and christological terms, and the five cosmic mediations that are accomplished by Christ and realized through the church. I then analyze the way Moltmann envisages Trinitarian-christocentric praxis, particularly through his teaching on God's human image in creation as: the *imago Dei*, the original designation of human beings; the *imago Christi*, the messianic alignment of human beings; and the *gloria Dei*, the eschatological glorification of human beings. Following this, I review Moltmann's Trinitarian and christologically rooted vision of the messianic fellowship of service for the kingdom of God. According to this perspective, I show how Moltmann speaks of fulfilling the doxological calling as worshipers of the triune God, the call to discipleship as followers of the crucified Christ, and the call to mission as Spirit-empowered servants of the kingdom of God.

The fifth chapter concludes with a reflection on the primacy of love in both Maximus and Moltmann's understanding of the human calling. I indicate that for both theologians, love is at the center of the human vocation. Moreover, love for God and neighbor is the foundation and goal of this vocation. I demonstrate this in Maximus's *Mystagogy*, where he explains that the church, as the image of God in creation, works the effects of God, including the unification of diverse people (while preserving their differences), bringing together male and female in Christ, bringing creatures to rest in the embrace of the Holy Trinity, all within the spirit of love for God and others. According to Moltmann's teaching, I show how the church is called to be Spirit-empowered servants of the kingdom of God, participating in Christ's messianic mission, the liberation and uniting of humanity in Christ, and the restoration of all creation in the fellowship of love. Additionally, Moltmann envisions God's nature as love (rather than almighty power), a Trinitarian love that does not rule through division and separation, but through healing and uniting what has been separated. Human beings, consequently, created in the image of the triune God and recreated in Christ through the energies of the Spirit, are called to unite with one another in Christian community, to embody love for all of God's creation, and to fulfill the divine command to love God and neighbor.

The sixth chapter, the conclusion, considers the implications of my argument for how we do theology today. To begin, I discuss the way Maximus and Moltmann start their theological anthropologies by meditating upon and trying to understand Christ and the Trinity, then contrast this approach with the tendency of modern theologies to devise an account of human being first, and then try to find ways in which Christ and the Trinity are somehow relevant to this human being. To illustrate these different approaches to theological anthropology, I take two key representatives of modern theology, Immanuel Kant and Friedrich Schleiermacher, contrast them with Maximus and Moltmann, and demonstrate how the theological anthropologies of Maximus and Moltmann provide insights that lead to important implications for contemporary theology. Further, I consider the constructive alternatives to the anthropocentrism of modernity offered by Maximus and Moltmann. Correcting this anthropocentric tendency, Maximus and Moltmann offer theocentric views of human being, underscoring that humanity is rooted both in God and in the broader community of creation. I suggest, additionally, that a critical retrieval of ancient texts and practices, as this book illustrates, can help us reenvision our understanding of humanity and creation. Finally, I demonstrate the approach to knowledge in Maximus and Moltmann that is different from those who view knowledge in objectifying and reductionistic ways. For Maximus and Moltmann, knowledge of God, humanity, and creation is contemplative and participatory.

Why Maximus and Moltmann?

As noted previously, one reason for exploring Maximus and Moltmann's Trinitarian and christologically structured anthropology *together* stems from an ecumenical motivation. My intent is to dialogue across Orthodox and Reformed traditions[8] through critical analysis of each theologian's conception of the human calling in creation.

A second reason is that my intuitions regarding the intriguing parallels between Maximus and Moltmann have been confirmed by leading scholars from various traditions, including Lars Thunberg (Lutheran), Hans Urs von Balthasar (Catholic), Joy Ann McDougall (Episcopalian), and Anestis Keselopoulos (Orthodox).[9]

A third reason for examining Maximus and Moltmann's Trinitarian-christocentric anthropology in conjunction is that, as the above scholars indicate, both theologians are "hub" figures that bring together a number of seemingly disparate realms in their theological anthropology. For example, Balthasar notes how Maximus reaches inside and opens up a host of intellectual worlds that appeared to have lost contact, bringing light out of each one that illumines the others, leading to new connections and

---

8. That Moltmann has deeply engaged Orthodox theology, including Maximus and Maximian scholarship, is well known. See Constas, "Eschatology and Christology," 191–99; Volf, *After Our Likeness*, 4. Moreover, in a personal letter from December 2007, Moltmann told me that Maximus is his favorite among all Orthodox theologians.

9. For a sampling of how these theologians have discerned interesting correlations, see: Thunberg, *MaC*, 147; Balthasar, *CL*, 343; McDougall, *PL*, 143; and Keselopoulos, *ME*, 93.

surprising similarities and relationships.[10] He explains that Maximus unites these worlds in his own approach to theology, as a contemplative biblical theologian, a philosopher trained in Aristotelian thought, a mystic in the Neoplatonic tradition of Gregory of Nyssa and Pseudo-Dionysius, a devout monk of the Evagrian tradition, and a man of the church who gave his life for the orthodox Christology of Chalcedon and for a church centered in Rome.[11]

Likewise, Moltmann is a theologian who brings together a number of seemingly disparate spheres of thought, including: biblical theology from a German Lutheran perspective; Dutch "apostolate theology" with its eschatological perspective of the church's universal mission toward the coming kingdom of God; concern for social ethics (fueled by his pioneering research into Dietrich Bonhoeffer's work), and the church's involvement in secular society (through Ernst Wolf); Barthian theology; Karl Rahner and Vatican II; Balthasar and DeLubac (*Resourcement*); Orthodox theology (including Maximus, John of Damascus, and Dimitru Stăniloae); Hegelian thought (which through Hans Joachim Iwand informed his dialectical interpretation of the cross and resurrection); through his *Theology of Hope*, he brings together Ernst's Bloch's Marxist philosophy and Jewish messianic theology (Franz Rosenzweig and Abraham Heschel); pastoral concern (having served as a pastor in Wasserhorst), seeking to do "the theology of the people," bridging academic and pastoral theology; an increasing openness to other traditions and movements, including Roman Catholic, Orthodox, Liberation theologies, and Pentecostal/Charismatic; and finally, his experience of the world-wide church has shaped his ecclesiology in particular.[12]

---

10. Balthasar, *CL*, 57. See Pelikan's reflections on the "bilingual" approach of Maximus, one that speaks both languages of spirituality and theology, as well as bridges Eastern and Western Christianity (introduction to *CWS*, 11). Although in different ways, Moltmann's theology also seeks to bridge Eastern and Western Christianity, as I will show throughout this study.

11. Balthasar, *CL*, 57. Balthasar even suggests that Maximus's eschatological vision not only makes him the teacher of the Celtic speculative theologian Erigena, but also through Erigena and a long line of thinkers, the intellectual ancestor of the German idealists (*CL*, 343).

12. See Bauckham, *TJM*, 1–3. Moltmann has engaged numerous traditions and movements, including Christian-Marxist dialogue, Black, Feminist, and Latino/a theology, Catholic and Orthodox theology, and Pentecostal/Charismatic theology. He has moved in many theological circles, engaged and integrated insights from diverse traditions, and sought, through his ecumenical theology, to bridge various traditions including Eastern and Western Christianity.

Introduction

Therefore, in view of these reasons—ecumenical, intutions confirmed by other scholars, and synthesizing approaches—this study proceeds to demonstrate how Maximus and Moltmann root their understanding of the human calling in their Trinitarian-christocentric visions.

Method

My methodological approach to this project is informed and influenced by an ecumenical group of scholars.[13] First, David Tracy's recent work, in which he juxtaposes Pseudo-Dionysius and Martin Luther on the incomprehensibility and the hiddenness of God, has been a paradigmatic and constructive model of theology that dialogues across traditions and engenders fruitful conversation between Orthodox and Lutheran theology.[14] Second, John Meyendorff's historical and systematic approach—as seen in such works as *Byzantine Theology*, with its judicious and constructive exposition—is exemplary for my own work here.[15] Finally, I employ Moltmann's ecumenical method, in which he critically and constructively draws from and integrates Catholic, Orthodox, and Protestant sources.[16]

---

13. Rowan Williams's reflection on theological methodologies has been informative. His proposal of a typology of theological activity suggests that we clarify the ways that the *celebratory* (poetic), *communicative* (rhetorical), and *critical* (scientific) styles interact. Williams's overall point, that one often displays various modes of arguing and interpreting rather than advancing a single system, is well taken (and applied) (prologue to *On Christian Theology*, xii-xvi). See also Moltmann's discussion of metaphorical language, including his reflection on Gregory of Nyssa and theological language. Moltmann's thoughts further explain how collating his work with that of Maximus, including the similarities and differences in language and concepts, is feasible, *ET*, 162. He also directs his readers to Sally McFague's work, *Metaphorical Theology*, 19n134, 364n138.

14. See the interesting and provocative interview by Lois Malcolm in which Tracy discusses some of the trajectories within his current research, "Interview with David Tracy," 24–30. In addition to the methodological influences mentioned in this section, I have also been informed by Bernard Lonergan's approach to theology, a method that functions as a framework for collaborative, critical reflection, creativity, and conversation between different thinkers and their particular areas (*Method in Theology*, xiff.).

15. Meyendorff, *Byzantine Theology*, viiff.

16. Moltmann, *God in Creation*, xv. See McIntosh, *Divine Teaching*, for excellent examples of correlating theologians from diverse backgrounds. For example, McIntosh compares and contrasts Origen of Alexandria, Thomas Aquinas, and Karl Barth on "basic points of commonality" in their accounts of the fundamental biblical story of the universe (40ff.). McIntosh also considers the various treatments of salvation in such theologians as Origen of Alexandria, John Calvin, and Elizabeth Johnson (65ff.).

One final note regarding method: while this project seeks to highlight certain correlations (a conceptual common ground of sorts) between Maximus and Moltmann, I understand that they come from distinct historical, geographical, and traditional backgrounds. I do not intend to ignore the irreducible differences between them, even while I seek to demonstrate elements of the conceptual common ground in which they root the human calling.[17] In other words, this book places Maximus and Moltmann in conversation, and listens to their constructive insights on humanity and creation, without homogenizing their unique theological visions.

Sources

On the note of sources, the following analysis of Maximus and Moltmann's theological anthropology focuses on their primary texts, including Maximus's *Mystagogy, Centuries on Love, Ad Thalassium*, and *Ambigua*,[18] and Moltmann's six "systematic contributions to theology."[19] Of course, I consider a number of their other texts, due to the immensity of their oeuvre, including many essays, articles, and chapters written by Moltmann over the past four decades. Additionally, I utilize critical secondary literature on Maximus and Moltmann, such as the work of Maximian scholars Polycarp Sherwood, Hans Urs von Balthasar,[20] Lars Thunberg, Vladimir Lossky,

---

17. While there are many correlations between Maximus and Moltmann's theology, throughout the study I do my best to view them in the light of their own particular contexts. Keeping the correlations *and* differences in mind will, I think, strengthen my argument as I seek to talk across traditions on the human calling in creation.

18. I want to be clear from the beginning: This is not a patristics study per se; it is a constructive project that utilizes patristic sources. It seeks to interface Orthodox patristic theology with contemporary constructive theology, in the spirit of what Florovsky calls "neopatristic synthesis." Ware, commenting on Stăniloae's *Dogmatic Theology*, explains that the "patristic writers are treated by Fr. Dumitru always as contemporaries, as living witnesses whose testimony requires on our side a continual self-examination and rethinking, with present day concerns in view. Faithful to the past, responsible to the present [Stăniloae's work] is . . . prophetic . . . open to the future, creative, pointing towards paths as yet unexplored" (foreword to Stăniloae, *Experience of God*, 1:ix).

19. Regarding Moltmann, his six systematic contributions are: *Trinity and the Kingdom of God* (1981); *God in Creation* (1985); *Way of Jesus Christ* (1990); *Spirit of Life* (1992); *Coming of God* (1996); *Experiences in Theology* (2001).

20. Balthasar's groundbreaking work in Maximus is widely acknowledged and appreciated, yet scholars have indicated some of its weaknesses, including: the notion that the questions he asks of Maximus are mostly modern questions (many related to Hegelian thought), issues important to French and German Catholic theology in the

Introduction

and Moltmannian scholars, Richard Bauckham, Joy Ann McDougall, and Geiko Müller-Fahrenhotz.²¹

Questions and Critiques

The overall question this study seeks to answer concerns how human beings, created in the image of God, fulfill their vocation in God's creation, and how this occurs, according to Maximus and Moltmann, in vital connection to Trinitarian and christological thinking. The study, therefore, shows how Maximus and Moltmann's theological anthropology springs to life from their Trinitarian and christological visions

Furthermore, as the argument develops, I will address certain questions and critiques related to Maximus and Moltmann's Trinitarian and christologically based understanding of the human vocation. One of the issues that lingered in my mind while working on this project was Lewis Ayres's pointed criticism of contemporary Trinitarian and christological teaching, with its use of what he calls "totalizing meta-narratives."²² Further matters concern Moltmann's methodology and his Trinitarian theology. In short, some theologians have questioned the methodological rigor of Moltmann's theology,²³ while others have voiced particular concerns regarding Moltmann's Trinitarian theology, including patripassionism and tritheism.²⁴ Another question concerns the universalizing, by Maximus, of the

---

mid-twentieth century; and the claim that his portrayal of Maximus blends authentic elements of Maximus's theology with shades of his own theological enterprise (see Daley's foreword to Balthasar, *CL*, 16–17).

21. The following resources provide a broad perspective on developments in Maximian and Moltmannian scholarship: Blowers, *Exegesis and Spiritual Pedagogy*, 1ff.; Louth, "Recent Research on St. Maximus," 67–84; Thunberg covers the five periods of research from 1930 to today (*MM*, 12–20); Bauckham details studies of Moltmann's theology (*TJM*, 262–74); the following two, in their extensive notes and bibliographies, engage recent Moltmannian scholarship: McDougall, *PL*, 165–99; Müller-Fahrenholz, *KP*, 245–62.

22. Ayres, *Nicaea and Its Legacy*, 384–429. One chief misconception I will steer clear of is the basic division between eastern and western Trinitarian theologies and the use of meta-narrative strategies, such as Theodore de Régnon's history of Trinitarian theology in the late nineteenth century, in which both of these misconstructions occur. See Barnes, "De Régnon Reconsidered," 51–79; cf. Marshall's comments regarding the emerging scholarship on Latin and Greek Trinitarian theology, which is unbound by de Régnon's views, in "Trinity," 199ff.

23. In the foreword to McDougall, *PL*, xiii, Moltmann responds to criticism regarding his methodology (xiii–xiv), something he addresses further in *ET*, ch. 2.

24. Bauckham addresses five particular issues which have been raised in criticism of Moltman (*TJM*, 23–26).

particular human being Jesus of Nazareth and Maximus's proclivity to find christological meaning in all things.[25] A final question and critique, which is actually raised by Moltmann, concerns the "spiritualizing" of creation in Orthodox soteriology (especially in the doctrine of *theosis*), rather than speaking in terms of "new creation."[26] Throughout the study I address these specific questions and critiques, along with other critical issues related to Maximus and Moltmann's theological anthropology.

---

25. See Norris, "Logos Christology," 194, and Yeago, "Jesus of Nazareth," 163–93.

26. This is addressed in ch. 3. See Moltmann, *CoG*, where he traces the historical development of the doctrine of *theosis*, then provides a critical evaluation (272–74). See also Stăniloae, Moltmann's Orthodox friend and frequent interlocutor, on Rev 21:5, where he reflects on God making "all things new," as humanity and the cosmos realize their full potential through unification with the Holy Trinity (*Experience of God*, 2:193–94).

2

The Trinitarian Matrix of the Human Calling

THE GOAL OF THIS CHAPTER IS TO DEMONSTRATE THE TRINITARIAN matrix in which Maximus and Moltmann develop their understanding of the human vocation. I begin with Maximus, analyzing the Trinity as source and goal of creation, the divine ideas tradition, the adumbrations of the Trinity within humanity and creation, and his reflections on the church and Trinity in the *Mystagogy*. After this, I explore the Trinitarian matrix in Moltmann, the perichoretic dimension within the Trinity and within creation, and the missional feature of his Trinitarian reflection.

What becomes increasingly evident, I suggest, as we consider the way Maximus and Moltmann root their understanding of the human calling in their Trinitarian (and christological) reflection, is how they demonstrate the fertility[1] and value of Trinitarian thinking.[2] In the following sections, I illustrate how the doctrine of the Trinity informs how Maximus and Moltmann conceive of what it means to participate in the life of God through Jesus Christ in the Spirit, and provides a heuristic framework for contemplating the mystery of God and ourselves in relation to God. What Rowan Williams says in his rumination on the doctrine of the Trinity—that

---

1. Norris refers to the criterion of "fruitfulness" used to test various theses (based on Popper's *Logic of Scientific Discovery*), something that applies to both Maximus and Moltmann's Trinitarian-christocentric visions as heuristic paradigms that disclose new insights into the relationship between God and the world ("Logos Christology," 201).

2. As a number of contemporary Trinitarian theologians have cogently argued (based on Maximus, Moltmann, and others), the doctrine of the Trinity is not simply abstract speculation about the inner-life of God (which in itself is not useless), but offers a bountiful harvest for Christian life and concrete practice in the world (see Cunningham, *These Three Are One*, 6), and is "an eminently practical doctrine with far-reaching consequences for Christian life" (LaCugna, *God for Us*, ix; cf. Williams, *On Christian Theology*, 162).

it appears as a comprehensive model for making sense of human spirituality—suggests what I aim to elucidate in the following.[3]

The Trinitarian Matrix in Maximus

What does the Trinitarian matrix look like in Maximus's theology? What are the main features of the Trinitarian context in which he works out his ideas on the human calling in creation? In the following sections, I succinctly explore these features of Maximus's Trinitarian-based theology in order to pave the way for a better understanding of his teaching on the human vocation.

The Trinity as Source and Goal of Creation

The first feature pertains to the Holy Trinity as the *source* and *goal* of creation. According to Maximus, creation is the "Trinity's creation," the joint work of the three (as described in other Eastern Fathers such as Irenaeus and Basil), so that "effects comprise all created things in heaven and on earth, while the causes that have brought them into being are the three Persons of the Holy Trinity."[4]

On this note, Moltmann speaks of God's history with the world as a Trinitarian history. He emphasizes "the co-efficacy of the divine Persons in concurrence," so that we understand that "all three Persons of the Trinity are always involved," whether we are speaking about the creation of the world, its preservation, or its preparation for the coming of God's kingdom. Moltmann suggests that this kind of Trinitarian thinking leads to two perspectives. According to the first, "the triune God empties [Godself] in creation, its preservation and redemption, in order to finally dwell there with [God's] eternal glory—as [God's] temple—so that we can say with Paul

---

3. Of course, "human spirituality" is an integral part of realizing the human calling in creation (Williams, "Trinity and Pluralism," in *On Christian Theology*, 168). Williams's essays on the Trinity (in relation to revelation, ontology, and pluralism) shed a good amount of light on various ways that the doctrine of the Trinity provides a fruitful paradigm for thinking about God, creation, community, and the human vocation. Moreover, in certain chapters Williams engages Moltmann's Trinitarian and christological thinking, exploring how it informs his anthropology. See, e.g., his analysis of Moltmann and Balthasar, and the way Moltmann's Christology becomes the means for him to address the question of what it means to be a human being, especially after such atrocities as the Holocaust, Vietnam, or Rwanda ("Word and Spirit," in *On Christian Theology*, 108ff.).

4. Maximus, *CC* II, par. 98; *VT*, par. 67; both in *Philokalia*, 82, 276.

The Trinitarian Matrix of the Human Calling

that in the end 'God will be all in all' (I Cor. 15:28)." The other perspective sees God's history with the world played out between the divine Persons. "Out of love for the Son/Logos, who is at the same time the Daughter/Wisdom, the Father creates a world of living beings who are meant to correspond to him." And "out of love for the Father, the Son himself becomes human and Wisdom becomes flesh, in order to redeem humanity and all the living; while the Holy Spirit fills everything that is with life, and holds all created being together." Thus, if "through the Logos/Wisdom the Father in the power of the Spirit creates a world differentiated from God, then this world derives 'from God.' The goal of its redemption is 'that they also may be in us' (John 17:21)." Moltmann concludes that these perspectives can be intertwined so that "we can say that the triune God will indwell the world in a divine way—the world will indwell God in a creaturely way."[5] In these reflections, we see how Moltmann shares elements of Maximus's perspective on the notions of the Trinitarian creation, preservation, redemption, and consummation of the world, and the goal of creation as dwelling in the Trinity.

Along with the perspective of the Trinity as the source of creation, is the notion that the Holy Trinity is the goal of creation. Maximus explains that God "is the origin, intermediary state and consummation of all things," and that God "is origin as Creator, intermediate state as provident ruler, and consummation as final end. For, as Scripture says, 'All things are from Him and through Him, and have Him as their goal'" (Rom 11:36).[6] On this theme of the Trinity as source and goal, Maximus is heir to his past, reaching back and bringing together the Trinitarian theology of Paul, Origen, the Cappadocians, Evagrius, and Pseudo-Dionysius.[7] More particularly, the notion of God as source and goal, or as beginning, middle, and end stems from Platonic and neo-Platonic philosophical tradition, as mediated through Pseudo-Dionysius.[8]

---

5. Moltmann, *ET*, 310–11.

6. Maximus, *CC* II, par. 98; *VT* par. 67; *Centuries on Theology* I, par. 10; from *Philokalia*, 82, 276, 116; cf. Thunberg, *MM*, 72, where he unpacks the notion that the "constitution of beings, is, however, a work not only of the Father but also of all three persons of the Holy Trinity . . . God, the eternal Creator, when He wills and acts because of infinite goodness, creates by His consubstantial Word and Spirit"; Argárate, "Maximus the Confessor's Criticism," 1037–41.

7. See Balthasar's comments on Maximus as heir to his past, *CL*, 98ff.

8. See Louth, *Origins of the Christian Mystical Tradition*, 156ff.; cf. Radde-Gallwitz, "Plato's *Parmenides.*"

The Divine Ideas Tradition

Related to Maximus's portrayal of the Trinity as source and goal is his use of the "divine ideas" tradition. A brief analysis of Maximus's reflection on divine ideas (as well as adumbrations of the Trinity in creation in the following section) reveals the pervasive Trinitarian-christocentric structure of his overall thinking, and consequently, his theological anthropology. What I will do here is sketch out the Trinitarian and christological contours of Maximus's thought, then flesh it out in the following chapters, where I look more closely at the christological basis, the redemptive goal, and the Trinitarian-christocentric practice of the human vocation.

One chief way Maximus expresses the relationship between the Creator and creatures is through earlier Logos theology developed by his predecessors. Based on the Stoic idea of *logos spermatikos*, merged with this early Christian Logos theology, Maximus draws from Origen, who appears to be the first Christian thinker to devise a more comprehensive theology of the *logoi* of creation, the ideas and basic outlines that reveal God's plan for the world.[9] According to this tradition, the Logos is the center and living unity of the *logoi* of creation. For Origen, the *logoi* exist only in an essential unity with the one, foundational Logos of creation. As a result of the fall, Origen suggests, the visible creation is diversified and must be reunited to its unified, divine source. This is one significant place where Maximus disagrees with Origen, modifies Origen's view,[10] and establishes a more world-affirming position. Accordingly, Maximus argues that the "goodness" of creation resides in creation itself, not solely in its unity with the divine essence and source. Maximus does say, however, that this "good" creation is fully realized and reaches its God-given potential, as its differentiated *logoi* (those preexistent "thoughts" and "wills" of God) are fixed and centered on God. This centering on God is, for Maximus, at the heart of

---

9. Thunberg provides a concise summary of the divine ideas tradition, including Origen's innovative teaching, as well as the development of the tradition in Athanasius, Augustine, Evagrius, Pseudo-Dionysius, John of Scythopolis, and Maximus (Thunberg, "Human Person as Image of God," 303). Also informative is the article by McIntosh, "Maker's Meaning," 365–84.

10. Balthasar argues, in his analysis of Maximus on the divine ideas, that Maximus brings "Origen's Logos-theology to its fulfillment," laying hold of "all the human powers, theoretical as well as practical, speculative as well as spiritual and mystical, powers of thought as well as those of prayer, in order to find Christ in all things and to find the triune God in him" (*CL*, 66).

the human endeavor of cultivating unceasing communion with the "super-essential" divine Logos.[11]

As we will see, especially in chapters 4 and 5, Maximus uses Origen, Evagrius, and Pseudo-Dionysius to adjust and refine one another on this notion of the *logoi* and their relationship to the Logos.[12] I will show, in more specific detail, how Maximus speaks of three different kinds of *logoi*—those in creation, in Scripture, and in Christ's incarnation—as well as the calling for humanity to discern these divine whispers of the Logos.[13] For now, my intention has been to introduce Maximus's teaching on the *logoi*, to show briefly how they represent the Trinitarian (and christological) structure of Maximus's thought, and how this factors into Maximus's view that all of creation is destined to "return" to God, its true source. Moreover, according to Maximus, human beings, "on account of their rational, 'logical' constitution, are able, *through contemplation of things* in their *logoi*, to keep the created universe together and to refer it to its primary cause, that is, in Christ and under God."[14] In Maximus's words, those "who look carefully at the present world, making the most of their learning, and wisely tease out with their minds the *logos* that folds together the bodies that harmoniously constitute it in various ways,"[15] are the ones who discover the divine structures of creation and begin to understand their role as mediators within the universe.

Adumbrations of the Holy Trinity in Humanity and Creation

In addition to the source/goal feature of Maximus's Trinitarian thought, and the related Logos/*logoi* teaching, is another crucial feature—the notion of

---

11. Meyendorff, *Byzantine Theology*, 132ff. Meyendorff explains how Maximus combines apophatic, anti-pantheistic tendencies, and builds on the Athanasian distinction between *nature* and *will*, so that an authentically Christian ontology of creation is established. He says, "This ontology presupposes a distinction in God between 'nature' (or 'essence') and 'energy,' a distinction which will later be called 'Palamism.' It presumes a personal and dynamic understanding of God, as well as a dynamic, or 'energetic,' conception of created nature" (132).

12. The following are particularly informative on the *logoi*/divine ideas teaching: Meyendorff, *Byzantine Theology*, 132ff.; Thunberg, *MM*, 73ff.; Kelley, *Early Christian Doctrines*, 18, 96, 145; Balthasar, *CL*, 116ff.

13. See McIntosh, *MT*, 57.

14. Thunberg, "Human Person as Image of God," 1:303.

15. Maximus, *Amb.* 10, 32C; in Louth, *MC*, 134.

adumbrations of the Trinity within human beings and the wider creation. Here I briefly sketch Maximus's ideas on Trinitarian adumbrations within humanity, outlines that will be filled in as my argument develops, especially in the later exploration of the doctrine of *theosis*. For now, what I aim to do is give a specific example in which Maximus parallels theological triads with anthropological triads. Then, I show how these traces of the Trinity in human beings are critical in understanding the human calling in creation.

No Traces—Negative Theology?

First, in particular places, it appears to some scholars, such as Balthasar, that Maximus states that the Godhead has left no traces of itself within creation. Balthasar points to what he thinks is the clearest expression of Maximus's tendency "to remove the triune life of God from any sort of rational speculation." In his *Ambigua*, Maximus assigns the Trinity to negative theology, assumes that positive theology concerns the God of "salvation history," and discusses how God rules the world by providence and judgment. Through an allegorical interpretation of the Lord's Transfiguration on Mt. Tabor,

Maximus describes the radiance of Christ's face a metaphor for apophatic theology, while his robes (along with Moses and Elijah representing "providence" and "judgment"), represent cataphatic theology. Concerning the first metaphor, Maximus says:

> The radiance of the Lord's face [is an image] ... of negative, mystical theology; according to this approach, the blessed and holy Godhead is essentially and supremely ineffable, unknowable, elevated an infinite number of times beyond all infinity. It does not provide the beings below it with the least trace [ἴκνος: lit., footprint], with the cloudiest conception of itself, nor does it offer any being at all a notion—even a dark hint—of how it can be at once unity and trinity. For it is not for the creature to grasp the uncreated, nor for limited beings to embrace the unlimited in their thought.[16]

Nevertheless, even though passages like this express the inability of creatures to grasp the transcendent mystery of the Trinity apart from divine revelation, Balthasar explains that because of "the history of the triune God in the world, a history of salvation and sanctification, [as] the real restoration of the creature to the Father through the Son and the Spirit, the

---

16. Maximus, *Amb.*; *PG* 91, 1168A; in Balthasar, *CL*, 99ff.

The Trinitarian Matrix of the Human Calling

Christian finds [him/herself] truly '*in*' the Trinity."[17] For the Trinity, according to Maximus, "moves in the spirit that can make it its own, whether angel or human—the spirit that searches through it and *in it* for what it really is [sic.]."[18] Further, if one's searching mind should attain to God, then it "shares not only in a unity *with* the holiness of the Trinity, but even in the unity that belongs to the Trinity in itself."[19] Thus, while the essence of God is supremely unknowable, by grace humans can participate in the life and energies of the Trinity.

Traces in Creation?

In other places, however, it appears that Maximus suggests that there *are* "adumbrations of the Trinity" in creation, as Polycarp Sherwood's seminal scholarship has demonstrated. Some passages, such as *Amb.* 10, intimate traces of the Trinity in the cosmos. In short, within this passage that deals with Origenist, Evagrian, and Dionysian themes, Maximus explains that God can be recognized as maker, provident, and judge through the "natural consideration" of substance, motion, difference, composition (*krasis*), and position (*thesis*). The point here is that for Maximus we *can* perceive (in the cosmos) the cause by the caused, and understand that God exists, though not what God is in Godself. By taking these triads from Origenist-Evagrian and Dionysian sources, Maximus "adapts them to his own thought—an express Trinitarian thought, not a mere Proclean triadism."[20]

Traces in Human Beings

Additionally, Maximus insinuates that there are adumbrations of the Trinity within human beings. Based on a Trinitarian image used by Gregory of Nazianzus, Maximus says, in *Amb.* 7, that our mind (*nous*), word (*logos*), and spirit (*pneuma*) are to be conformed to the archetype, the great Mind and Word and Spirit.[21] While there are other passages that evince the notion of adumbrations of the Trinity in human beings, this one is particularly important because of its ramifications for the human vocation. If traces of

---

17. Balthasar, *CL*, 100.
18. Maximus, *Amb.*; PG 91, 1260; in Balthasar, *CL*, 100.
19. Maximus, *Amb.*; PG 91, 1196B; in Balthasar, *CL*, 100.
20. Sherwood, *SMC*, 41.
21. Maximus, *Amb.* 7; 1088A; cf. 10; 1196A; cf. Sherwood, *SMC*, 41ff.

the Trinity are found within humans, and if humans are destined to be conformed to the archetypal Trinity, then humans are also called, Maximus argues, to participate in the unifying work of the triune God. This means, first, that the apex of the spiritual life is union with the Holy Trinity, a "unity that is understood in the Holy Trinity."[22] There are three elements in this Trinitarian based unity: simplicity, goodness, and freedom from division. Second, the human calling to be conformed to the archetypal Trinity means that we are called to participate in and reflect the unifying work of God in the cosmos. One cannot overstress, on this point, the central role that the church (and its liturgical and sacramental life) plays in Maximus's Trinitarian vision of cosmic and human life.

The Mystagogy: Church and Trinity

One of the more vivid places where this can be seen is in Maximus's *Mystagogy*.[23] The thrust of Maximus's thought in the *Mystagogy* is that the highest vocation of humanity is to eucharistically present creation back to and into the Holy Trinity, thereby fulfilling God's destiny for humanity and all of creation. While I will reserve the full analysis of this for chapter 4, I offer here a few salient passages that demonstrate the Trinitarian structure of Maximus's portrayal of the human vocation.

First, Maximus speaks of the holy Church as that which "bears the imprint and image of God," and engages in the "same activity as [God] does by imitation and in figure."[24] Second, Maximus says:

> For God who made and brought into existence all things by his infinite power contains, gathers, and limits them and in his Providence binds both intelligible sensible beings to himself and to one another. Maintaining about himself as cause, beginning, and end all beings which are by nature distant from one another, he makes

---

22. Maximus, *Amb.* 10; 1196B; cf. Sherwood, *SMC*, 42. Ware asserts that "life begins with the Trinity, and its end and aim is the Trinity." Ware goes on to develop an illuminating essay on how the Trinity is the beginning, foundation, final hope, and heart of the Christian life. He also considers ways that Trinitarian doctrine shapes our understanding of human personhood, the human vocation, and human participation in the unifying presence of the Trinity ("Human Person," 8:2, 6–23).

23. See Dragas, "Church in St. Maximus' Mystagogy"; cf. Louth, "St. Denys the Areopagite," 172ff.

24. Maximus, *Mystagogia* 1; in *CWS*, 186.

The Trinitarian Matrix of the Human Calling

them converge in each other by the singular force of their relationship to him as origin.²⁵

Third, Maximus expounds on the Trinity, in whose image the church is made, explaining that the "same unity and trinity has a unity without composition or confusion and a distinction without separation or division."²⁶ Fourth, Maximus considers the contemplative and liturgical life of the church, emphasizing that through the mystery of the Eucharist that is accomplished on the divine altar, God's church brings together and reunites the cosmos and humanity with the Holy Trinity.²⁷ In these passages, Maximus weaves together interrelated themes regarding humanity. Human beings are created in the image of the Trinity and called to participate in the unifying work of God, a work mediated through the church's contemplative and liturgical life. For Maximus, therefore, the human calling in creation is rooted and spelled out in Trinitarian terms.

The Trinitarian Matrix in Moltmann

Having examined facets of Maximus's Trinitarian shaped anthropology, I now turn to the question, what does the Trinitarian matrix of the human calling look like in Moltmann? Like Maximus, Moltmann roots his teaching on the human vocation within his Trinitarian vision. In *The Trinity and the Kingdom*, his initial systematic volume on the doctrine of God, Moltmann asks "whether the doctrine of the Trinity itself cannot provide us with the matrix for a new kind of thinking about God, the world and [humanity]."²⁸

25. Ibid.

26. Maximus, *Mystagogia* 23; in *CWS*, 205. Polycarp Sherwood says that "for Maximus the ultimate mystery of Christianity and of mystical theology is simply 'the unity understood in Trinity': 'The Trinity is truly triad completed by no divisive number . . . , but the substantial existence of three-personed monad. For the Trinity is truly monad, because so it is; and the monad truly triad, because so it objectively exists—one Godhead that is being as monad and objectively exists as triad.'" (*Amb.* 1; 1036B.13–C.5; in *SMC*, 44).

27. Maximus, *Mystagogia* 6; in *CWS*, 194.

28. Moltmann, *TK*, 16ff. In his development of fresh thinking within a Trinitarian matrix, Moltmann proposes a Trinitarian understanding of history. In his book *Experiences in Theology*, where he speaks of ways, forms, and methods of theology, he says, "God's history with the world is a trinitarian history. . . . All three persons of the Trinity are always involved" (310). See also McIntosh's discussion on particular questions in Trinitarian theology today, including inquiries regarding: the Holy Spirit, the problem of "Persons," gender and society, Trinitarian self-abandon and divine suffering, and relationality.

In view of Moltmann's intent to cultivate fresh, Trinitarian based thinking, I suggest that there are two main features of the Trinitarian matrix within which Moltmann develops his thoughts on the human calling in creation.

The Perichoretic Dimension: Within the Trinity

The first is the *perichoretic* dimension. Within this perichoretic dimension are two aspects. The first is the *perichoresis* within the Trinity.[29] Moltmann, stemming from his analysis of biblical texts—especially in the Gospel of John: "Whoever has seen me has seen the Father" (14:9), "Believe me that I am in the Father and the Father is in me" (14:11), "The Father and I are one" (10:30)—thinks that the perichoretic form of unity "is the only conceivable *trinitarian concept of the unity* of the triune God, because it combines threeness and oneness in such a way that they cannot be reduced to each other, so that both the danger of modalism and the danger of 'tritheism' are excluded."[30]

Moltmann finds in John of Damascus (c. 678–749), whose theology accords with Maximus at several points, a clear articulation of this profound doctrine of the eternal *perichoresis* of the Trinitarian Persons. In short, Moltmann understands the Damascene to say that *perichoresis* describes the circulatory character of the eternal divine life, a dynamic activity that takes place through the exchange of energies. Moltmann explains that "by virtue of their eternal love they live in one another to such an extent, and dwell in one another to such an extent, that they are one." It is precisely "through the personal characteristics that distinguish them from one another, [that] the Father, the Son and the Spirit dwell in one another and communicate eternal life to one another." For in "the perichoresis, the very thing that divides them becomes that which binds them together."[31] This

---

29. Moltmann is careful to explain that the Trinitarian perichoresis must not be viewed as a rigid pattern, but we "should see it as at once the most intense excitement and the absolute rest of the love which is the wellspring of everything that lives, the keynote of all resonances, and the source of the rhythmically dancing and vibrating worlds" (*GC*, 16).

30. Moltmann, *ET*, 322. It is important to note Moltmann's regular disavowal of all tritheistic theology. Concurring with Bauckham, I think Moltmann is often misunderstood by those who do not read enough of his theological corpus. They are all too quick to label him "tritheistic," supporting their claims with sound bites from his work, rather than reading (and citing) in a more contextual, holistic, and thorough manner; cf. Bauckhaum, *TJM*, xff.; Rusch, *Trinitarian Controversy*, 1–27; cf. Coakley, "'Persons' in the 'Social' Doctrine," 123–44.

31. Moltmann, *TK*, 174–75. Moltmann adds that in "their perichoresis and because

The Trinitarian Matrix of the Human Calling

perichoretic vision of God helps clarify the way that Moltmann roots the human vocation in the triune life.

The Perichoretic Dimension: Within Creation

This leads to the second aspect in Moltmann's perichoretic dimension, the *perichoresis* of creation.[32] According to Moltmann, the Trinitarian perichoresis is the wellspring of love from which everything flows, the keynote of all resonances, and the source of the world with all its rhythms and vibrations.[33] He asserts that "all relationships which are analogous to God reflect the primal, reciprocal indwelling and mutual interpenetration of the trinitarian perichoresis." This includes "God *in* the world and the world *in* God; heaven and earth *in* the kingdom of God, pervaded by his glory; soul and body united *in* the life-giving Spirit to a human whole; woman and man *in* the kingdom of unconditional and unconditioned love," who are "freed to be true and complete human beings."[34]

Some might wonder if Moltmann's use of this analogy is ontological or merely structural. In a key section in *God in Creation*, Moltmann makes several important points, points that suggest the analogy above is both

---

of it, the trinitarian persons are not to be understood as three different individuals, who only subsequently enter into relationship with one another (which is the customary reproach, under the name of 'tritheism'). But they are not, either, three modes of being or three repetitions of the One God, as the modalistic interpretation suggests. The doctrine of the perichoresis links together in a brilliant way the threeness to the unity, without reducing the threeness to the unity, or dissolving the unity in the threeness. The unity of the triunity lies in the eternal perichoresis of the trinitarian persons" (*TK*, 175). Karen Kilby presents a vigorous critique of Moltmann (and others) on this point, arguing that this kind of thinking "projects" human experience onto God, and proposing that trinitarian doctrine be seen as "a kind of structuring principle of Christianity rather than its central focus" ("Perichoresis and Projection," 432–45).

32. See Moltmann, "Cosmic Community," 93–105; cf. Maximus's use of *perichoresis* regarding the cosmos, *Amb.* 41:1308B5; in Louth, *MTC*, 213n10; Cunningham provides a helpful analysis of *perichoresis* in the Trinity and creation, in *These Three Are One*, 180ff.

33. Moltmann, *GC*, 16. Cf. Cunningham, *These Three Are One*, 121ff., a book that has received mixed reviews, but nevertheless, contains some creative, illuminating reflections on the Trinity.

34. Moltmann, *GC*, 17. See also Moltmann's sermon "Triune God," 5, where he says that the Trinity is the basis for all relationships: men and women in the Spirit of Christ, the church unified in the Spirit, and the whole world—a creation community. Cf. Clayton, "God and World," who critiques Colin Gunton's theology and suggests appropriating Orthodox tradition, as Moltmann does here, in *Cambridge Companion to Postmodern Theology*, 214n20; Moltmann, "Theology in the Project of Modernity," 232–33.

ontological and structural.[35] First, based on the creation narrative in Genesis, Moltmann explains that to say God "created" the world indicates God's self-distinction from that world, as well as emphasizes that God desired it. Contrary to other ancient accounts of creation, the biblical narrative suggests that the world in itself is not divine, nor an emanation from God's eternal being. Rather, it is the result of God's will and decision to create. All of creation is neither divine nor evil, nor is it eternal like its Creator. Creation is contingent. God creates (אָרָב, *bara*), bringing forth something new out of nothing (*ex nihilo*).

Further, Moltmann argues that God's creative activity is not supremely a manifestation of almighty power, but divine "love, which means the self-communication of the good." If "God creates the world out of freedom, then [God] creates it out of love. Creation is not a demonstration of [God's] boundless power; it is the communication of [God's] love, which knows neither premises nor preconditions: *creatio ex amore Dei*." Regarding this, Moltmann quotes Dante: "From the Creator's love came forth in glory the world . . ."[36] Out of God's free love, [God] both creates and sustains the universe. Moltmann says that God's "love is literally ecstatic love: it leads [God] to go out of [Godself] and to create something which is different from [Godself] but which none the less corresponds to [God]." The "delight with which the Creator celebrates the feast of creation . . . makes it unequivocally plain that creation was called into being out of the inner love which the eternal God . . . *is*."[37] Through these interrelated ideas on divine love, freedom, and power, Moltmann seeks to demonstrate the fecundity of Trinitarian, perichoretic thinking.

---

35. Moltmann says that God's creative activity employs God's inner life, communicating divine love to God's creatures, giving human beings a share in the productivity of God's will and in God's very nature (2 Pet 1:4). Humans, created to be God's image, are of God's race, God's offspring (Acts 17:28). "To be God's creature and [God's] image means being more than merely a work of [God's] hands. It means being actually 'rooted' in the creative ground of the divine life. This becomes especially clear if we understand creation pneumatologically, in the light of the Creator Spirit who dwells in [God's] creation" (*GC*, 85).

36. Moltmann, *GC*, 76. For further critical comments on Moltmann regarding this point, see Kilby's essay, "Perichoresis and Projection," 441ff.

37. Moltmann, *GC*, 76. On this point, Moltmann references Kallistos Ware, *Orthodox Way*, 56ff. McDougall reflects on Moltmann's engagement of Maximus. She notes Moltmann's work in the Greek church fathers, particularly Maximus, and his use of *eros* to describe the overflowing love within the triune community, a creative force that joins human beings to God and one another (*PL*, 143).

Additionally, after looking at Aristotelian and medieval ontology, with its notion of the cause actually communicating its own being to the effect, Moltmann briefly discusses the image of God in humanity. He argues that as "God's *work*, creation is not essentially similar to the Creator; it is the expression of [God's] will." But "as *image*, men and women correspond to the Creator in their very essence, because in these created beings God corresponds to [Godself]. It is an *analogia relationis*." As "the image of God on earth, human beings correspond first of all to the relationship of God to themselves and to the whole of creation." But "they also correspond to the inner relationships of God to [Godself]—to the eternal, inner love of God which expresses and manifests itself in creation." As "God's image, men and women are beings who correspond to God, beings who can give the seeking love of God the sought-for-response, and who are intended to do just that." As "God's image, men and women are [God's] counterpart in the work of creation. The human being is the Other who resembles God (Ps. 8:5)." Moltmann is careful to explain that this "seeking love of God" does not imply need on God's part, as I explain below. This perichoretic thinking about the image of God in humanity, which underscores the correspondence and relationship of human beings to God, has practical implications for the human calling in creation. Humans are created to function as God's counterpart in creation, the other who comes into being out of the overflow of the inner relationships of the triune God. For Moltmann, this means humans are created for intimacy with God, and destined to cooperate with God in bringing all of creation into full communion with the Trinitarian, perichoretic relationships.

The Missional Feature

THE OPEN TRINITY: COMMUNITY OF EROTIC LOVE

Linked with this perichoretic feature of Moltmann's Trinitarian theology, in which he roots the human calling, is a second: what I refer to as the *missional* feature. For Moltmann, the Trinity is *open* toward the world and humanity, moved by seeking love, intent on gathering, unifying, and glorifying humanity and creation.[38] As we saw, according to Moltmann, God's "seeking love" does not mean that God is unfulfilled within Godself.

---

38. Moltmann, *Trinitarian History of God*, 642. Interestingly, Moltmann quotes Adrienne von Speyer, Hans Urs von Balthasar's dear friend and colleague: "The relationship of the divine persons to each is so wide that the whole world has room within it" (642).

Moltmann is careful to emphasize this within his work, often repeating that "God need not have created the world." There "are no inner reasons and no outward compulsions for his action. God is self-sufficient. [God's] bliss is self-complete." God is perfect and does not need a creative expression of Godself nor a creation. But "it was [God's] good pleasure to create a world with which [God] could be 'well pleased.' That is why [God] created a reality corresponding to [Godself]."[39] Along these lines, Moltmann points to Maximus who also suggests, as noted above, that the community of divine love is a community of *Eros*, a community overflowing with a seeking, uniting, and intermingling force.[40]

Regarding Moltmann's interaction with Maximus on divine *Eros*, the Trinity's overflowing and uniting love in the cosmos, and the return of creatures to their Creator, McDougall reflects: "Appealing to the Greek church Fathers (particularly Maximus the Confessor), Moltmann uses the . . . term *eros* to describe both divine and human loves." *Eros* "signifies both God's fellowship with humankind and the force that joins human beings into community with one another."[41] She references a relevant text in Moltmann: "The community of love is an *erotic community*: God's loving community with [God's] beloved creation is erotic." It is "the [erotic] force which differentiates and unites all [God's] creatures . . . the rapturous delight of lovers in one another."[42] As McDougall adds, Moltmann identifies *eros* "with the creative Spirit of life who infuses love—an affirmation of life—into all of creation. *Eros* imparts to human beings a share in the divine life and enables them to reflect this same love in the sphere of earthly relations."[43] For Moltmann, therefore, the notion of the Trinity as a community of erotic love that is open to the world, does not suggest in any way that God is unfilled with Godself or compelled to create and seek creatures out of need. Rather, the work of creation and recreation is a result of God's overflowing, evocative love, an erotic force that draws all of creation back into God's embrace.

---

39. Moltmann, *TK*, 105; cf. 108, where Moltmann says that "the idea of the world is already inherent in the Father's love for the Son . . ."

40. Moltmann, *SL*, 261; quoting from Yannaras, *Person and Eros* (Göltlingen, 1982), 122ff. (*PG* 4, 268 CD–269 A).

41. McDougall, *PL*, 143ff.

42. Moltmann, *SL*, 261; in McDougall, *PL*, 143.

43. McDougall, *PL*, 143.

The Trinitarian Matrix of the Human Calling

THE CROSS OF CHRIST

At the heart of the Trinitarian community of seeking love, Moltmann argues, is the cross of Christ.[44] In *The Crucified God*, Moltmann offers a detailed and nuanced exposition of the idea of the "crucified God." The two sections that are particularly relevant to my argument deal with the doctrine of the two natures and the suffering of Christ, and the Trinitarian theology of the cross. These specific areas are critical because they influence and shape Moltmann's theological anthropology, especially in his consideration of the divine image in humanity and the church's identification with Christ's Passion in discipleship.

For Moltmann, the notion that the Trinitarian God of love "seeks" does not imply need, but expresses that God is a community overflowing with the force of love that saves, redeems, transforms, and reunites humanity with its Maker.[45] Moltmann unpacks this in the two aforementioned sections of *The Crucified God*, in which he makes a number of key points. First, Moltmann affirms what he understands to be the Nicene stance against Arius, that God is not changeable. He also supports the church's position against the Syrian monophysites that it was impossible for God to suffer. While Moltmann agrees that God does not suffer like creatures, he raises the question, "But must God therefore be thought of as being incapable of suffering in any respect?"[46] In an intriguing discussion of *apatheia*, Moltmann suggests that

---

44. See where McIntosh raises questions about theologies that emphasize the Trinitarian relationality of God read against the background of radically cross-oriented theologies (as in Moltmann). Citing Rowan Williams, McIntosh says that "what seems to develop are problematic 'forms of trinitarian pluralism that threaten to become mythological—the divine life as interactive drama . . . a highly anthropomorphic plurality of agencies.'" McIntosh argues that in Moltmann's *Crucified God*, the "concept of the divine Persons seems to have donned the apparel of modern Cartesian subjectivity . . . as if the *relational structure* of the divine life has been metamorphosed into divided *autonomous selves*, trapped in their private griefs and sorrows even while they may struggle along in the drama of the relationship with each other" (*MT*, 154.)

45. McIntosh, in conversation with Rowan Williams's work, provides a stirring commentary on Trinitarian *kenosis*, *sapientia*, and divine, ecstatic love that reaches out and transforms humanity and creation, Williams, "*Sapientia* and the Trinity," 317–32; quoted in McIntosh, *Mystical Theology*, 166.

46. Moltmann, *CG*, 229, 230. Balthasar points out that Maximus speaks of *the God who suffers*. In his discussion of Trinitarian and christological perichoresis, the mutual exchange of properties in Christ, and salvation, Balthasar reflects on and quotes Maximus: "This symbiotic interpenetration is the basis for the possibility of an 'interconnected exchange' of the names that belong to the two natures; thus one can 'call *God one who suffers*' and man 'Son of God' and 'God'" (*CL*, 258, italics mine); Maximus, *Opusc*.;

there are other forms of suffering between "unwilling suffering as a result of an alien cause and being essentially unable to suffer, namely active suffering, the suffering of love, in which one voluntarily opens himself to the possibility of being affected by another." Moltmann argues that if God is incapable of suffering in any respect, "and therefore in an absolute sense, then [God] would also be incapable of love."[47] These ideas are important because, as I have been demonstrating, Moltmann's vision of the triune God shapes his understanding of the human person and his or her fulfillment of the human calling. As I will explain below, the ideas of *apatheia*, active suffering, identifying with Christ's Passion, and the love that flows from the Trinity through the crucified Christ into the church, are vital for both Moltmann and Maximus's understanding of the human vocation.

The Crucified within the Trinity

Further, Moltmann develops a Trinitarian theology of the cross. Critiquing patripassion and theopaschite views, he asserts that in order "to understand what happened between Jesus and his God and Father on the cross, it is necessary to talk in trinitarian terms."[48] Moltmann shows the vital connections between the form of the crucified Christ, the doctrine of the Trinity, and the saving work of the triune God that brings about the new creation of humanity and the cosmos.[49] The work of the triune God through Christ's crucifixion and resurrection, as Moltmann indicates, directly informs and shapes theological anthropology. Not only does a Trinitarian theology of

---

PG 91, 121A. Balthasar adds that through his voluntary incarnation and *kenosis*, Christ transforms weakness and suffering into redemption and power (*CL*, 259).

47. Moltmann, *CG*, 230. In his informative study *Suffering of the Impassible God*, Paul L. Gavrilyuk explains that Moltmann's position "is not easily classifiable, since he rightly recognizes that *apatheia* for the Greek authors denoted God's freedom and self-sufficiency, rather than apathy and indifference" (178).

48. Moltmann, *CG*, 235ff. Here, as he often does, Moltmann references Balthasar: "The scandal of the cross is tolerable for believers only as the action of the triune God, indeed it is the only thing in which the believer can boast" (*CG*, 286n102).

49. Moltmann, *CG*, 246–47. Noting parallels between Maximus and Thomas Traherne, McIntosh traces the links between the overflowing, creating Trinitarian abundance, the sharing of the Trinitarian life through the cross of Christ, and the receiving and giving of this life by God's creatures (*Divine Teaching*, 11); Traherne, *Centuries*, 28–29 (from passage I.58–60). This perspective on the cross, as *the* revelation of divine self-giving, is found in Moltmann's Trinitarian understanding of Christ's crucifixion. As with Maximus, Moltmann explains that the cross is the expression of the triune God's abundant, seeking love, a window into the ineffable mystery of the Holy Trinity.

the cross help articulate the new creation of God's creatures, it also exemplifies the spirit of Christian ethics lived and taught by Christ. Moltmann explains, "What Jesus commanded in the Sermon on the Mount as love of one's enemy has taken place on the cross through Jesus' dying and the grief of the Father in the power of the Spirit, for the godless and the loveless." Additionally, Moltmann describes how the love of the Father, the free act of Christ on the cross, and the resurrecting Spirit lift believing humanity "into the inner life of God." For the Trinity is "an event of love in the suffering and the death of Jesus," and "is no self-contained group in heaven," but an overflowing community of love "open for [humanity] on earth, which stems from the cross of Christ."[50] Therefore, the notion of a Trinitarian theology of the cross, according to Moltmann, informs Christian ethics, and clarifies how human beings in Christ, as God's new creation, are to extend the love of the crucified Christ to the world.[51]

Before turning to the next chapter, it might help to summarize briefly the main features of the Trinitarian matrix in which Maximus develops his understanding of the human vocation. The first considered the notions of the Trinity as the source and goal of creation and the divine ideas tradition. Maximus uses these concepts to express that creatures are present in the mind of God, that they proceed from God through Christ in the energies of the Spirit, and that they return to God through union with the incarnate Logos. Second, is the idea of adumbrations or traces of the Trinity in humanity and wider creation, an image that Maximus employs to portray the deep Trinitarian structures and divine whispers within all of creation. Further, I analyzed features of the Trinitarian matrix in which Moltmann forms his teaching on the human calling. The first was the perichoretic dimension, within both the Trinity and creation. Secondly, was the missional feature, which entails the notion of the Trinity as a community of erotic love that seeks and evokes creatures back into the divine embrace, as well as the aspect of the crucified within the Trinity. Having considered these features of the Trinitarian matrix in which Maximus and Moltmann develop their teaching on the human vocation, I turn now to the christological basis.[52]

---

50. Moltmann, *CG*, 249.

51. Concerning Moltmann's reflection on "concrete ethical suggestions," see his foreword to McDougall, *PL*, xiiiff.; cf. Moltmann, *ET*, 129ff.

52. See David Tracy, whose thoughts on the inseparability of Trinitarian theology and Christology are particularly illuminating here. Tracy, "Trinitarian Speculation," 286.

3

The Christological Basis of the Human Calling

BOTH MAXIMUS AND MOLTMANN, AS I AM DEMONSTRATING, SITUATE THE human calling within their Trinitarian and christological reflections. For Maximus and Moltmann, we understand what it means to be authentically and fully human as we contemplatively seek the Trinity, live in faithful communion with Christ and the church, and serve as God's redemptive agents in the world. In the previous chapter, I examined the ways that both theologians develop their portrayal of the human vocation within the soil of Trinitarian theology. In this chapter, my aim is to explore the christological roots from which their theological anthropology springs. Moroever, I will demonstrate how their christological thinking shapes and informs their teaching on the human vocation.

Aspects of Maximus's Christology

The Absolute Centrality of Christ

In Maximus, I demonstrate how his Christology influences his theological anthropology by delving into three aspects of his Christology. The first is the absolute *centrality* of Christ in every dimension of Maximus's work. According to Maximus, the person of Christ is *the* fundamental mystery of the universe. He explains: "Of all divine mysteries, the mystery of Christ is the most significant, for it teaches us how to situate every present or future perfection of every being, in every kind of intellectual investigation."[1] Balthasar, consequently, says that Maximus's great achievement is the way he uses christological terminology as the cornerstone of his understanding

---

1. Maximus, *Amb.*; *PG* 91, 1332C; from *CL*, 208–9; Cf. Meyendorff, *Christ in Eastern Christian Thought*, 131–51; cf. McFarland, "Developing an Apophatic Christocentrism."

The Christological Basis of the Human Calling

of the world.² Paul Blowers, citing Thunberg and Balthasar, underscores Maximus's visionary understanding of Christ's person, that the Second Person of the Holy Trinity in Jesus of Nazareth unlocks the secrets to the foundations and transcendent end of humanity and all creation. He explains that "Maximus' achievement, from one angle, is a panoramic commentary on the first chapter of Ephesians and on Colossians 1:15–23, the Apostle Paul's reflections on the mystery of Christ as the mystery of the world."³

That Christ is the sun around which all things orbit in Maximus's theology is evident. As we saw in chapter 2, the centrality of Christ as the fundamental mystery of the universe is expressed by Maximus in his appropriation of Alexandrian Logos Christology, which takes on more human and evangelical features in Maximus.⁴

This christocentric core of Maximus's sweeping cosmic vision,⁵ in which all *logoi* are clearly understood and ultimately rest in the divine Logos, leads to a further aspect of Maximus's christological basis of the human calling, its *incarnational context*. In order to adequately demonstrate the importance of the incarnational context in Maximus's christologically-grounded anthropology, I will point out a few particular strands. Maximus weaves these christological strands together, giving a nuanced portrait of the incarnate Word, which in turn serves as the pattern for his theological anthropology.⁶

The first of these strands is that Christ's incarnation is the central turning point in the history of the cosmos. Commenting on a passage from one of Gregory of Nazianzus's *Sermons*—"and the natures are instituted afresh, and God becomes man"⁷—Maximus develops his thoughts on the incarnation as the pivotal event in world history. One of the main areas where Maximus develops his ideas on this is in *Amb.* 41, a text where he

---

2. Balthasar, *CL*, 208. He asserts, further, that Maximus's christological vision of the world parallels that of the greatest Christian minds, including Augustine and Aquinas. See Stăniloae, "Christology of St. Maximus."

3. Blowers, *CMJC*, 20.

4. Balthasar, *CL*, 207.

5. See Blowers, *CMJC*, 19.

6. At various points, I discuss how Maximus envisions three incarnations of Christ: his own embodiment; in Scripture; and in the church. The ongoing nature of Christ's incarnation is a key concept in Maximus's understanding of the human vocation, as we will see below.

7. From St. Gregory Nazianzus's *Sermon* 39.13, on the Feast of Lights (i.e., the Theophany/Epiphany), *PG* 36.348D); cf. Louth, *MC*, 52, 156ff.

describes the way that Christ's incarnation brings together and heals five major divisions in the cosmos. According to this text, it is through Christ's role as incarnate mediator that humanity (and all of creation) is healed, and the divinely intended vocation of humanity is made clear.

A second strand that informs Maximus's theological anthropology is that the incarnation of the Word is that which makes God knowable. As a faithful interpreter of Pseudo-Dionysius, Maximus is committed to "divine unknowing" and the notion of God as a "ray of darkness." Accordingly, Maximus asserts, "Whoever has seen God and has understood what he saw, has seen nothing."[8] Maximus brings together the Evagrian notion of *ekdemia* ("migration" from the world and all created reality toward God) and the Dionysian emphasis on God's transcendence and the necessity of *ekstasis* ("ecstasy," being transported beyond all creation into the inconceivable reality of God) in his understanding of Christ's incarnation. In short, Maximus enhances and completes the Evagrian and Dionysian traditions by placing them within a more thoroughly incarnational context. Surprisingly, Maximus explains that while the incarnation of the Word reveals the Unknowable One, our ignorance of God is not abolished but actually increased, in a mysterious way. He says:

> he was not subjected to nature or made a slave by becoming human; rather, he has elevated nature to himself, by transforming it into a second mystery, while he him himself remains completely inconceivable and has revealed his own becoming flesh as something beyond all intelligible being, more inconceivable than any other mystery. He became comprehensible in [human] nature to the very same degree as he has been revealed more fully, through this nature, as the incomprehensible One. "He remained the hidden God, even after this epiphany," says the Teacher [Gregory of Nazianzus], "or, to put it in a more theological way, even *in* this epiphany. . . ." Even when uttered he remains unspoken, even when seen he remains unknown.[9]

This apophatic, incarnational perspective determines Maximus's teaching on the human vocation. Furthermore, we will see how the soteriological effects of Christ's incarnation do not mitigate divine transcendence

---

8. Maximus, *In Ep.* I; *PG* 4, 529A; in Balthasar, *CL*, 91.
9. Maximus, *Amb.*; *PG* 91, 1048D—1049A; in *CL*, 96-97.

The Christological Basis of the Human Calling

and unknowability, but disclose how the otherness of God becomes the very ground of humanity's reunification with God.[10]

A third strand regarding the incarnational context in which Maximus speaks of the human calling concerns the incarnation as the key to human salvation, or better, the recapitulation of all creation. A closer look reveals that this strand consists of several entwined, interconnected ideas. One is the way that Maximus portrays the incarnation of the Word in terms of the ancient concept of "synthesis."[11] To illustrate, I need to give an extended quote in which these ideas are linked, where Maximus discusses the *mysterium magnum*, of which Paul speaks:

> Here is the great and hidden mystery. This is the blessed end, the goal, for whose sake everything was created. This was the divine purpose that lay before the beginning of all things. . . . With this goal in mind, God called the natures of things into existence. This is the limit toward which providence and all the things it protects are moving, where creatures realize their reentry into God. This is the mystery spanning all the ages, revealing the supremely infinite and infinitely inconceivable plan of God, which exists in all its greatness before all the ages. . . . For Christ's sake, or for the sake of the mystery of Christ, all the ages and all the beings they contain took their beginning and their end in Christ. For that *synthesis* was already conceived before all ages: the *synthesis* of limit and the unlimited, of measure and the unmeasurable, of circumcision and the uncircumcised, of the Creator with the creature, of rest with movement—that *synthesis* which, in these last days, has become visible in Christ, bringing the plan of God to its fulfillment through itself.[12]

The synthesis of Christ's person, according to this text, reveals the divine plan for the restoration of humanity and all of creation. The great

---

10. As Balthasar says, "The highest union with God is not realized 'in spite of' our lasting difference from [God], but rather 'in' and 'through' it" (*CL*, 96).

11. "In his most general of intellectual laws," explains Balthasar, "Maximus discovers the truth behind the ancient Gnostic theory of paired beings, or *syzigies*: 'By syzygy, I mean the [synthesis] of theoretical and practical reason, of wisdom and prudence, of contemplation and action, of knowledge and virtue, of immediate vision and faith.' *Mystagogia* 5; *PG* 91, 676A; cf. *CL*, where Balthasar comments on Christ as the supreme synthesis of all, and how for Maximus, all things "had become organic parts of ever-more comprehensive syntheses, and had become themselves syntheses pointing to the final synthesis of Christ, which explained them all" (66–67).

12. Maximus, *QT* 60; CCG 22, 75, 32–56; *PG* 90, 621AB; in *CL*, 272.

and hidden mystery, the divine purpose and goal for humanity and all of creation, is that creatures are to reenter God. In other texts, such as the aforementioned *Amb.* 41, Maximus carefully explains how this occurs, the graced role thay humans play in bringing creation to rest in God. Of course, Maximus does not merely assent to the importance of the doctrine of the incarnation in the divine plan. He demonstrates how Christ, as the embodiment of God's purposes for human being, shows us how to fulfill the human vocation through a life of ascetic discipline, contemplation, and loving union with God.

In addition to this thread of synthesis in Maximus's incarnational thought, is the notion of what Maximus calls the "blessed conversion."[13] In the spirit of Cappadocian theology, Maximus says that in the incarnation a divine-human exchange occurs, which makes God human through the divinization of man and makes man God through the humanization of God. For the divine Logos, who is God, wants to see the mystery of his Incarnation brought to realization constantly, and in all of us.[14]

> Man has become God to the degree that God has become man, for he [man] has been led by God, through the stages of divine ascent, into the highest regions to the same degree that God has descended down to the farthest reaches of our nature, by means of a man and through a destruction of his own self that nevertheless implies no change.[15]

This incarnational, theotic interplay—the incarnation of God and the deification of humanity—is a major motif in Maximus's vision of the human person. Precisely because Christ, the Word, the second person of the Holy Trinity, has taken on human flesh, humanity is enabled by grace to partake of the divine nature (2 Pet 1:4). Accordingly, Maximus's Chalcedonian vision of Christ and incarnational grounding shed light on precisely what it means to be human, how one is deified by grace, and how human beings can actually function as microcosms and mediators within God's creation.

Another important thread within this strand on human and cosmic recapitulation relates to the interconnected themes of incarnation, crucifixion, and resurrection. For Maximus, these three christological motifs

---

13. Cf. Moltmann's discussion of "the merry exchange" in Luther's theology, *ET*, 107ff.

14. Maximus, *Amb. PG* 91, 1084CD; in *CL*, 280; cf. Thunberg, *Man and the Cosmos*, 51ff.

15. Maximus, *Amb. PG* 91, 1385BC; 280; cf. Stăniloae, *Experience of God*, 1:25ff.

The Christological Basis of the Human Calling

provide the hermeneutical key to unlock the secrets of Scripture, and the *logoi* and telos of creation. Maximus asserts that the

> mystery of the Incarnation of the Word bears the power of all the hidden meanings and figures of Scripture as well as the knowledge of visible and intelligible creatures. The one who knows the mystery of the cross and tomb knows the principles of these creatures. And the one who has been initiated into the ineffable power of the Resurrection knows the purpose for which God originally made all things.[16]

According to Maximus, the incarnation of the Word discloses the meaning of the written Word, and enables human beings to understand their purpose in God, an understanding that informs their fulfillment of the human vocation as they follow Christ's living example of love and obedience to God. What's more, passages like the following evince Maximus's staurocentric (a term Moltmann uses) or cross-centered perspective on the cosmos:

> Everything visible needs the cross—needs a condition that holds in check our appetite for the sensible things that the world itself has produced; but everything intelligible must descend into the grave—into the complete motionless of our intellectual response to the world. For if not only that sensible appetite but also our natural activity and stimulation in response to all things is eliminated, then the Word arises by himself alone, as if from the dead, and includes and possesses in himself everything that takes its origin from him, even though no single thing is related to him by natural connection or relationship. For it is by grace, not by nature that the elect attain salvation.[17]

Like Moltmann, Maximus's theology is thoroughly cruciform. In Moltmann, I showed how the cross stands at the center of his Trinitarian shaped theology. As Moltmann argues in *The Crucified God*, the cross of Christ is the foundation and criticism of Christian theology. In the message of Christ crucified, the essence of God's self-revelation and saving activity is made known, as well as the heart of Christian discipleship for the church. Moltmann's theology is inspired, accordingly, by the cross oriented

---

16. Maximus, *Centuries on Theology* I, 66; in *CWS*, 139–40. See also Reed, "Redemption," 228–29. On "divine ideas," see Louth, *Origins of the Christian Mystical Tradition*, 60ff.; Balthasar, *CL*, 115–36.

17. Maximus, *Centuries on Theology* I, 67; *PG* 90, 1108B; in *CWS*, 140; Balthasar, *CL*, 279.

theology of Augustine, Luther, Barth, Rahner, and Balthasar. While Maximus may use different parlance from a different tradition, like Moltmann he views the world in the shadow (and light!) of the cross. The above passage illustrates the central role of the cross in Maximus's view of the world. It also exemplifies how Maximus entwines the subjects of the (incarnate) Word, the cross, and the resurrection, and how these events are living realities within the spiritual life of the church. For Maximus, the cross paves the way for and epitomizes the Christian ascetic life. As believers freely participate in death to the allurements of the world, they enter experientially into the dynamics of the crucifixion, entombment, and resurrection.

In another key passage, Maximus elaborates on how Christ, through the blood of his cross (Col 1:20), establishes peace, both for those who dwell in heaven and on earth.[18] Further, in a passage that manifests a mysticism of cross-oriented suffering, Maximus says:

> Every individual who believes in Christ is nailed to the Cross with Christ, according to the measure of his own strength and the type and condition of his virtue; *at the same time, he nails Christ to the Cross with himself*, precisely in that he is crucified with Christ in a spiritual way.[19]

Stemming from the Apostle's mystical theology in Galatians 2:20, Maximus speaks of a twofold dynamic that occurs in the Christian spiritual life. First, through faith in Christ, believers are nailed to the cross with Christ, a reality experienced according to the degree of virtue in his or her life. Second, the believer nails Christ to the cross with him/herself, manifesting the reality of the spiritual crucifixion of which Paul speaks in Galatians. These various meditations on cross oriented mysticism, as well as the themes of synthesis, "blessed conversion," and the incarnation/cross/

---

18. Maximus, *Lord's Prayer*, in *CWS*; CCSG 23, 33, 116–20; *PG* 90, 877AB; in Balthasar, *CL*, 273ff. Also worth mentioning is how Maximus speaks of four forms of abandonment that occur within Christian spiritual life, each one represented in the life of a biblical character (Jesus, Job and Joseph, Paul, and the Jewish people), *CC* IV, in the *Philokalia*, 112–13, par. 96.

19. Maximus, *Amb.*; *PG* 91, 1360AB; in Balthasar, *CL*, 278. Interestingly, Balthasar notes the uniqueness of this notion in Maximus: "Outside of Origen . . . Pseudo-Macarius . . . this kind of mysticism of suffering, which reminds us of Pascal, does not exist in the East" (278). I am not sure, however, that this claim is supported by enough evidence. For example, one finds a cross-oriented mysticism of suffering in St. Mark the Monk, *To Nicolas* 3; *PG* 65: 1033AB; and St. Isaac the Syrian, *Ascetical Homilies* 36 (34), 59, 74 (79), tr. Holy Transfiguration Monastery, 161, 289–90, 364; in Ware, *Orthodox Way*, 129.

resurrection, demonstrate the incarnational context in which Maximus develops his understanding of the human calling. They also lay the groundwork for his more detailed teaching on the Christian ascetic life, one of the primary means by which human beings fulfill the human vocation by embodying the power of the life and death of Jesus.

In Chalcedonian Terms

This leads to the third aspect of the christological basis of the human vocation: How Maximus articulates his vision in *Chalcedonian terms*. That the Council of Chalcedon is a principal source of and formative influence on Maximus's theology, and thereby his anthropology, is underscored by many leading Maximus scholars.[20]

Scholarship on Maximus has proposed that Chalcedon is so influential on Maximus that one can discern a certain "Chalcedonian logic" or "Chalcedonian attitude" within his work.[21] As I will point out in this section, one does find the language and concepts of Chalcedon running through much of Maximus's theology and anthropology. In this section, I will underscore how this Chalcedonian perspective brings together many of the aforementioned elements regarding the incarnational context of Maximus's thought, as well as develops further insights into a christologically based understanding of the human vocation.

In his dealings with the Monothelite controversy,[22] Maximus articulates a thoroughly nuanced Christology drawing from a number of theological sources. Chief among these is the christological definition of the Council of Chalcedon (451), which maintained the unity of Christ, who is one and the same [i.e., one of the Trinity], perfect in divinity and humanity,

---

20. Examples of the influence of Chalcedon on Maximus's theology are noted by: Balthasar, *CL*, 46, 48–49, 211; Thunberg, *MM*, 21–36; Louth, *MC*, 27, 49–51, 57, 214. Citing Cyril O'Regan's research, Blowers comments that O'Regan, "again using the analogy of a 'symphonic' theology, has suggested that Maximus' work is an extended and richly textured gloss on the Chalcedonian Definition, which functions for him as 'dense knot of implication, both visionary and interpretive,' that holds the mysterious key to the world and its salvation" (*CMJC*, 16); cf. O'Regan, "Von Balthasar and Thick Retrieval," 246–47.

21. Louth, *MC*, 57; Thunberg, *MM*, 426.

22. The Monothelite doctrine, proposed in the seventh century, taught that Jesus Christ had only one will, and was an attempt to reconcile Monophysite and orthodox parties in the Byzantine Empire. It was condemned as a heresy at the Third Council of Constantinople (the Sixth Ecumenical Council, 680–681). See Tsirpanlis, "Dyothelitic Christology," 10–13.

like us in all respects except for sin.[23] The Council utilized language shaped in Trinitarian discussion in its reflection on Christ,[24] including such terms as *ousia* and *physis*, something I will consider in subsequent sections. What is key for our consideration here is the way that Maximus employs the four key adverbs from the Council's definition: *asynchtôs, atreptôs, adiairetôs, achôristôs*. Chalcedon's description of Christ—without confusion, change, division, or separation—becomes for Maximus a grid through which he envisions the recapitulation of humanity and the entire cosmos.

Synthesized with his other theological sources, Chalcedon structures Maximus's Christ-centered view of all things, including his understanding of the human calling in creation. Paul Blowers notes the way Maximus brings together Chalcedonian Christology, Cappadocian theology, Irenaeus's principle of cosmic recapitulation (*anakephalaiosis*), and a critical rehabilitation of Origen's insight into the divine permeation of all things (1 Cor 15:28).[25] This Christ-centered vision of the world, what Louth calls Maximus's "Chalcedonian logic," enables the Confessor to safeguard the integrity of the natural, so that the confusion and division brought about by humanity's fall is restored by and within Christ's "unconfused" person. Thus, the synthesis of Christ's person becomes the paradigm for the restoration of the cosmos and the pattern for the Christian life.[26] I will demonstrate this below with examples from Maximus, but before doing so a few things should be clarified.

---

23. Ware asserts that when Maximus "opposed Monothelitism, this was not because of some technicality, but because such a view subverted the understanding of the full reality of man's salvation and deification in Christ." The Monothelites wished to "reconcile the supporters of the Council of Chalcedon (451), who ascribed two natures to the incarnate Christ, with the Monophysites, who believed that He has only one nature; and so they proposed as a compromise the theory that Christ has two natures, the one divine and the other human, but only a single will." Countering this, Maximus "maintained that human nature without a human will is an unreal abstraction: if Christ does not have a human will as well as a divine will, He is not truly man; and if He is not truly man, the Christian message of salvation is rendered void," (*Philokalia*, 48–49).

24. See Aidan Nichols regarding Pierre Piret's analysis of Maximus's use of Trinitarian language in Christology (*Byzantine Gospel*, 77ff.).

25. Blowers, *CMJC*, 21.

26. Balthasar explains that "synthesis," not "confusion," is "the first structural principle of all created being," and that Maximus's ontology and cosmology "are extensions of his Christology, in that the synthesis of Christ's concrete person is not only God's final thought for the world but also his original plan" (*CL*, 207); cf. Balthasar on Christ's hypostatic union, *CL*, 235–36; cf. Williams, "Pseudo-Dionysius," 193ff.

The Christological Basis of the Human Calling

First, Maximus's dealings with Chalcedon are not merely repetitions of the Council's decrees, but evince creative reflection on its christological and anthropological content.[27] On this note, the way that Maximus creatively engages and works out the implications of Chalcedon illustrates precisely what Moltmann calls for in his own christological contributions. Maximus illustrates Moltmann's call for newer thinking that picks up previous thinking, refines it in a creative and judicious fashion, and sets it in a more thoroughly nuanced cosmological context.[28]

Further, this creative engagement can be seen in Maximus's ruminations on the concepts of *communicatio idiomatum* and *perichoresis*. Thunberg suggests the way that Maximus uses the christological content of Chalcedon as the underpinning for his elaborate theology of deification and spiritual perfection is one of Maximus's pioneering and primary contributions to Christian theology.[29]

As we have seen in other places, the concepts that Maximus takes up have a long, rich history (which is often complicated and controversial, as in Origen). This is also the case with his development of *communicatio idiomatum*. This concept, known as the principle of the "exchange of properties" (*antidosis idiomaton*), is found in early Christian thinkers such as Irenaeus and Origen.[30] It is expanded in the *Tome of Leo* (449), based on its usage in Tertullian and Augustine. To explore the development of this idea would take us off course, so I will focus on the way that Maximus appropriates the *communicatio idiomatum* in order to make a significant contribution through his theological anthropology.[31] Even more specifically, I will look at the way Maximus employs the term *perichoresis* to express the way that divinity and humanity relate, in the person of Christ and in a more general sense. Again, grasping these Chalcedonian terms, concepts, and themes will help make better sense of Maximus's christologically-grounded anthropology as my argument develops.

---

27. Thunberg's chapter on the Chalcedonian heritage of Maximus's theology has been particularly helpful here (*MM*, 21–36).

28. Moltmann, *WJC*, xviff.

29. Thunberg, *MM*, 22.

30. See Thunberg, *MM*, 22ff.; cf. McGuckin, *Westminster Handbook*, 70–71.

31. One can also trace Maximus's dealings with neo-Chalcedonian theology, a topic that Balthasar argues needs further exploration (*CL*, 13ff.). Thunberg does offer some preliminary observations along these lines. He discusses such things as the position of Cyril of Alexandria in Maximus's theology, including the positive evaluation of Cyril's expression "one incarnate nature of the God Logos" (*MM*, 36ff.).

As I pointed out above in my discussion of the perichoretic dimension of Moltmann's Trinitarian thought, the notion of *perichoresis* appears to have crystallized in the theology of John Damascene (ca. 675–749). However, Thunberg posits that the term *perichoresis*, used to describe the relationship between the divine and human natures in Christ, seems to have been first used precisely by Maximus. Moreover, in light of a long line of Maximus scholarship (H. Weser, G. L. Prestige, H. A. Wolfson, and V. Lossky), Thunberg reasons that Maximus is probably the first Christian theologian to give *perichoresis* such a primary position within orthodox Christology.[32] Thus, this perichoretic emphasis is another intriguing reason for juxtaposing Maximus and Moltmann's Trinitarian-christocentric visions in which they root their teaching on the human vocation, since it figures prominently in both theologians' work.

Based on his deliberation of Pseudo-Dionysius and Gregory of Nazianzus, Maximus forms his own conception of *perichoresis*. For example, in *Amb.* 42, Maximus considers Gregory of Nazianzus's teaching on the two natures of Christ and their characteristics, where Gregory speaks of these natures as "... penetrating (περιχωρῶν) into each other on account of their mutual adhesion (συμφυΐα)."[33] What is especially important here is how Maximus goes on to develop a conception of *perichoresis* as an expression of *activity*, rather than an idea that simply reflects the interrelation between the two attributes in Christ.[34]

In his own development of the notion of *perichoresis*, one can discern several features. The first emphasizes the divine penetration into the human level. In *QT* 59, which deals with the ongoing incarnation that takes place in Christians, Maximus speaks of the ineffable penetration (*perichoresis*) of the object of faith in relation to the amount of faith present in the believer. Also, in *Myst.* 2, one finds a similar idea of a reciprocal relationship between the intelligible and sensible levels of creation, where the different elements remain unconfused (*asugkutos*) in their contact with one another.[35] This is yet another place where Maximus's Chalcedonian logic comes into play, as he stresses the various "unconfused" relations within the cosmos. It also plays an important role within Maximus's vision of humanity in Christ serv-

---

32. Thunberg, *MM*, 25ff.

33. Gregory of Nazianzus, *Ep.* 101; *PG* 37, 181 C; as indicated in Thunberg, *MM*, 26.

34. See Thunberg, *MM*, 26ff.; cf. McIntosh, *MT*, 56–62; and McIntosh, *Christology from Within*, 4–5, 40–44.

35. See Thunberg, *MM*, 27.

The Christological Basis of the Human Calling

ing as mediators that bring together the various elements within creation, while their individuality is maintained in an "unconfused" manner.

A further feature of Maximus's conception of *perichoresis* in his Chalcedonian perspective deals with the human penetration into the realm of the divine. An illustration of this is found in *Amb.* 5, where Maximus says that, based on the union without confusion (*asugkutos*) in Christ's incarnation, human nature is enabled to penetrate (*perichorein*) into the divine nature. A text like this combines the notions of *perichoresis* and *asugkutos*, so that the dynamics of union without confusion and reciprocity correspond with one another.[36]

Another feature of *perichoresis* in Maximus's Chalcedonian vision, which stems from the previous one, deals with the reciprocity of the divine-human relationship, as Maximus speaks of it in terms of a double penetration. As indicated earlier, Maximus constructs his understanding of this on Gregory of Nazianzus's theology, where Gregory retools Stoic ideas of "mixture" for their use in christological reflection. In *Amb.* 17, Maximus speaks of the penetration of opposites into each other in virtue of their mixture (*kata ten krasin eis allela perichoresis*).[37] While there are numerous implications radiating from this, the main point I want to stress is that, for Maximus, the idea of a double penetration reinforces his perspective on an *active perichoresis*. Moreover, within his ongoing consideration of an active *perichoresis*, in the framework of Chalcedonian Christology, Maximus asserts that the two energies of Christ are joined, in order to clarify that the divine energy and the human energy are united into one subject. In other words, the divine energy in Christ at work in the economy of salvation, and the human energy in Christ which co-operates with the divine energy, are entirely united "through their mutual adhesion and penetration" (*té pros allelés sumphia kai perichosei*).[38] Hence, Thunberg asserts that through "*perichoresis*, which is an activity of the natures towards each other, a common activity and a unified direction of intention is affected." The "purpose of Maximus' stress on reciprocity is," Thunberg adds, "thus, first of all to underline the unified activity, which it expresses and of which it is an expression." However, "according to Maximus it belongs to the character of this unity, that it is in all respects 'unconfused' (ἀσύγχτοσ)."[39]

---

36. See ibid., 28.
37. Maximus, *Amb.* 17; *PG* 91, 1228 C; in Thunberg, *MM*, 29.
38. Maximus, *Opusc.* 7; *PG* 91, 85 D–88 A; in Thunberg, *MM*, 30.
39. Thunberg, *MM*, 30. Thunberg elaborates: "Therefore it is, of course, never 'of

Maximus employs the image of iron and fire, a recurring metaphor in the Patristic tradition,[40] in order to illustrate this notion of unconfused perichoretic activity. Maximus explains that when iron is placed in the fire, it remains what it is in itself. In the one hypostasis of iron, both iron and fire are found together, but the iron is simply doing what is in accordance with its own nature, along with the effect of glowing, which belongs to both natures.[41]

This notion of unconfused *perichoresis* in Christ is important, not some unwarranted focus on minutia or the clanking of ghostly chains from the Conciliar past, without vital implications for contemporary theology (as Balthasar humorously puts it).[42] These christological details and insights, expressed as they are in Chalcedonian language and concepts, lay the groundwork for Maximus's vision of humanity realizing its graced potential through union with Christ. As both Thunberg and Lossky demonstrate, Maximus's Chalcedonian language and iron-fire metaphor are crucial. They are crucial because, through them, Maximus is striving to elucidate how human nature is adopted into the sphere of the divine, an adoption towards which human nature naturally tends, and within which it develops what is inherent in and proper to itself.[43] In two key passages, Lossky says:

---

nature' (κατὰ φύσιν). There is 'a newness of modes' (τῶν τρόπων καινότησ) but never 'an alteration of *logos*' (κατὰ τὸν λόγον ἀλλοίωσις)" (30).

40. Louth notes how this analogy of the iron in the fire, used to illustrate the union of the two natures in Christ's Incarnation, is classic in Christian theology (*MC*, 216n22). He cites Origen, *On First Principles* II.6.6.

41. Maximus says, regarding the image of a sword plunged into the fire, that neither "suffers any change by the exchange with the other in union, but each remains unchanged in its own being as it acquires the property of its partner in union. So also is the mystery of the divine Incarnation: the Godhead and the humanity are united hypostatically, but neither of the natural energies is displaced by the union, nor are they unrelated to each other after the union, but they are distinguished in their conjecture and embrace" (*Amb.* 5, 1060A; in Louth, *MC*, 178–79).

42. Balthasar says: "Many of the descriptions that have been given [in the past] leave the impression that the debates about the being of Christ were simply a verbal joust—ghosts clanking their chains!—without vital implications for our own time.... I hope to convey a different impression. Much that Maximus said about the form of Christ seems all too abstract; other things seem inexact, and still others seem long since to have become common Christian parlance. Still, his synthetic thought, taken as a whole, remains a classic example of Christianity's lively struggle to give expression to the world's central mystery" (*CL*, 212).

43. Thunberg, *MM*, 30–31.

The Christological Basis of the Human Calling

> The two natures of Christ remain distinct and unmixed with one another. However, being united hypostatically without being transformed into one another, they permeate one another (περιχώρησις εἰς ἀλλήλας), according to St. Maximus who reproduces here, in the framework of the Christological dogma, the Eastern conception of energies or processions of the nature.[44]
>
> The humanity of Christ is a deified nature that is permeated by the divine energies from the moment of the Incarnation. St. Maximus uses here the example of iron penetrated by fire, becoming fire, though remaining iron by nature—an example which the Greek Fathers habitually use in expressing the state of deified nature. In each act of Christ one can see two distinct operations, for Christ acts in conformity to both His natures, and by both His natures—as the sword reddened by the fire cuts and burns at the same time: "as iron cuts, as fire it burns."[45]

When we consider *theosis*, the union between creature and Creator that is made possible through Christ's incarnation, the import of this doctrine will become even clearer.

A further feature of Maximus's teaching on *perichoresis* expresses a twofold idea. Maximus emphasizes, first, the "newness" of the redemptive union of Christ's human and divine natures, and, second, the idea that this union implies a genuine development of what is distinct to human nature. Thunberg and Balthasar suggest that this christological understanding, based upon the insights of Chalcedon, could be his most important contribution to theology. Thunberg says:

> In accordance with this double purpose [i.e., the "newness" and true development of the redemptive union of Christ's two natures] Maximus makes his most important contribution, not only by emphasizing the continuing difference between the two natures as well as the unity of the hypostasis, but above all by making the one aspect directly related to and dependent on one another. The union of the two natures is based on a certain *polarity* between them in virtue of the very fact that they are human and divine. Maximus obviously regards such a positive polarity as being the decisive insight of the Council of Chalcedon...[46]

---

44. Lossky, *Mystical Theology*, 145.

45. Ibid., 146; cf. Maximus, *Disputatio cum Pyrrho*, in *PG* 91, 337 C; *Amb.*, in *PG* 91, 1060 A.

46. Thunberg, *MM*, 31.

Balthasar concurs on the importance of Maximus's appropriation of Chalcedon's insights. Tying together Maximus's ideas on Christ's freedom, the divine-human synthesis that occurs in him, the synthesis based on the difference between God and humanity, Balthasar says:

> The person of the Redeemer is both the divine act of being and the unlimited personal freedom of the Son; both of them, as a unity, form the synthesis, and so both also give hypostatic form to the synthesis' human side, without being "confused" with it.[47]
>
> Maximus builds his whole doctrine of salvation, with great consistency, on the basis of his formal Christology. There the unconfused but continued existence of the two natures provided the foundation for the decisive synthesis . . . [he quotes Maximus:] "Precisely *because* Christ was the mediator between God and man, he had to preserve completely his natural kinship with the two poles he brings together, by being them both himself." . . . In the synthesis, the mutual difference of the poles is precisely what is underlined and confirmed.[48]

These Chalcedonian insights that Maximus applies, particularly this last one regarding the redemptive synthesis of human and divine in Christ that brings together polarities, lay the foundations for his teaching on deification. While the full discussion of deification occurs in the following chapters, it might be helpful at this point, before looking into Moltmann's christological basis for the human vocation, to briefly summarize the aspects of Maximus's Christology I have analyzed. First, I underscored the absolute centrality of Christ in Maximus's theological vision, then considered the incarnational context in which he conceptualizes the human vocation. I looked, finally, at how Maximus utilizes Chalcedonian terms to express the christological basis of the human calling. With these aspects of Maximus's Christology in mind, we now transition to Moltmann, whose Christology also structures and forms his conception of the human calling.

47. Balthasar, *CL*, 254.

48. Balthasar continues: "This does not imply any kind of natural communication between the two [divine and human poles]: 'nature and nature do not share a common nature' [Maximus states] . . . 'for it is only by denial of opposition, as some think, that a mediating position is affirmed.' In fact, what happened is something unexpected, yet perfectly logical: in the synthesis, the mutual difference of the poles is precisely what is underlined and confirmed. . . . It is only then, when God and man come closest to each other and meet in a single person that it becomes obvious before our very eyes that God is eternally, irreducibly other than man and that man may therefore not seek his salvation in a direction that implies abandonment of his own nature" (*CL*, 254–57).

The Christological Framework of Moltmann

Moltmann, though often using different language than Maximus, also constructs his understanding of the human calling based on a christological framework. In this section, I examine the aim of Moltmann's Christology, showing how his work proposes the development of a new paradigm for christological reflection. Moreover, I review some of the salient features of Moltmann's christological vision that will enable us to grasp his portrayal of the human calling.

The Christological Center

The first is what Moltmann scholar and New Testament theologian Richard Bauckham calls the "christological center" of Moltmann's work.[49] Pertaining to this, one of Moltmann's primary objectives in his Christology, particularly in *The Way of Jesus Christ*, is to propose the development of a new christological paradigm.[50] In *The Way of Jesus Christ*, Moltmann brings together many of the key christological insights laced through his other works, adding new light, and presenting a new synthesis. In his proposal toward a new model of doing Christology, Moltmann deeply engages what he thinks are two predominant christological paradigms of the past.[51] The first is what he terms "the cosmological paradigm of the patristic age," and the second is "the anthropological paradigm of the modern period." Moltmann argues that our postmodern context calls for a fresh christological paradigm. One main reason for this, Moltmann says, is because new questions about humanity and salvation have arisen. Therefore, within a changing milieu,

---

49. Bauckham, "Jürgen Moltmann," 157ff. I elaborate on this below.

50. Bauckham's chapter "Messianic Christology" has been helpful in locating and illuminating the aim, historical context, and main features of Moltmann's Christology (*TJM*, 199–212). This instructive chapter is the reworking of an article he published previously: "Moltmann's Messianic Christology," *Scottish Journal of Theology* 44 (1991) 519–31. What makes Bauckham's elucidation of Moltmann particularly valuable is his working knowledge of Moltmann's theological corpus and his willingness to critique him at several junctures. Consequently, I will reference a number of these insights and critiques throughout my analysis.

51. While I do not fully agree with this kind of "paradigmatic" thinking and evaluation on the whole, I do see how it can be used as a heuristic device for making some general observations regarding broader trends and themes. Perhaps this is what Moltmann intends. It seems that this is an example of the use of meta-narrative thinking and strategies that troubles Lewis Ayres, as I mentioned in the introduction.

where new anthropological, christological, and soteriological questions are emerging, the need for a new christological paradigm, a new synthesis, also surfaces.[52] As indicated above, Maximus is an excellent classical example of how one constructs a fresh christological synthesis that addresses contemporary issues, by appropriating and refining one's theological, philosophical, and spiritual sources. Moltmann's call for a new christological paradigm seeks to answer current christological (and anthropological and soteriological) questions based on a methodology that balances genuine Christian identity and contemporary relevance. Thus, Moltmann attempts to do this by addressing these themes of identity and relevance based on a hermeneutic of biblical origins and a hermeneutic of the modern/postmodern context, within which its answers must sufficiently address current questions with timely answers. Moltmann maintains that these concerns of Christian identity and contemporary relevance are intrinsically linked and must, therefore, lead to christological reflection that attends to both the biblical witness *and* the pressing issues of the current situation.[53]

Moltmann's quest to develop this new christological paradigm that mutually relates its biblical origins and its contemporary relevance, intends to take up the "strengths" of the cosmological and anthropological paradigms and form a more comprehensive one. Accordingly, Moltmann offers a constructive critique of the "cosmological christology of the patristic period." Within the largely cosmocentric view of reality, Moltmann says, one primary soteriological question concerned the transience of the finite and the eternity of the divine. In response, the church developed its Christology of two natures, explaining (as we saw with the Cappadocians) that God became human in order to divinize human nature and the whole cosmos.[54]

---

52. Maximus is a prime example of this, a theologian who crafted a fresh christological synthesis that integrated past insights with emerging christological, anthropological, and soteriological issues.

53. Below I consider how Moltmann builds on Bonhoeffer's questions and insights regarding the concerns of Christian identity and contemporary relevance. For example, in his discussion on Christology in the contradictions of scientific and technological civilization, Moltmann seeks to explore various fundamental problems in order "to align the soteriological aspect of christology towards the total misery of the present." He argues that every theology has to "enter into the changing conditions of the culture in which it is pursued, perceiving and developing its own concern in those conditions . . . [and] in this case our concern is christology." He highlights Bonhoeffer's question: "*Who really is Christ for us today?*" He also asks the related anthropological question: "Who really are we today?" (*WJC*, 63–64).

54. Regarding the knowledge of the humanity and divinity of Jesus Christ, Moltmann

The Christological Basis of the Human Calling

While Moltmann does critique this view's emphasis on the redemption of the physical and the accompanying doctrine of *theosis*,[55] he does include certain key elements of this "cosmological christology" within his proposal. Before looking at these elements, however, I would like to consider Moltmann's thoughts on *theosis*, primarily because Moltmann discusses it in the context of Christology.

To begin, it seems that Moltmann holds contradictory views on *theosis*. On one hand, he demonstrates deep appreciation for the doctrine of deification, employing the concept at various points.[56] To illustrate, in *The Trinity and the Kingdom*, Moltmann contemplates the inner links between creation, the Trinity and incarnation, and deification. He explains: "The creation of the world is nothing other than 'a history of the divine love between God and [God's] Other self.'" For this "means that God's love for the Son also potentially presupposes the Son's *incarnation*." Thus, the "incarnation of God's Son is not an answer to sin. It is the fulfillment of God's eternal longing to become man and to make of every man a god out of grace; an 'Other' to participate in the divine life and return the divine love."[57] Like-

---

reflects: We "have to look at Jesus' humanity in order to know his divinity, and we have to contemplate his divinity so as to know his humanity. Anyone who resolves this dialectical process of perception into dogmatic alternatives, is resolving—or dissolving—christology altogether. That person will end up with a theological christology without Jesus, or with an anthropological Jesuology without God" (*WJC*, 69). Moreover, Moltmann refers to Meyendorff's *Christ in Eastern Christian Thought* as he considers the development of "two-nature christology." While Moltmann mentions the considerable criticism lodged against two-nature Christology, especially by nineteenth-century liberal Protestant theologians, he says that one must "remember that it developed out of the dual New Testament definitions: crucified—raised; died—rose again; humiliated—exalted; past—present; and that it was in substance well able to retain the sense of these original definitions" (*WJC*, 48–49).

55. These various and contradictory views on *theosis* can be seen in *GC*, 228–29, *CG*, 272–74, *WJC*, 47.

56. In addition to the examples I give above, there are other places where Moltmann critically appropriates the concept of *theosis*. In *CG*, over the course of Moltmann's reflection on the doctrine of Christ's two natures, viewing the cross in Trinitarian terms, and understanding human history, he argues: "To think of 'God in history' always leads to theism and to atheism. To think of 'history in God' leads beyond that, into new creation and *theopoiesis* [i.e., *theosis*]. To think of 'history in God' however, first means to understand humanity in the suffering and dying of Christ, and that means all humanity, with its dilemmas and its despairs" (246–47).

57. Moltmann, *TK*, 46. Another example, where Moltmann blends critical appropriation and historical analysis, is in *WJC*, where he reflects on Teilhard de Chardin's ideas on *Christus evolutor*, cosmic eucharistization, and deification (294). As I demonstrate

wise, in his reflection on the Trinitarian doctrine of the kingdom (creation, liberation, glorification) and its relation to the incarnation, Moltmann says that through the divine energies of the Spirit, people become God's dwelling and home. "They participate in the new creation." The determinations of the history of God's kingdom—its creation by the Father, its liberation through the Son, and its glorification in the Spirit—"point towards the eschatological kingdom of glory in which people will finally, wholly and completely be gathered into the eternal life of the triune God and—as the early church put it—be 'deified' (θέωσις)."[58] Moreover, in *The Spirit of Life*, Moltmann discusses the overflowing, seeking love of God, and how "the passion history of Christ reveals the suffering of the passionate love of God." He goes on to say that "God's suffering history in Christ's passion serves the history of God's joy in the Spirit over the homecoming of human beings and all other creatures into the kingdom of God." He references Athanasius, explaining that "Athanasius summed this up in a statement which was accepted as authoritative in the patristic church: 'God became human so that human beings should be deified.'"[59] And, in his eschatological study, *The Coming of God*, Moltmann considers the cosmic significance and linking of Christ's death and resurrection with the salvation of sinners and the transfiguration of the body and of the earth. He reflects: "The new creation will not only manifest the liberty of the children of God. It will also bring 'the deification of the cosmos' through the unhindered participation of all created beings in the livingness of God."[60] Here as well as other places in *The Coming of God*, Moltmann references Stăniloae, who says: "The world as the work of God's love, is destined to be deified."[61] These are just a few examples of Moltmann's appropriation of *theosis*.

---

in various places when considering Maximus's *Mystagogy*, similar ideas emerge when Maximus reflects on the liturgy, the "mystery that is accomplished on the divine altar," and the eucharistization and transfiguration of humanity and the cosmos.

58. Moltmann, *TK*, 212ff. Furthermore, in *GC*, where Moltmann considers the messianic calling of human beings to be conformed to the likeness of Jesus the Messiah, Moltmann speaks of the "eschatological becoming-one-with-God of human beings (*theosis*) is inherent in the concept of 'seeing,' for the seeing face to face and the seeing him as he is transforms the seer into the One seen and allows him to participate in the divine life and beauty" (*GC*, 229).

59. Moltmann, *SL*, 299; from Athanasius, *De incarnatione*, cap. 54.

60. Moltmann, *CG*, 92.

61. Moltmann, *CG*, 375n18; from Stăniloae, *Orthodox Dogmatik* I, 293ff.

The Christological Basis of the Human Calling

At other junctures, Moltmann simply reports the historical development of the doctrine of *theosis*, without approving or disapproving it. In *The Way of Jesus Christ*, Moltmann merely traces the connections between cosmological Christology and *theosis*. He explains the growth of ideas regarding human participation in and correspondence to the divine glory, saying that human participation in the glory of the divine being entails receiving a life which knows no death but is unfading and immortal. Furthermore, it is not only human beings which undergo this participation and correspondence to the divine glory, but "the whole cosmos will be drawn into the glory with him." For the "Fathers of the church saw this all-embracing goal of salvation as 'the deification of the human being' and 'the deification of creation.'"[62] Thus, Moltmann is objectively sketching the development of the doctrine.

Finally, in other places, Moltmann offers a robust critique of *theosis*. It is in *The Coming of God* where Moltmann most fully develops his "critical evaluation of the Orthodox idea about deification." He suggests that the idea of the hypostatic unity of nature and person offers a solution for the tendency in modern thinking to divide the person as subject and nature as object. For whatever "happens to the person touches nature too; whatever redeems the person, also redeems nature. Any redemption of human beings without the redemption of cosmic nature is therefore inconceivable."[63] But

> the deification of the cosmos is not thought of as being a new creation of heaven and earth. It is seen as a spiritualization of the cosmos and its interpenetration by the radiance of the Spirit. That lends an element of docetism to the doctrine of cosmic deification held by the Orthodox churches, and to their spirituality. But is the "completely spiritualized world" brought about through the union of human beings with God already "the new earth" and the new bodiliness of God's Shekinah?[64]

---

62. Moltmann, *WJC*, 47. As in other places, here Moltmann references Stăniloae (see 348n14). See Moltmann's further comments on the famous axiom of Athanasius, "God became human so that human beings might be deified" (*CG*, 272). Moltmann turns, again, to Stăniloae's remarks concerning *theosis*, where the Romanian theologian asserts that the maximal union with God [of which deification speaks], "in which the person is interpenetrated by God's fullness without being absorbed into it, means at the same time the deification of the human being" (376n35; from Stăniloae, *Orthodox Dogmatik* I, 359).

63. Moltmann, *CoG*, 274.

64. Ibid.; cf. Janet Williams's comments regarding deification and humanization. Williams argues, essentially, that some commentators see deification as the central theme of Maximus's theology, a view that neglects the double aspect of the Incarnation. She

All Things New

Stemming from this critical analysis, Moltmann proceeds to explore Lutheran, Orthodox, and Calvinist ideas about the end of the world, how these traditions emphasize different points within the christological framework of Christ's death and resurrection, and the ramifications for anthropology. Again, briefly touching on these points is important for understanding how Moltmann's anthropology is formed by his christological thinking. It will also lay further groundwork for the following two chapters.

In short, Moltmann argues that the Lutheran doctrine of the world's annihilation seems to have as its premise a one-sided theology of the cross, whereas the Orthdox doctrine of deification is consistent with a one-sided theology of the resurrection. The Calvinist theory of transformation, Moltmann proposes, could "be the mediation between perspectives directed severally towards the end of 'this world,' and the genesis of a 'new world' that will accord with God and thus be deified."[65] As Moltmann explains, however, Calvinist theology has not attained the depths of the Lutheran theology of the cross, as well as the heights of the Orthodox theology of deification. Consequently, Moltmann argues that the ideas of reduction to nothingness (*reductio in nihilum*) and the elevation to God (*elevatio ad Deum*), belong together, balance one another, and are mutually complementary.[66] Therefore, in his treatment of *theosis*—its appropriation, historical development, and critique—Moltmann offers intriguing insights that will illumine my later discussion on *theosis* in Maximus.

Turning back to what I was considering before these thoughts on *theosis*, I continue by showing how Moltmann includes elements of cosmological Christology in his proposal. For example, Moltmann's Christology addresses the ancient soteriological question of transience and death with his cross/resurrection dialectic, underscoring how how Christ's death and

---

proposes that it is more accurate to say that humanization *and* deification together are the central theme in Maximus's Chalcedonian understanding of Christ, a notion that resonates with Moltmann's critique of deification (Williams, "Pseudo-Dionysius," 194).

65. Moltmann, *CoG*, 274. See also Moltmann's related commentary on medieval mysticism, divinization, and Luther's perspective: "Whereas medieval mysticism understood the way of suffering and the *meditatio crucis* as a way to the divinization of man by means of the *via negationis*, Luther reverses this approach and sees in the cross God's descent to the level of our sinful nature and our death, not so that man is divinized, but so that he is de-divinized and given new humanity in the community of the crucified Christ" (*CG*, 213).

66. Moltmann, *CoG*, 274. While some might think that these observations are "generalizations" that lack nuance, they seem to be helpful, heuristic foci for developing a constructive perspective on *theosis*.

resurrection destroys death (1 Cor 15:54–56),[67] ushers in the new creation when the triune God indwells all of creation. Throughout Moltmann's work, he is careful to glean and emphasize the high value placed on physical and material redemption found in the patristic period, in such thinkers as Maximus. This high regard for physical creation, as evinced in his appropriation of Orthodox creation theologies, plays a vital role in his various books, including his ecological doctrine of creation which flows from his Trinitarian and christological reflection. The way Moltmann draws from Orthodox creation wisdom profoundly influences his understanding of the human calling in creation.

In addition to Moltmann's constructive critique of the "cosmological christology of the patristic period," is his evaluation of the "anthropological christology of the modern period." Once more, it is important to point out elements of these basic evaluations because they set up Moltmann's own christological proposal, which in turn, gives rise to his theological anthropology. In short, Moltmann suggests that the emphasis on human subjectivity and detachment of human beings from nature, fomented soteriological questions dealing less with the divinization of human beings (as in the cosmological Christology of the patristic period) and more with their humanization and full realization. Consequently, notions of metaphysical incarnation were considered outdated, and modern Christology shifted its focus to the human "historical Jesus" who served as the model for true humanity.

In an insightful analysis of the development of this anthropological Christology, Moltmann discusses such figures as Melanchthon, Kant, Schleiermacher, and Rahner.[68] He asserts that, in spite of certain positive outcomes of the modern turn to the subject, the anthropological Christology (or "modern Jesuology") falls short in its attempt to answer christological and soteriological questions. Modern Christology, moreover, only exacerbates modern humanity's sense of dislocation and identity crisis by seeking a salvation that is localized in the human heart and expressed in language centered on an individual's "existence," subjectivity, and inner self-transcendence. Moltmann argues that this emphasis on the inward,

---

67. "When this perishable body puts on imperishability, and this mortal body puts on immortality, then the saying that is written will be fulfilled: 'Death has been swallowed up in victory.' 'Where, O death, is your victory? Where, O death, is your sting?' The sting of death is sin, and the power of sin is the law" (1 Cor 15:54–56).

68. Moltmann, *WJC*, 63ff.; cf. Moltmann's earlier reflections on Kant and Schleiermacher's Christology and the ramifications for anthropology, *CG*, 92–98.

individual self has neglected the external conditions and connections to society. He explains:

> This relegation of salvation to the inward realm of "the heart" (and its presupposition in modern Jesuology) finds its sociological equivalent in the privatization of religion: "religion is a private affair." This theology fits without any conflict into the requirements of the "civil religion" of modern society. As the "civil religion" of that society, it ministers to its educated and ruling classes, but not to its victims. Schleiermacher proclaimed the gospel of Christ to the "cultured among Christianity's despisers," but not to "poor sinners," remarked the poet Immermann, after hearing him preach.[69]

This critique plays an important part in Moltmann's own construction of theological anthropology. Based on his constructive critiques of the cosmological and anthropological paradigms of Christology, Moltmann seeks a new paradigm, a synthesis that critically retrieves vital elements of each previous paradigm. As indicated above, Moltmann aims to construct a Christology that finds "its authentic Christian identity in a hermeneutic of biblical origins and its contemporary relevance in a hermeneutic of its biblical origins to which it must prove soteriologically relevant."[70] In the remainder of this section, I intend to examine notable features of Moltmann's Christology and how they shape and inform his anthropology.

The first feature, already referenced in the previous paragraphs, is the "christological center" of Moltmann's entire project.[71] Like Maximus, Moltmann asserts that Christ is the foundation, mediator, and goal of the whole creation.[72] Yet this christological focus must be expanded, Moltmann

---

69. Moltmann, *WJC*, 63; cf. Moltmann's other analysis of Schleiermacher, where he discusses the development of a Christology of the personal relationship of faith to Jesus, Christ's essential sinlessness, and the redeeming effect of Christ's archetypal God-consciousness (i.e., how he draws believers into the constant potency of his own consciousness of God). In the face of Schleiermacher's reasonings, Moltmann called for a reorientation of Christology that grapples with the crucifixion, and the profound implications for soteriology and anthropology (*CG*, 94–98).

70. Bauckham, *TJM*, 200.

71. Bauckham, "Jürgen Moltmann," 157ff.; cf. Müller-Fahrenholz, *Kingdom and the Power*, 31.

72. Moltmann, *TK*, 102. Moltmann calls for Protestant theology's "christological concentration" to be matched by an extension of theology's horizon to cosmic breadth (*GC*, xiv). McIntosh points out, in conversation with James Alison, the implications of understanding creation through the lens of Christ's dying and rising: how creation comes from God, how it realizes its true destiny, and how we are intended to live in this world so

The Christological Basis of the Human Calling

contends. He explains: "The salutary 'christological concentration' in Protestant theology . . . must be matched today by an extension of theology's horizon to cosmic breadth, so that it takes in the whole of God's creation."[73] This extension of theology's horizon encompasses his theological anthropology. Thus, the christological basis, along with a cosmic perspective leads Moltmann to emphasize a holistic understanding of the human vocation. According to Moltmann, the human calling is realized through active discipleship, extending the fellowship of Christ's church to all people, and ethical living as stewards of God's creation.

Moltmann says, further, that his proposal for a new christological synthesis attempts to place this christocentric focus into a wider Trinitarian framework.[74] Therefore, in support of my overall argument, one discerns in Moltmann a christological center, placed in a wider Trinitarian framework, enabling him to construct a theological anthropology based on this Trinitarian-christocentric vision of all things. This interweaving of christological, Trinitarian, anthropological, soteriological, and cosmological threads also reinforces why reading Maximus and Moltmann alongside one another mutually illuminates each theologian's work and sheds more light on the idea of the human calling in creation.

Another aspect of the christological center in Moltmann's theology and anthropology, concerns the way he builds on his earlier Christology, with its cross and resurrection dialectic and its emphasis on the Old Testament/Jewish framework. In line with his objective (in *The Way of Jesus Christ*) to retrace Christology to its biblical origins, and from there reconstruct it, Moltmann offers fresh treatment of the Old Testament messianic hope. In conversation with Christian Old Testament scholarship and contemporary Jewish theologians, Moltmann develops an eschatological Christology in continuity with the Old Testament history of messianic promise.

The metaphor of "the way" he employs in his Christology illustrates this Old Testament notion of "the coming One," who fulfills God's redemptive purposes for humanity and all of creation. It also conveys the

---

as to participate in bringing it to fulfillment in the new creation (*DT*, 184).

73. Moltmann, *GC*, xiv.

74. Moltmann, *SL*, x. Regarding this expansion of Moltmann's Christology, Bauckham comments: "In *The Way of Jesus Christ*, Moltmann returned to Christology, which had been at the centre of his early work, but was now able to develop a much more comprehensive Christology. The dialectic of cross and resurrection, interpreted in eschatological perspective and trinitarian context, is retained from the early work" (*TJM*, 19–20).

provisional nature of every Christology and the narrative dimension of Christology's subject, Jesus Christ as he is portrayed in Scripture.[75] The way that Moltmann expands his eschatological Christology into a more distinctively messianic form will help us better understand the graced role that humanity in Christ is allowed to play in the divine restoration of the world, a world that is to viewed in light of its messianic future in Christ.[76]

The Earthly Life and Ministry of Jesus

Another feature of Moltmann's Christology that is important for grasping his christologically-based anthropology, is the way that he pays particular attention to *the earthly life and ministry of Jesus*. There are two ramifications of this perspective. One is Moltmann's development of a "Spirit Christology," in which he accentuates the presence and power of the Holy Spirit in the life and ministry of Jesus. For Moltmann, Spirit Christology is not a replacement of nor an alternative to incarnation Christology, nor does it lead to a degree Christology, as Bauckham rightly argues.[77] Moltmann's attention to the pneumatological themes within Christology has significant repercussions for the human vocation. For example, the Spirit-empowered messianic mission of Jesus (Luke 4:18–19),[78] according to Moltmann, forms the mission of his followers (Matt 10:7–8),[79] so that the "church participates

---

75. See Bauckham, *TJM*, 205ff.

76. See Vanhoozer, "Theology and the Condition of Postmodernity," in *Cambridge Companion*, 16ff.; cf. Moltmann, "Jesus between Jews and Christians," 63ff.; cf. Norris, *Christological Controversy*, 2.

77. Bauckham, *TJM*, 207. Regarding degree Christology, that he alleges is found in Rahner's theology, Paul D. Molnar writes: "Degree Christology . . . is distinguished by the view that Jesus is different from us not in kind but in the degree of self-transcendence which he experienced in his life and this view results from Rahner's attempt to reconcile traditional Christology with what he calls an evolutionary view of the world in his 'neo-Chalcedonian' Christology. Rahner certainly attempts to uphold Jesus' uniqueness in kind by stressing that he also is different from us as the Logos or Word. But even his explanation of that difference . . . does not convincingly overcome the appearance that Rahner has fallen prey to a type of degree Christology by conceiving Jesus as a uniquely divinized human being. This issue . . . leads him and a number of his followers to equate Jesus' divinity with his humanity" (*Incarnation and Resurrection*, 69).

78. "The Spirit of the Lord is upon me, because he has anointed me to bring good news to the poor. He has sent me to proclaim release to the captives and recovery of sight to the blind, to let the oppressed go free, to proclaim the year of the Lord's favor" (Luke 4:18–19).

79. "As you go, proclaim the good news, 'The kingdom of heaven has come near.'

in Christ's messianic mission." What's more, as we find in Maximus's christologically-grounded vision of the human calling, Moltmann discusses the notion that the church is the continuation of the incarnation of the divine Logos as it is indwelt by the Spirit.[80]

A second consequence of Moltmann's attention to the earthly life of Jesus in his Christology, is his discussion of the ethical way of life that Jesus taught and modeled for his disciples. Moltmann contends that Christology and christopraxis are to be done together, so that Christ's disciples, those who "follow him on the way," embody and manifest the fruits of the redemptive kingdom of God that has broken into human history. Moltmann's attention to Jesus' ethical teaching and action generates a vision for the Christian community. This vision for christopraxis that emerges from and interacts with christological reflection, corrects aberrant notions of praxis as a kind of moralism that lacks anchoring in Christian discipleship. Moreover, Moltmann's ethical vision, based as it is on the biblical account of Christ's person and mission, offers an alternative program for social and ecological reform. In response to the violence and injustice that run rampant in today's world, Moltmann articulates a vision for the Christian community, one that calls for Christ's followers to embody and manifest the compassion and justice of the triune God through non-violent action and creative love.[81]

A Holistic Christology

A further feature of Moltmann's Christology that informs and shapes his anthropology is its *holistic emphasis*. Moltmann's christologically-based

---

Cure the sick, raise the dead, cleanse the lepers, cast out demons. You received without payment; give without payment" (Matt 10:7–8).

80. Moltmann, *CPS*, 76, 73, 65. Moltmann does say, however, that the doctrine of *Christus prolongatus* must be carefully nuanced so that Christ's freedom with regard to his church is not blurred. Furthermore, Christology and pneumatology must be integrated within a balanced Trinitarian perspective (73).

81. Moltmann, *WJC*, 72; cf. Bauckham, *TJM*, 209. Müller-Fahrenholz, in his broader discussion of the links between Christology, ethics, and the church's mission, points to an earlier, lesser known text in which Moltmann says: "The Son of Man . . . transcends other human beings by understanding himself in the sickness and transgressions of the inhuman. He is the Son of Man in that he accepts the lost and the untouchables. . . . His rule has nothing to do with the nature of the world ruler. It consists in the reversal of rule to become service, of power to become love, and of demands to become vicarious suffering" ("*Mensch,*" 11; in *KP*, 115).

anthropology attempts to counter trends of Cartesian dualism, especially within his own Protestant German Reformed tradition. What he proposes as a counter-argument and remedy to such dualistic tendencies is a critical retrieval of biblical and patristic concepts that stress a holistic perspective on Christ and how humanity is saved and transformed in Christ.

This holistic understanding of humanity and the world renewed in Christ, is a key motif in Maximus as well, as Keselopoulos and Ware assert.[82] In his proposal toward a more holistic Christology and anthropology, Moltmann begins with a succinct analysis of dualistic developments and trends in Western thought. In short, Moltmann examines how the patristic church ran counter to particular Platonic influences that attempted to subsume biblical accounts of Christ and salvation, namely the liberation of the soul from the body. I will amplify this idea below. Next, Moltmann reviews medieval theology and the way that the Aristotelian notion of how the body is formed by the soul shaped medieval anthropology. Moltmann then explores how modern European anthropology is governed by the idea that the conscious mind exerts its power over the instrument of the body, following the trajectory set by Descartes and La Mettrie.[83] Moltmann goes on to critique, in greater detail, the notion of the primacy of the soul in Plato, Descartes's ideas on the mechanistic body, and Karl Barth's teaching on "the ministering body of a ruling soul."[84]

---

82. See Keselopoulos, *Man and the Environment*, 163; and Ware, *Orthodox Church*, 232. Moltmann references Maximus (this very text) on the holistic understanding of Christ and redemption: see *SL*, 94, where Moltmann comments on Maximus and Gregory Palamas: Countering Platonic and gnostic tendencies, and building on Paul's insistence of the resurrection of the body, Maximus asserts that "'by nature man remains wholly human in soul and body, but by grace he becomes wholly God both in his soul and in his body' . . . [and] according to the Orthodoxy mysticism of Gregory Palamas—the light that shone on Tabor transfigured Jesus' body and his clothing as well as his soul, and was a visble anticipation of the 'transfigured body' of the risen Christ, to which our bodies are to be conformed (Phil. 3:21)."

83. Moltmann, *GC*, 245ff. See Sherrard's trenchant analysis, where he discusses the roles of thinkers such as Hobbes, Descartes, Kant, and La Mettrie in the development of modern anthropology and cosmology, "Fetish of Mathematics and the Iconoclasm of Modern Science," in *Human Image*, 41ff.

84. Moltmann, *GC*, 247–55. Moltmann does appreciate the way that Barth counters certain Platonic and Cartesian trends through his exposition of anthropology centered on the human being Jesus Christ and the experience of God's Spirit. However, Moltmann offers an insightful critique of Barth's emphasis on sovereignty and how this shapes his entire theology, cosmology, and anthropology. Thus, as God rules over creation, and man rules over woman and the earth, human beings are to rule over their bodies, without any notion of harmony or reciprocity (252–54).

In response to these influences and trends, Moltmann proposes a retrieval of biblical and patristic anthropology that is rooted in Christology, sources that stress the holistic dimension of creation and life in Christ. In an intriguing move, Moltmann uses German mystic Friedrich Oetinger's (1702–1782) thesis that "embodiment is the end of all God's works," to set the course for his exposition of a christologically-grounded anthropology. Put concisely, Moltmann's holistic alternative asserts that according to the biblical traditions and patristic doctrine, embodiment is the end of God's work in *creation*. Stemming from thoughts on Genesis 1:28, Moltmann says that what makes men and women God's image on earth is not their spiritual existence, but their whole and particular bodily existence.[85]

Further, Moltmann explains that embodiment is also the end of God's work in *reconciliation*. Based on the theology flowing out of the Gospel of John's statement—"The Word became flesh . . ." (1:14)—Moltmann asserts that it is in Christ's bodily form that God brings about the reconciliation of the world (Rom 8:3).[86] It is through Christ's incarnation, death on the cross, and bodily resurrection that human beings are reconciled with God.

Finally, Moltmann's holistic treatment of Christology and anthropology states that embodiment is the end of the *redemption* of the world. As Moltmann explains, "the new earth" completes God's redemptive activity (Rev 21). The new "transfigured" embodiment of humanity is the fulfillment of the Spirit's yearning within creation (Rom 8). Moltmann says:

> That is why the patristic church ran counter to the general Platonic trend of its cultural environment which I have already mentioned, and introduced into the Apostles' Creed: I believe in "resurrection of the body and a life everlasting." Redemption begins with the gift of the Spirit and ends with the transfiguration of the body. It begins with the new righteousness "of the heart" and ends in the new, just and righteous world. It begins in faith and ends in the new, sensory experience of God which is called "seeing."[87]

---

85. Moltmann, *GC*, 245; cf. Johnson's incisive discussion regarding living bodily, community and connectedness, and the image of God in human beings, *She Who Is*, 68ff.

86. "For God has done what the law, weakened by the flesh, could not do: by sending his own Son in the likeness of sinful flesh, and to deal with sin, he condemned sin in the flesh" (Rom 8:3).

87. Moltmann, *GC*, 246. See Moltmann's comments in *CoG*, 65–67, where he asserts that the resurrection of the body is not to be reduced to "a life after death," but is to be understood as an event that belongs to the whole of life. Hope for the resurrection of the body "permits no disdain and debasement of bodily life and sensory experiences; it affirms them profoundly, and gives greatest honour to 'the flesh,' which people have made

Thus, one recognizes how Moltmann's proposal brings together various threads seen in both his and Maximus's understanding of the human calling and how it is established on christological grounds. It is the embodied, incarnate Word who brings the hope of salvation and bodily resurrection to the church, a salvation that ultimately transfigures all of creation in the Spirit.

In the christologically-structured vision that he presents, as an alternative to ancient and modern dualistic tendencies, Moltmann's holistic understanding of Christ, salvation, and anthropology resonates with Maximus's own vision. In addition to themes in the biblical and patristic traditions that inform Maximus and Moltmann's holistic Christology—including those expounded by Origen, Athanasius, Irenaeus, and Basil—is an interesting parallel worth mentioning. In Maximus's holistic vision, unity in diversity is based upon and proceeds from the hypostatic union in Christ. Humanity's reunification with the Trinity and with one another occurs in such a way that safeguards the differentiated characteristics of the individual, as we saw in the *Mystagogy*.

Likewise, Moltmann's holistic Christology emphasizes that reconciliation and redemption, cooperative works of the Father, through the Son, by the Spirit, reunite humanity with God, with one another, and with all creation, in a manner that preserves differentiation. Moltmann explains that "we theologically understand being human" as part of God's history with the world. "What is human is not revealed in isolation from the history of God and the encirclement of his Spirit; it is manifested through *integration*, and through *differentiated correspondences* to these things [God's creative, reconciling, and redemptive activity in Christ]."[88] The way that Maximus and Moltmann stress the integration of creatures with God and one another, while preserving their differences, is a recurring theme in their Trinitarian and christologically-based visions of renewal in Christ.[89]

---

something to be despised" (cf. 1 Cor 15:42–44).

88. Moltmann, *GC*, 246ff., italics mine.

89. Balthasar regularly points this out in his study of Maximus, suggesting that the idea of the balance and reciprocity of universal and particular is among the most important contributions of Maximus's theology. He cites a key text in *QT*: "In his providence . . . God brings about an increasing similarity between the individual and the universal, until finally he identifies the self-expressive drive of the person with the general law of intellectual being as such, by means of the instinctive drive of each individual drives into harmony and unity of motion both with each other and with the all, because their personal efforts are no longer focused on particular interests that separate them from the whole but are now found as the realization of a single idea in all of them" (*QT*

The Christological Basis of the Human Calling

Another issue related to Moltmann's proposal for holistic Christology and anthropology concerns the perilous situation of life on our planet. Moltmann contends that this holistic Christology is particularly necessary for the present situation of life on our planet, one that lives under the real threat of nuclear annihilation and ecological destruction. The "crisis of life on this planet," Moltmann argues, "is so comprehensive and so irreversible that it can not unjustly be described as apocalyptic."[90] Within this apocalyptically understood context, Moltmann seeks "to open up new dimensions of the eschatological dialectic of the cross and the resurrection." Through "his cross, Jesus enters and suffers vicariously the end-time sufferings that threaten the whole creation. He identifies with dying nature as well as with abandoned humans." Christ, moreover, undergoes "the birth pangs of the new creation, and his resurrection is the eschatological springtime of all nature."[91]

Once again, this holistic understanding of Christ's earthly life, suffering and death on the cross, and life-giving resurrection structures Moltmann's view of what it means to be human, and how women and men in Christ are called to bring healing and hope to a world threatened by such destruction. As I have sought to demonstrate repeatedly in Maximus and Moltmann, christological reflection undergirds, envisions, and propels the Christian community to mediate God's redemptive love to all creatures.

A Developing Christology

This brings us to one final feature of Moltmann's christological framework upon which he structures the human vocation, that it is a *developing Christology*. While I have already touched on this to some degree, I think it is important to fill out a few more details that will shed light on the following

---

2; CCG 7, 51, 12–19; *PG* 90, 272AB; in *CL*, 161).

90. Moltmann, *GC*, xiiiff.; cf. Moltmann, "Ecological Crisis," 5–18. See also Sherrard's bracing analysis in the opening pages of *Human Image*, where he argues that the real answer to the current ecological crisis is to recover our true identity and dignity, our self-image as sacred beings, and a sense of the holiness of the world. This recovery, he argues, leads to an awakening of the true destiny of humanity and creation (8–10). Like Moltmann, Sherrard sees the importance of a holistic understanding of Christology and anthropology if these very real threats of destruction are to be overcome.

91. Bauckham, "Jürgen Moltmann," 158. See *WJC*, where Moltmann spells this out (xvff.), as well as the overall structure of his Christology, based on the messianic mission of Christ, the apocalyptic sufferings of Christ, and the eschatological resurrection of Christ, the cosmic Christ, and the parousia of Christ (vii-xi).

chapters. As noted above, Moltmann intends to inspire fresh christological reflection through a new synthesis, one that reinvigorates, expands, and realigns christological teaching of the past.[92] Moltmann is concerned with developing a Christology for the modern/postmodern world.

Stemming from Bonhoeffer's formulation, as noted above, Moltmann asks: "Who really is Christ for us today? And who really are we today?"[93] This probing spirit is what leads Moltmann to call for fresh christological thinking in an effort to construct a "christology in the contradictions of scientific and technological civilization."[94] Moltmann is not content to simply restate christological formulations from the past. He subscribes to the church's creeds, often working through them and relying on their assertions in his christological reflections, yet he searches for new ways to converse with and apply the creedal statements in the contemporary context.

Further, Moltmann offers careful readings and constructive critiques of the two significant christological paradigms: the cosmological Christology of the patristic church and modern anthropological Christology. He is very appreciative of the cosmological Christology of the ancients, as evidenced in his ongoing engagement of Orthodox theology, including Irenaeus, Origen, Basil, Athanasius, John Chrysostom, Gregory of Nazianzus, Gregory of Nyssa, and Maximus, to name a few.[95] Yet Moltmann does raise specific questions regarding particular developments in the tradition. An example of this is Moltmann's analysis of the shift in Christology from Christ's cross and resurrection to the incarnation and birth of Christ as the divine human being, something that he finds rather puzzling.[96]

---

92. Bauckham, *TJM*, 199. See Nichols's insightful commentary on Pierre Piret's exposition of the various ways that Maximus exemplifies this integrative approach to Christology, one that synthesizes, expands, and refines the christological thinking of his predecessors, "Pierre Piret on the Trinity," in *Byzantine Gospel*, 64–110.

93. Moltmann, *WJC*, 64.

94. Ibid., 63.

95. A few examples of his reflections on Orthodox Christology are found in *WJC*. These include his thinking on the resurrection of Christ, nature, and the new creation in the Orthodox Easter Liturgy, and the cosmic bond between Christ's resurrection and the new creation in Gregory of Nyssa's interpretation of Holy Saturday, *De tridua inter mortem et resurrectionem Domini nostri Jesus Christi spatio*, opera 9, ed. Gebhardt, *Sermones* 1, 274, in *WJC*, 252–54. Moltmann consistently looks to Orthodox theology for inspiration and insights. He finds in these "earliest traditions of Christian theology" some of "the most pregnant ideas" for revolution in our thinking and actions (*GC*, xv).

96. *WJC*, 49. See Moltmann's reflections on the shift of center from Easter to Christmas. He explains that a "christology which traces the path from Christ's death on the

The Christological Basis of the Human Calling

As we have seen, this appreciation for and appropriation of Orthodox theology has notably influenced Moltmann's Trinitarian and christological constructions, as well as his theological anthropology. Moreover, Moltmann critiques what he thinks are weaknesses in modern anthropological Christology, especially its dissolving of Christ into a mere human teacher of ethics, its relegation of salvation to an inward and individualistic affair, and its lack of attention to the poor and victimized.

In dialectical fashion, Moltmann intends to provoke new christological reflection that is informed by the past, but seeks to address current questions and issues. Thus, it is a *developing* Christology that "implies the transition from the metaphysical christology of the 'ancients' to the historical christological of modern times," which "places human history ecologically in the framework of nature." Moltmann notes that modern "historical thinking" shoved aside the ancient "metaphysical thinking." But, he asserts that "newer thinking takes up the old metaphysical thinking again, under the conditions of 'historical thinking,' and in a cosmological perspective." For a "transition does not have to be a breach. Transitions can also place traditions within wider horizons, and preserve older perceptions by translating them into new situations." Where "modern historical thinking set human history over against a nature without history," newer thinking "integrates human history in the natural conditions in which it is embedded."[97] This dialectical thinking is crucial in Moltmann's developing Christology, as well as his theological anthropology which springs out of his Christology.

Again, his effort to construct a developing Christology is a primary reason for employing "the way" metaphor that sets the tone for his Christology. This "transitional christology" that constructively critiques and builds on the past, symbolizes: the idea of "process," that Christology is aligned toward the eschatological goal of Christ's parousia; the notion that every human Christology is historically limited and conditioned; and that "the way of Jesus Christ" is not merely a christological category, but an ethical category, a call to both believe in and follow Christ.[98] This linking of dog-

---

cross to his resurrection presents a kind of '*ascendence*' christology, from below upwards; whereas every incarnation christology pursues the path of the eternal Son of God from above downwards, and is a '*descendence*' christology." He adds that this reversal of perspective began early, as evidenced in the hymn about Christ in Phil 2:5–11, 49.

97. Moltmann, *WJC*, xvi. Moltmann acknowledges that his christological thinking, particularly this aspect of embodiment, has been enriched by certain feminist theologians, especially his wife, Elisabeth Moltmann-Wendel.

98. Moltmann, *WJC*, xiv.

matics and ethics, or Christology and christopraxis, becomes an important filament in Moltmann's work. As in Maximus, the context and role of the church is crucial in properly understanding Christ, following him on his way, and serving as his redemptive emissaries in the world. We will look more closely (in the next two chapters) at the ecclesial dimension of the spiritual life, discipleship, and the Christian community's part in mediating the redemptive love of Christ. Because, for both Maximus and Moltmann, the human vocation is worked out and realized within the context of the Body of Christ.

Finally, this developing Christology seeks to take into account the dynamic nature of Christ, viewing him on the way to his goal. Thus, for Moltmann this means constructing a Christology against the horizon of eschatology. As noted above, Moltmann pays careful attention to the earthly life of Jesus Christ. What I did not mention is how he roots his entire christological work in the unfolding of the dynamic events of Christ's life. As Moltmann says, this portrayal envisions Christ in the movement of God's eschatological history.[99] Bauckhum points out that Moltmann's *The Way of Jesus Christ* is organized not as a discussion of the humanity and divinity of Christ, as some are. Rather, after the two preliminary chapters on the messianic perspective and various trends and transmutations in Christology, it is organized as five chapters on the five stages of Jesus' way: his earthly mission, his cross, his resurrection, his present cosmic role, and his parousia.[100]

Therefore, to summarize my argument in this chapter, I have attempted to demonstrate the christological basis of the human vocation, pointing out correlations and distinctives between these two theologians. For Maximus, the christological basis entails a portrayal of the human calling that emphasizes the absolute centrality of Christ, an incarnational context, and thinking shaped by Chalcedonian Christology. According to Moltmann, the christological basis of the human vocation involves a christological center that is attentive to Christ's earthly life, as well as holistic, cosmic, and dynamic elements, and the connection between Christology and christopraxis. Having considered the christological foundations of their anthropology, we proceed to investigate the redemptive goal of the human calling.

---

99. Moltmann, *WJC*, 33.

100. Bauckham, *TJM*, 205; cf. Müller-Fahrenholz's analysis on these elements within Moltmann's Christology, and the consequences of this for his anthropology, *KP*, 173ff.

4

The Redemptive Goal of the Human Calling

SO FAR I HAVE SOUGHT TO DEMONSTRATE SPECIFIC WAYS THAT MAXIMUS and Moltmann's Trinitarian and christological reflection shapes their understanding of the human person and calling. We have looked at ways that their theological anthropology is developed within a Trinitarian matrix, as well as how it springs out of their Christology. In this chapter, I intend to explore the redemptive goal of the human calling. That is, since humanity is created in the image of the triune God, is made new through faith in Christ, and is called to cooperate with God in the renewal of creation, we consider the question: What is the salvific objective for humanity and the cosmos? How do Maximus and Moltmann envision the Trinitarian and christological shaped design for creation? And how does each theologian portray the human calling in an eschatological orientation?

I have chosen to consider the redemptive goal of the human vocation *before* the practices so as to give a preview of the end result. This will serve as a preview that, I think, will make better sense of the actual theologically grounded practices (in the next chapter) that seek to work toward that end.

In both Maximus and Moltmann's visions of the human vocation, there is an eschatological alignment, a dimension in which anthropology and soteriology are portrayed in eschatological terms. In the following chapter, I begin by analyzing the biblical and patristic background of *theosis* in Maximus, the primary image he uses to speak about the redemptive goal of humanity and the world. Then, I consider Maximus's appropriation of *theosis*, pointing out certain adjustments and contributions he makes to the tradition that utilizes this concept. As an example, I take a closer look at Maximus's *Fourth Century on Love*, a text that illustrates Maximus's understanding of *theosis* and its intrinsic connections to Trinitarian and christological reflection. Next, I probe the notion of adumbrations of the Trinity in humanity, and touch on the concept of eschatological rest, a metaphor taken up by Moltmann, as I will explain in the following sections.

Theosis in Maximus

Background

An exploration of Maximus's teaching on *theosis* further reinforces my overall claim—that his understanding of the human person emerges from his Trinitarian and christological reflection. Moreover, though Maximus and Moltmann come from distinct backgrounds and have irreducible differences, I am demonstrating points of correlation between their visions of the human calling. One of these significant points of correlation is found in their teaching on the redemptive goal of the human calling. While I began to discern these congruencies in Maximus and Moltmann's eschatologically phrased soteriology, my discoveries were confirmed by particular scholarship. For example, in his study of Maximus, *Man and the Cosmos*, Thunberg discusses the eschatological dimension of Maximus's theology, noting its accordant elements with "existential" and "modern" thought. Thunberg also goes on to speak of how congruent Maximus's eschatological-soteriology is with Moltmann's work. He finds this congruence, particularly in Moltmann's *Theology of Hope*, where Moltmann articulates his argument that "Christianity is eschatology," that the eschatological "is the medium of Christian faith as such, the key in which everything in it is set, the glow that suffuses everything here in the dawn of an expected new day."[1] We will reflect further on these congruencies, especially when dealing with Maximus and Moltmann's teaching on eschatological rest, and how this shapes their understanding of the human calling. In mentioning them, my intention is to set the course for my discussion in the remainder of this chapter.

As I suggested, the doctrine of *theosis* (also known as *theopoiesis*, deification, and divinization) is the primary image Maximus uses to speak about the redemptive goal of humanity and the world. In a key text on *theosis*, Maximus writes:

> A sure warrant for looking forward with hope to the deification of human nature is provided by the incarnation of God, which makes man god to the same degree as God Himself became man. For it is clear that He who became man without sin (cf. Hebrews 4:15)

---

1. Thunberg, *MaC*, 147ff.; Moltmann, *Theology of Hope*, 16.

The Redemptive Goal of the Human Calling

will divinize human nature without changing it into the divine nature, and will raise it up for His own sake to the same degree as He lowered Himself for man's sake. This is what St. Paul teaches mystically when he says, "... that in the ages to come He might display the overflowing richness of His grace" (Ephesians 2:7).[2]

This text raises a number of issues and points of discussion related to *theosis*, especially its Trinitarian, christological, soteriological, and eschatological implications for Maximus's anthropology. For Maximus, the redemptive goal of the human vocation engenders hope, an assurance of our transformation based on the reality of Christ's incarnation. These notions, according to Maximus, are rooted firmly in Scripture and the Fathers.

Scripture

The stunning notion that through faith in Christ human beings can become partakers of the divine nature is a thread that runs through all of Maximus's work. It is a thread that is anchored within Christian Scripture. In the spirit of mystical theology,[3] Maximus forms his thoughts on *theosis* within the "womb" of biblical meditation. Some of the principal biblical texts that present aspects of *theosis*, passages upon which Maximus appears to have regularly meditated[4] as evidenced in their presence in his writings, are:

> Thus he has given us, through these things, his precious and very great promises, so that through them you may escape from the corruption that is in the world because of lust, and may become participants of the divine nature (ἵνα διὰ τούτων γένησθε θείας κοινωνοὶ φύσεως) (2 Pet 1:4).[5]

---

2. Maximus, *First Century of Various Texts* 62, in *Philokalia*, 177–78.

3. See Bernard McGinn's commentary on Pseudo-Dionysius, his pioneering role in mystical theology, and his systematic expression of a dialectical view of the relation of God and the world that influenced theologians for over a thousand years, *Foundations of Mysticism*, 158.

4. The importance of "continuous meditation on the divine Scriptures" is stressed and exemplified in Maximus, *AL*, 18; in Sherwood, *SMC*, 113. For an example of Maximus's reflection on a text related to *theosis* (e.g., 2 Pet 1:4), see *Ep.* 24; *PG* 91, 609 C; cf. Thunberg, *MM*, 430n545. Balthasar underscores the scriptural emphasis in Maximus's work, noting that scriptural meditation is the "the vehicle and medium of all his thought" (*CL*, 52–54).

5. *Greek New Testament*, 4th rev. ed., ed. Aland et al., 799.

> . . . and to know the love of Christ that surpasses knowledge, so that you may be filled with all the fullness of God (Eph 3:19).
>
> And the Word became flesh and lived among us, and we have seen his glory, the glory as of a father's only son, full of grace and truth. . . . From his fullness we have all received, grace upon grace (John 1:14, 16).
>
> The glory that you have given me I have given them, so that they be one, as we are one, I in them and you in me, that they become completely one, so that the world may know that you have sent me and have loved them even as you have loved me (John 17:22–23).
>
> Now the Lord is the Spirit, and where the Spirit of the Lord is, there is freedom. And all of us, with unveiled faces, seeing the glory of the Lord as though reflected in a mirror, are being transformed into the same image from one degree of glory to another; for this comes from the Lord, the Spirit (2 Cor 3:17–18).
>
> My little children, for whom I am again in the pain of childbirth until Christ is formed in you (Gal 4:19).
>
> Beloved, we are God's children now; what we will be has not yet been revealed. What we do know is this: when he is revealed, we will be like him, for we will see him as he is (1 John 3:2).[6]

Along with these select biblical passages are many others that communicate the idea that human beings in Christ are taken up into the very fellowship of the Holy Trinity. By God's grace, believers participate in God's nature, become dwelling places of the Holy Spirit, are increasingly transfigured into Christ's image, and guaranteed that one day this transformative process will be consummated so that they will be like God and fulfill their God-given potential.

Through reflection on biblical passages like the ones mentioned above, the Fathers developed a vital tradition of *theosis*. Drawing from these biblical and patristic sources, Maximus makes his own significant contributions to the tradition, as I will demonstrate. Before that, however, I would like to outline a few important figures and note the strokes they added to the church's portrayal of *theosis*. Examining these developments on *theosis*, and ways that Maximus appropriates them in his own theology,

---

6. See Stephen Finlan and Vladimir Kharlamov's introductory chapter, in which they outline the grouping of biblical passages in order to trace the development of the idea in Scripture, in *Theosis*, 2–3.

The Redemptive Goal of the Human Calling

will offer further insight into how this concept informs and shapes Maximus's Trinitarian-christocentric based anthropology.[7]

Patristic Sources

In order to succinctly summarize the concept of *theosis* in the Greek Fathers before Maximus, I point out a handful of the major thinkers.[8] Utilizing ideas found within pagan and biblical thought, earlier Greek Fathers augmented the concept of *theosis*. John McGuckin has pointed out the bold use of language related to *theosis* and deification that evoked the pagan language of *apotheosis*, the notion that human beings, especially emperors, are advanced to the rank of deity, although the term *apotheosis* was avoided because of the skewed implications of creatures transgressing on divine prerogative.[9]

Theologians such as Irenaeus, Clement of Alexandria, and Origen worked with concepts related to *theosis*. These concepts often dealt with the notion of the divine image in humanity and how human beings become children ("adopted sons" as Scripture says) of God. For example, Irenaeus says that "the Word of God, our Lord Jesus Christ, who did, through his transcendent love, become what we are, that He might bring us to be even what He is Himself."[10] Thunberg posits that it is not until Athanasius, though, that a "real theology of deification was developed."[11] As indicated in chapter 3, the Athanasian aphorism—"For the Word (Logos) was made man that we might be made God"[12]—can be seen as a seminal idea from which a more fully developed doctrine of *theosis* emerged. Moreover, Athanasius's statement includes the notion of reciprocity, a theme taken up by Maximus and others, especially in the expansion of the *tantum—quantum* formula,[13] something we will consider in the following sections.

---

7. Ware gives one of the more helpful summaries of *theosis* in which he outlines six critical points, in *Orthodox Church*, 236–37.

8. Helpful treatments of *theosis* can also be found in: Lot-Borrodine, *La Deification de l'homme*; Lossky, *Vision of God*; Ladner, *Idea of Reform*, 96ff.; Russell, *Doctrine of Deification*.

9. McGuckin, *Westminster Handbook*, 98. Ladner's comments on *theosis* are also very helpful, in *Idea of Reform*, 98ff.

10. Irenaeus, *Adversus Haereses*, bk. 3, 19:1.

11. Thunberg, *MM*, 428.

12. Athanasius, *On the Incarnation*, 107.

13. Thunberg, *MM*, 428.

For the most part, the Cappadocians follow Athanasius's basic line of teaching on *theosis*. Basil and Gregory of Nazianzus deal with the doctrine of *theosis*, though in a more restrictive sense due to the possibilities of misunderstanding.[14] Gregory of Nyssa, while somewhat cautious in his treatment of *theosis*, develops certain elements of deification within an explicit eucharistic and sacramental context. Ladner takes note of this, explaining how Gregory of Nyssa "fits the eucharistic sacrament into the doctrine of spiritual image-likeness, assimilation, vision, and deification." Since human beings are a "corporeal-spiritual compound, not only [their] soul but also [their] body must become united with [their] Saviour." For "Christ's body and blood . . . which have the power to blend with our bodies under the guise of bread and wine which we can assimilate to ourselves." Therefore, the God-Man, "transforming (μεταστοιχειώσας) the nature of the visible elements, 'mingled' (κατέμιξεν) Himself with our mortal nature in order that by communion with His godhead humanity might at the same time be deified (συναποθεωθῇ)."[15]

Additionally, the way that Gregory of Nyssa emphasizes the distinction that exists between human beings and God is an important theme taken up by Maximus in his own expansion of the doctrine of *theosis*, as we saw in Maximus's use of Chalcedonian language in chapter 3. Thunberg has also indicated the significance of Gregory's treatment of the difference between God's immutability and humanity's "ever-moving" character. Gregory's teaching on these distinctions is crucial for understanding Maximus's appropriation of *theosis* doctrine. Thunberg explains that by accepting human mutability, Christ liberates human beings from death, an important notion intimated from the earliest teaching on *theosis*.

Therefore, according to Athanasius and the Cappadocian Fathers's treatment of *theosis*,[16] humans are divinized based on the reciprocity in Christ, while the clear distinction between God and creature is maintained,

---

14. Based on Dalmais, Divinisation, II, Patristique grecque, *Dictionnaire de spiritualité* III, 1957, col. 1376–1389, and Plagnieux, *Grégoire de Nazianze*, 186, 427, Thunberg speaks of Basil and Gregory of Nazianzus's explicit treatment of *theosis*. However, they do so in a limited way because of possible misunderstandings (*MM*, 428).

15. Ladner, *Idea of Reform*, 97–98; Gregory of Nyssa, *Catechetical Oration*, 11ff. Ladner also details the essential connections between *theosis* and *theoria*, particulary in Origen, Evagrius, and Gregory of Nyssa, in *Idea of Reform*, 98–99.

16. See the informative essay by Lewis Ayres, "Deification and the Dynamics of Nicene Theology."

The Redemptive Goal of the Human Calling

within a sacramental and eucharistic vision.[17] Maximus, as we will see, incorporates these elements into his own understanding of deification, elements that are crucial in the development of his wider theological anthropology.

Working with the ideas developed by Irenaeus, Athanasius, and Gregory of Nyssa, Cyril of Alexandria adds his own nuances. Where Athanasius focused on Christ's incarnation as a physical atonement, a mystical reconciliation of the divergent natures of God and humanity,[18] Cyril takes the notion further. The "natural" reconciliation of divinity and humanity, something that could not happen without divine intervention, was demonstrated in the incarnation of the Logos as the God-man, Jesus Christ. Cyril adds that the mystical reconciliation that occurs in Christ's two natures, extends beyond Christ himself to the entire human race. Thus, in Christ's person (consisting of two natures), the divine re-creation of human nature takes place. As McGuckin has indicated, the Greek Fathers's teaching envisaged "the incarnation as having reconstituted the human person as a divinely graced mystery: *deification* was the term chosen to represent this." Moreover, Cyril connects this "dynamic approach of incarnational theology" with eucharistic theology, and gradually this stream was diffused into broader Christian thought.[19]

One last key figure worth mentioning because of his influence on Maximus's conception of *theosis*, is Pseudo-Dionysius.[20] In Denys's writings, influenced as they are by Neoplatonic thought, he underscores that *theosis* is the aim of creation, and that creation is realized in its likeness

---

17. Thunberg adds, in terms that accord with Ladner's comments above: "To the importance of Baptism, received by faith, he [Gregory of Nyssa] adds an understanding of the Eucharist as a unification of the deified flesh of Christ with ours. Thus deification is explicitly understood as the basis of the union of the Logos with the whole of man, through which human nature is deified in Him" (*MM*, 428).

18. McGuckin, *Westminster Handbook*, 98.

19. Ibid., 98–99.

20. Thunberg says that in Denys's writings, the term *theosis* finally replaces *theopoiesis*. He also details how the term *theosis* had been used earlier by theologians, but not as *the* technical term. Thunberg gives a number of helpful examples of its use within the speculation on deification in: Gregory of Nazianzus, *Oration* 39:16; in *MM*, 429n536. Louth, *Denys the Areopagite*, also sheds light on the role of *theosis* in Denys's liturgical vision of humanity and the universe.

and union with God.²¹ Moreover, *theosis* is a gift of divine grace,²² and is accomplished by means of baptism and the Eucharist,²³ thereby enabling human beings to ascend to divine virtue through the various hierarchies.²⁴ Maximus utilizes Denys's thoughts on *theosis* as he shapes a vast, synthetic vision of Christ and the cosmos, a vision in which human beings realize their divine purpose by ascending to the Trinity through Christ.

Maximus's Appropriation

This brief overview of *theosis* in Maximus's predecessors is essential in order to clearly understand Maximus's appropriation of their ideas into his own distinctive theological vision. It is also crucial in support of my overall claim—that Maximus's theological anthropology springs to life from his Trinitarian and christological reflection.

Having considered some of the key sources from which Maximus draws, I will now examine some of the ways that Maximus serves as a point of confluence for these elements of *theosis*. As we have seen in other places, Maximus carefully weaves together thematic threads from his spiritual teachers, in order to construct his own tapestry, a vivid image of the incarnate Word who unifies humanity and all creation within himself.

The Divine Purpose for Human Beings

In examining Maximus's portrayal of *theosis*, I point out a number of details, some of which harmonize richly with aspects of Moltmann's teaching. The first of these details is that the divine purpose for human beings is deification. As we saw in chapter 3, the *mysterium magnum*, the great mystery and divine purpose for humanity, is their reentry into God, their rest in God, their deification in Christ.²⁵ Elsewhere, in a meditation on God's pur-

---

21. Pseudo-Dionysius, *Ecclesiastical Hierarchy*, 1, 3; *PG* 3, 376 A; in *Complete Works*, 197.

22. Pseudo-Dionysius, *Ecclesiastical Hierarchy*, 1, 4; *PG* 376 B; in *Complete Works*, 198.

23. Pseudo-Dionysius, *Ecclesiastical Hierarchy*, 2, 1; *PG* 393 A and 6. 3, 5; 536 C; in *Complete Works*, 200, 246–47.

24. Pseudo-Dionysius, *Ecclesiastical Hierarchy*, 1, 2; *PG* 373 A; in *Complete Works*, 196.

25. Maximus, *QT* 60; see Blowers, *CMJC*, 123ff. Russel's study on *theosis* in Maximus is particularly helpful (*Doctrine of Deification*, 262–95).

poses for all of creation, Maximus explains that God created human beings to become partakers of the divine nature, an allusion to the foundational biblical text (2 Pet 1:4) in the doctrine of *theosis*.[26] And in language that echoes his meditation on the *mysterium magnum* just mentioned, Maximus describes "the great plan of God the Father" that is made known through the incarnation of the Son. The Son, as the messenger of the great plan of God and the incarnate Logos, descended into the lower parts of the earth through his incarnation and ascended above all the heavens in his resurrection. Maximus asserts that in these actions, Christ "underwent in himself through the incarnation as man *our future destiny* . . . the great destiny which he has promised to those who love the Lord." He explains, further, that through the incarnation of the Word, God is making human beings gods and sons of God, so that Christ has become in his nature a "forerunner to the Father on our behalf." Those who follow in Christ's steps, who are deified by grace, will meet the Father, so that "God will be in the 'assembly of the gods,' [Ps 82:1] that is, of those who are saved . . ."[27] This kind of thinking expresses the incredibly high calling placed before humanity. As those created from the infinite love and wisdom of God, followers of Christ become messengers of the great plan of God for all creation. Through their communion with Christ and one another, their virtuous living, and their loving service of others, women and men in Christ continue to flesh out the divine purpose for humanity.

The Gift of Divine Grace

Yet, in accord with Athanasius and the other predecessors referenced above, Maximus underscores the idea that human beings cannot attain to this participation in the divine nature by means of their own capabilities. As Maximus explains, *theosis* is the gift of divine grace:

> God made us so that we might become "partakers of the divine nature" (2 Peter 1:4) and sharers in His eternity, and so that we might come to be like Him (cf. 1 John 3:2) through deification by grace. It is through deification that all things are reconstituted and

---

26. Maximus, *Ep.* 24; *PG* 91, 609 C; cf. Thunberg, *MM*, 430n545: Maximus refers to 2 Pet 1:4, "an important Scripture passage in the Christian development of the idea of deification," as Thunberg notes.

27. Maximus, *Centuries on Theology* II, 23; *CWS*, 152.

achieve their permanence; and it is for its sake that what is not is brought into being and given existence.[28]

Linked to this notion of deification by divine grace, is the interesting language Maximus uses to describe what happens in deification. He says that God is "absolute existence, absolute goodness and absolute wisdom, or rather, to put it more exactly, since God is beyond all such things, there is nothing whatsoever that is opposite to Him." On the other hand, creatures "all exist through participation and grace, while those endowed with intelligence and intellect also have a capacity for goodness and wisdom."[29] We will further explore Maximus's use of these Aristotelian concepts below, when elaborating on his teaching regarding adumbrations of the Trinity. For now, I simply want to reinforce that for Maximus human existence and realization, is made possible by divine grace, by graced participation in God.

Therefore, in Maximus's estimation, the high calling that God places on humanity—to be partakers of the divine nature and to be reconstituted in Christ—is possible only by the grace of God. In a sense, this levels the playing field for Maximus. It is not because of someone's intellectual prowess or location in life that he or she realizes their potential. Maximus's insistence on the gift of divine grace knocks the legs out from under such thinking. For Maximus, God grants us the gift of existence, the gift of repentance and conversion, and the gift of growth in virtue as we cooperate with the energy of grace, enabling us to participate in the divine life.

God's Essence and Energies

This idea of partaking of or participating in the divine nature, leads to a further point regarding *theosis* in Maximus. For Maximus, and the tradition in which he works, deification is to be understood in the light of the distinction between God's essence and God's energies.[30] In his *Second Century on*

---

28. Maximus, *First Century of Various Texts* 42, in *Philokalia*, 173. The Trinitarian and christological structure of Maximus's teaching on *theosis* is evident in many texts. Moreover, the role of the Holy Spirit is central in the dynamic process of deification, as Maximus says in his treatise *Lord's Prayer*: "Then He leads us up still further on the supremse ascent of divine truth to the Father of lights, and makes us share in the divine nature (2 Pet. 1:4) through participation by grace in the Holy Spirit" (*Philokalia*, 304). Surprisingly, there is little scholarship focused on Maximus's pneumatology.

29. Maximus, *CC* III, 27; in *Philokalia*, 87.

30. See Papanikolau, *Being with God*, 24–27.

Theology, a text that interweaves the themes of the incarnation of the Logos, his coessential relationship with God and humanity, Christian growth in grace and virtue, and images of *theosis*, Maximus employs *energy/essence* language to convey that union with God signifies union with the divine energies, not the divine essence.[31]

These facets of Maximus's teaching on *theosis* support my claim, that his understanding of the human person is structured by his Trinitarian and Christological reflection. I have demonstrated this by highlighting the features of his teaching on *theosis* in the above: that deification is God's purpose for humanity, is effected by grace, and signifies union with God's energies, not God's essence. At this point, I want to consider a few more aspects of Maximus's teaching on *theosis*, before discussing the means or agents of deification within his Trinitarian-christocentric vision.

The Hypostatic Union in Christ

A further significant point in Maximus's understanding of *theosis* concerns how he bases his sweeping vision on the hypostatic union in Christ. As I pointed out in my analysis of Maximus's "Chalcedonian logic" in chapter 3, the hypostatic union between human nature and divine Logos is that which reforms the foundations of human existence, enabling humans to be united to God "without confusion" (*asynchtôs*). Thus, as Thunberg explains, "it is characteristic of deification, as Maximus understands it, that it is effected precisely under the conditions which are those of the hypostatic union in Christ, i.e. in perfect coherence and yet without any change or violation of the natures."[32] The importance of this point in Maximus's christologically-based understanding of *theosis* and the human vocation cannot be overemphasized. Through the hypostatic unity in Christ, the possibility for mystical union between God and human beings is made known and available.

---

31. Maximus, *Centuries on Theology* II, 76; in *Philokalia*, 156–57; cf. Ware, *Orthodox Church*, 232: "The idea of deification must always be understood in the light of the distinction between God's essence and His energies. Union with God means union with the divine energies, not the divine essence: the Orthodox Church, while speaking of deification and union, rejects all forms of pantheism." Moltmann also speaks about human participation in the divine energies, especially in his pneumatological work; see, e.g., *SL*, 196.

32. Thunberg, *MM*, 430.

Further, in contrast to other eastern religious teachings that suggest humans are swallowed up into the deity, Maximus contends that through the dynamics of *theosis* humans are brought into a real and mystical union with God, while retaining their full personal integrity. As Lossky argues, the human being who is divinized does not cease to be human: "We remain creatures while becoming god by grace, as Christ remained God when becoming man by the Incarnation."[33]

The Tantum-Quantum Formula

Closely linked to this, and tied in with his Chalcedonian rationale, Maximus utilizes the *tantum-quantum* (Latin, "insofar as") formula to convey the mutual penetration and communication that is possible within a hypostatic union.[34] In *Amb.* 10, Maximus brings together several important threads along these lines. Based on a lengthy exposition of Gregory of Nazianzus's *Sermon* 21 (a panegyric of St. Athanasius), Maximus addresses the constitution of the human person and meaning of God's providence.[35] More specifically, Maximus explains that while human beings are made in the image of God, they are not able to deify themselves. Rather, humans are to relate to God as their "archetype," so that God and human beings are actually "exemplars" of one another. In accord with the point noted above, this does not suggest an ontological unity, a unity with God's essence. As Thunberg indicates, the relationship between God as archetype and humans "lies in the field of imitation, of capacity for mutual adaptation of the modes of existence."[36]

---

33. Lossky, *Mystical Theology*, 87; cf. Ware, *Orthodox Church*, 232: "The human person, when deified, remains distinct (though not separate) from God. The mystery of the Trinity is a mystery of unity *in diversity*, and those who express the Trinity in themselves do not sacrifice their personal characteristics. When St. Maximus wrote 'God and those who are worthy of God have one and the same energy,' [*Amb.*, PG xci, 1076C] he did not mean that the saints lose their free will to the will of God.... The human being does not become God *by nature*, but is merely a 'created god,' a god *by grace* or *by status*."

34. Thunberg, *MM*, 431ff. Thunberg explains that Maximus "can say that God is incarnate *insofar as* man has deified himself." Thunberg goes on to explain more about some of the ways Maximus uses the *tantum quantum* formula, including the incarnation of Christ, the ongoing incarnation that occurs in individual believers, and the "two movements" that take place between God and humanity (the revelatory movement of God towards human beings and their movement towards God).

35. Louth, *MC*, 94ff.

36. Thunberg, *MM*, 431.

The Redemptive Goal of the Human Calling

In using the *tantum—quantum* rule, Maximus seeks to balance the notion that humans do not have the inherent power to deify themselves with the reality that God becomes human to the extent that humans deify themselves through the gift of charity.[37] This ongoing and progressive incarnation of the Word in the virtues of Christians, according to Maximus, is the essence of deification. And, as Thunberg has argued, Maximus's main personal contribution "lies in the way in which he combines the doctrines of Incarnation and deification by means of the *tantum—quantum* formula linked with the concepts of *communicatio idiomatum* and perichoresis." It "is this fact which at the same time makes it possible to present *his doctrine of deification as a summary of his whole theological anthropology*."[38]

Therefore, Maximus's teaching on *theosis* attempts to synthesize a number of crucial elements. Deification is God's purpose for humanity (and the cosmos). It is the work of the triune God in Christ. *Theosis*, moreover, effects a mystical union between God and creatures, through the workings of the divine energies. Divinization, in Chalcedonian terms, is based upon the hypostatic union of Christ's two natures, which reforms the foundations of human constitution and enables human beings to realize their full potential in Christ.[39] Finally, by using vital language from Trinitarian and christological formulations, Maximus asserts that while humans do not have the intrinsic capabilities to deify themselves, they are enabled by divine grace and charity to freely choose to avail themselves to the indwelling Logos.[40]

Means of Deification

With some of the central background features of Maximus's teaching on *theosis* in mind, as well as ways that Maximus adapts and articulates his own vision of *theosis*, I turn my attention to specific *means* of deification in Maximus. In this sketch of the agents of deification,[41] what I aim

37. See *Opusc.* 1; *PG* 91, 33 B; as Thunberg has pointed out, *MM*, 431.

38. Thunberg, *MM*, 430.

39. Sherwood says that deification is the ultimate fulfilling of human nature's capacity for God (*SMC*, 71).

40. Irénée-Henri Dalmais, in his preface to *CWS*, explains how Maximus assimilates the heritage of diverse currents in patristic theology to convey God's ultimate design [i.e., *theosis*] (*CWS*, xii-xiii).

41. See Sherwood, *SMC*, 70ff. Sherwood's pioneering work in Maximus sheds much light on the Trinitarian and christologically grounded vision of the human vocation, as

to do is demonstrate how these means of *theosis* are rooted in Maximus's Trinitarian and christological reflection, and the role they play in fleshing out his vision on the human vocation.

The Church

The first of these agents is the church.[42] The heart of Maximus's teaching on the church is found in his *Mystagogy*, a text considered in chapter 2. In this carefully structured work, Maximus details how the Holy Trinity reunifies humanity and all of creation through the church.[43] The *Mystagogy* evinces the Trinitarian matrix within which Maximus configures the human calling, as well as the christological basis on which the human vocation stands. Maximus explains that his treatise on the church and the synaxis (an assembly for liturgical purposes) aims to clarify Dionysius the Areopagite's reflections in his *Ecclesiastical Hierarchy*. The general problem Maximus addresses in the *Mystagogy* is how the divine image is restored to us, having been snatched away by the evil one through deception and disobedience. This restoration of the divine image is, as I have been showing, central to Maximus's teaching on *theosis*.[44]

In this prayerful exposition of the "sacred celebration," Maximus says that human reason alone cannot figure out how the image of God in human beings is restored. We must rely on the grace of God to illumine, to purify the mind to receive the rays of revelation, and to guide us into a better understanding of how the transcendent God restores the divine image and reunifies creation.[45] The church functions as an image of God, energized by divine power, to cooperate with God in effecting the reunification of all things with their Maker. This reunification with God, who is the cause,

---

evidenced in his elucidation of the agents of deification.

42. In his exposition of Maximus's teaching on the church, Sherwood highlights several interesting features including the role of the role of the Holy Spirit in the life and unity of the church, the church as imitator of God, and the the sources of authority in the church (*SMC*, 73–77).

43. See the helpful elucidation of this text by George Dion Dragas, "Church in St. Maximus's Mystagogy: The Problem and the Orthodox Perspective," *Theologia* (Athens), vol. 56:2 (1985) 385–403.

44. Maximus, *Mystagogia*; in *CWS*, 183–84.

45. Ibid., 184–86.

beginning, and end of all things, is articulated in the language of Chalcedonian language (i.e., "unconfused").[46]

In order for the work of the evil one to be overcome, resulting in the deification of human beings, we must transcend our own particular, fragmented existence, and be joined to God and one another in faithful and universal union. As Mark McIntosh explains in his consideration of the *Mystagogy*, Maximus portrays the church as the "ongoing communal event of Christ's reconciling activity."[47] Accordingly, the Body of Christ, as the image of God in the world (that reflects its divine archetype), builds a new communal structure in which divisions are overcome as they are brought into the very depths of the Trinitarian life. This new communal structure in which a divided humanity and cosmos are reconciled in Christ, does not entail homogeneous conformity. Rather, this reconciliation and unification means that all the features of men, women, and children who are distinct from one another by birth, appearance, nationality, language, customs, age, opinions, skills, manners, habits, pursuits, studies, reputation, fortune, characteristics, and connections, are brought together into a united whole that respects the integrity of each particular creature.[48]

Demonstrating again how his thinking on the church as an ongoing communal event of Christ's reconciling activity is formed in the womb of ongoing biblical meditation, Maximus grounds his argument in Galatians 3:28. He writes:

> All are born into the Church and through it are reborn and recreated in the Spirit. To all in equal measure it gives and bestows form and designation, to be Christ's and to carry his name. In accordance with faith it gives to all a single, simple, whole and indivisible condition which does not allow us to bring to mind the existence of the myriads of differences among them, even if they do exist, through the universal relationship and union of all things with it. It is through it that absolutely no one at all is in himself separated from the community since everyone converges with all the rest and joins together with them by the one, simple, and indivisible grace and power of faith. "For all," it is said, "had but one heart and one mind" [Acts 4:32]. Thus to be and to appear as one body formed of different members is really worthy of

---

46. Ibid., 186.

47. McIntosh, *DaT*, 252ff.

48. For an interesting treatment of the *Mystagogy* and Maximus's striking relevance for contemporary theology, see Carter, *Race*, 343–69.

> Christ himself, our true head, in whom says the divine Apostle, "there is neither male nor female, neither Jew nor Greek, neither circumcision nor uncircumcision, neither foreigner nor Scythian, neither slave nor freeman, but Christ is everything in all of you" [Gal 3:28].[49]

Hence, in this text Maximus describes how the church, as Christ's body, is graced to image and carry out the reintegration of all believing humanity into a glorious whole. As the human body has many diverse parts, but is brought together into an organic whole, so the church brings together all peoples into oneness with the Holy Trinity and with one another. And, what I am highlighting here in particular is how the deifying agency of the church is worked out for Maximus in thoroughly Trinitarian and christological terms.

McIntosh reinforces the deifying agency of the Christian community when he says that the divine power and activity in which the church cooperates with God is Trinitarian.[50] The church is the place where God's unifying activity is made visible in the world. The triune God is seen in this activity that causes every creature to "converge in each other by the singular force of their relationship to him . . ."[51] Through their mutual relationship to God, creatures are freed from their divisive interactions with one another, placing them in a new communion with each other. Maximus explains:

> This reality [the new relation to one another through their communion with God] abolishes and dims all their particular relations considered according to each one's nature, but not by dissolving or destroying them or putting an end to their existence. Rather it does so by transcending them and revealing them, as the whole reveals its parts . . .[52]

Here Maximus utilizes language and concepts forged in Trinitarian and christological formulations in order to describe the church's role as an agent of deification, a community that brings human beings together in a way that mirrors the inner Trinitarian relations. Through this distinction between nature and one's particular mode of existence, Maximus conveys how creatures can move beyond the divisive and limiting interactions at play in the world, into liberating and uniting relations to one another.

49. Maximus, *Mystagogia*, ch. 1; in *CWS*, 187.
50. McIntosh, *DaT*, 252–53.
51. Maximus, *Mystagogia*, ch. 1; in *CWS*, 186.
52. Ibid.

The Redemptive Goal of the Human Calling

As McIntosh explains, "God's activity is precisely to *release* the creatures from 'their particular relations considered to each one's nature,'" so that creatures "discover God bringing about relationships among them based not necessarily on the self-preserving instincts of *nature* but based on the development of *persons* whose identities are given in God."[53] In other words, as creatures are drawn out of themselves in response to the self-giving of God in Christ, they rediscover their own identities and those of their neighbors in the light of God's unifying love. "This sets up a divine pattern of life subverting the world's structures," asserts McIntosh, "a heavenly pattern in which a completely new mode of relation and personal identity can come to birth in the matrix of the divine unifying power."[54]

This subversion of the world's divisive structures, based on the Trinitarian life and divine self-giving in Christ, is what leads Moltmann to develop his understanding of egalitarian relations in the human community. Like Maximus, Moltmann demonstrates how a vision of the Trinity's overflowing community of love, made known in the free and loving self-emptying of Christ, overturns the world's alienating structures. Contemplating this reality, and living a communal life grounded upon it, is what brings humanity out of the tight, impeding alleyways of existence, into the "broad place" of life in God.[55]

As Maximus's meditation on the church proceeds, he unfurls the rich metaphor of the church functioning as God's living icon in the world. It is, as we have seen, the "holy Church of God" that "works for us the same effects of God" by realizing the union of the faithful with God. "As different as they are by language, places, and customs, they are made one by [the church] through faith." God "realizes this union among the natures of things," Maximus says, weaving together the many threads, "without confusing them but in lessening and bringing together their distinction . . . in a relationship and union with himself as cause, principle, and end."[56]

Additionally, Maximus explains why Christians are to "frequent God's holy Church." It is in the church, as believers present themselves to the triune God, that the grace of the Holy Spirit transforms and changes

---

53. McIntosh, *DaT*, 253.

54. Ibid.; cf. Carter's reflection on these emancipatory, egalitarian elements, in *Race*, 351–53.

55. While this theme appears in many places within Moltmann's works, ch. 24 in *ABP* traces the development of his Trinitarian and christological thinking in relation to egalitarian community before God (321–33).

56. Maximus, *Mystagogia*, ch. 1; in *CWS*, 188.

each person, remolding them in proportion to their sanctity and devotion to God.[57]

In addition to the church functioning as God's icon in the world, the place where God's gracious deifying power operates, is Maximus's intriguing notion that the church is like a human and the human is like "a mystical church."[58] While I do not want to get ahead of myself by discussing too many of the elements to be covered in chapter 5, following Maximus's reasonings in the *Mystagogy* introduces a number of themes we will explore more fully below. In short, Maximus explains in symbolic terms how the church and human beings share parallel realities: with the sanctuary representing the soul, the mind as the divine altar, and the body as the nave. He says that as the church symbolizes humanity, so humanity is a mystical church: with the body functioning as the nave where one observes the commandments in moral wisdom and ascetic activity (*praktike*), the soul as the sanctuary in which one engages in natural contemplation (*physike*), and the mind as the altar through which one "summons the silence abounding in song in the innermost recesses of the unseen and unknown utterance of divinity by another silence, rich in speech and tone."[59] According to Maximus, this holistic centering of the self on God brings one to dwell within mystical theology (*theologia*) and to be indwelt and marked by the dazzling splendor of God.

Moreover, it is through this purgative, illuminative, and unitive approach that human beings actually cooperate with God in the reordering, recapitulating, and restoring of all things. By cultivating the virtues of body and soul through asceticism, by discerning the *logoi* or traces of God within the fabric of creation through contemplation, and by silently and reverently worshiping God through the mediating and unifying Logos, the Christian is united to and indwelt by the glorious Creator. When Christians progress in the spiritual life along these lines, they become mediators of God's healing presence and a unifying fulcrum within creation. As I suggested, by laying out these interconnected themes, we will be better prepared to probe them in greater detail in the following sections. With this in mind, we turn to consider the next means of *theosis* in Maximus, the sacraments.

---

57. Maximus, *Mystagogia*, ch. 24; in *CWS*, 206.
58. Maximus, *Mystagogia*, ch. 4; in *CWS*, 189, 190.
59. Maximus, *Mystagogia*, ch. 4; in *CWS*, 189, 190.

The Redemptive Goal of the Human Calling

The Sacraments

Maximus's teaching on the sacraments is, of course, lodged deeply in his vision of the church. The sacraments are important in this study because, among other things, they play a crucial role in realizing the redemptive goal of the human calling. What I aim to do here is look specifically at how the sacraments function in Maximus's Trinitarian and christologically rooted theological anthropology.

As we have just seen, the church is for Maximus both an agent of deification and the milieu in which salvation and deification are apprehended.[60] For Maximus, the Holy Trinity brings about the salvation of human beings through the incarnate dispensation of the Son. Through baptism, Maximus asserts, Christians are reborn through faith in the God who took on human flesh. The gist of Maximus's teaching on baptism is found in six key texts.[61]

Essentially, and relevant to our consideration of the redemptive goal of the human calling, Maximus explains that the manner of birth from God is twofold (based on his understanding of 1 John 3:9 and John 3:5–6).[62] The first mode of birth "bestows the grace of adoption, which is entirely present in potency (δυνάμει) in those who are born of God," while the other "introduces, wholly by active exertion (κατ' ἐνέργειαν), that grace which deliberately (γνωμικῶς) reorients the entire free choice of the one being born of God toward the God who gives birth."[63] Blowers points out how Maximus's "'realized eschatology' informs his whole understanding of the 'potentiality' and 'actuality' of the grace of deification. The full fruition of the grace of adoption is already present, at least potentially, in the believer, before it becomes actually operative in the spiritual life." The Holy Spirit, Maximus

---

60. Sherwood, *SMC*, 77.

61. Sherwood points to these chief references in his analysis, *SMC*, 233n325.

62. 1 John 3:9 reads: "Those who have been born of God do not sin, because God's seed abides in them; they cannot sin, because they have been born of God." John 3:3–6 says: "Jesus answered him [Nicodemus, the Pharisee], 'Very truly I tell you, no one can see the kingdom of God without being born from above.' Nicodemus said to him, 'How can anyone be born after having grown old? Can one enter a second time into the mother's womb and be born?' Jesus answered, 'Very truly, I tell you, no one can enter the kingdom of God without being born of water and Spirit. What is born of flesh is flesh, and what is born of the Spirit is spirit.'"

63. Maximus, *QT* 6; cf. Blowers's comments: "Maximus' 'realized eschatology' [cf. *QT* 22] informs his whole understanding of the 'potentiality' and 'actuality' of the grace of deification. The full fruition of the grace of adoption is already present, at least potentially, in the believer, before it becomes actually operative in the spiritual life" (*CMJC*, 103).

argues, is the one who brings about the spiritual rebirth, the saving faith, and the reformation of the human γνώμη (will). Through the Incarnation, human powers and habits are renewed, so that by their proper use humans are enabled to realize to their full potential all that is made possible through the sacrament of baptism.[64]

Maximus explains, further, that through the renewing second birth of baptism the law of corruption brought about by Adam's sin is broken. The Holy Spirit engenders in the believing, baptized Christian a new state of sinlessness, restores a provisional incorruptibility, a graced manner of existence that is preserved by obedience to God's commandments. Maximus also teaches that through the incarnation, God provided another beginning (*arche*), a second nativity (*genesis*) for human nature. Because of Christ's sufferings and death, death itself has been condemned, so that the power of sin and death in the lives of baptized Christians has been broken.[65]

One key text synthesizes these various baptismal themes:

> Baptized in Christ through the Spirit, we receive the first incorruption according to the flesh. Keeping this original incorruption spotless by giving ourselves to good works and by dying to our own will, we await the final incorruption bestowed by Christ in the Spirit. No one who possesses this final incorruption fears the loss of the blessings he has obtained.[66]

This encapsulating text, moreover, introduces other elements that will be important for our analysis of Maximus's teaching on humanity's disintegration through the passions and reintegration through the virtues. At the pivotal moment of baptism, when a believer dies to sin and puts on Christ, she is on her way to becoming the person God intended. As she grows in her life of Christian virtue, with Christ's life taking shape in hers, she is graced to cooperate with God in the restoration of all things.

---

64. Maximus, *QT* 6–280C; *QT* 61–632A; *Amb.* 7–1097C; Sherwood, *SMC*, 78.

65. Maximus, *QT* 61–636D; cf. Blowers's comments on this multifaceted text and its resonances with Gregory of Nyssa, *CMJC*, 131–32. Blowers also notes the "sublime paradox" in *QT* 61 and its echoes in *Mystagogia* 8, where Maximus affirms that "in exchange for our passions [Christ] gives us his life-giving Passion as a salutary cure which saves the whole world" (*PG* 91:688C; *CWS*, 198).

66. Maximus, *Centuries on Theology* I, 87, in *Philokalia*, 133. Sherwood comments that "death voluntarily accepted must be understood in the light of Christ's death, and so the Christian's, being in condemnation not of nature but of sin" (*SMC*, 233n332).

Penance

In addition to the sacrament of baptism as an agent of deification in Maximus's teaching on the human calling, is his teaching on penance. While on might expect more teaching regarding penance, especially considering Maximus's monastic context, there are only a few texts in which Maximus deals with this theme. The essence of what he says regarding penance is that where baptism frees Christians from original sin, repentance releases from post-baptismal sin. By repentance, the ongoing conversion or turning of one's whole life towards God, and submission to hardship, believers overcome distorted sensual pleasure and the power of sin.[67] Though the deifying agent of penance is infrequently discussed by Maximus, it is nevertheless an important element in Maximus's spirituality.[68]

The Eucharist

Yet another crucial sacrament in Maximus's teaching on the redemptive goal of the human vocation is the Eucharist.[69] Like opening matryoshka (nesting) dolls, in order to get to the core of Maximus's teaching on the Eucharist as a deifying agent, we first had to look briefly at the church and its role as the vehicle of God's redemption. Now, what I would like to do is open up his teaching on the Eucharist as it is embedded within (and the climax of) the church's liturgy.

As we saw above in our discussion of the church, Maximus's ecclesiology is liturgical and sacramental. For Maximus, the church is a mystical body, as he suggests in the mystical ecclesiology of his *Mystagogy*. Moreover, this *Mystagogy* seeks to explain the many facets of the church's eucharistic liturgy, particularly the *Synaxis*. In the following, I will elucidate some of these features pertaining to the Eucharist, and in accordance with

---

67. Maximus, *AL* 44–956A; Sherwood, *SMC*, 134.

68. See the *Philokalia*, 386: "Repentance (μετάνοια—*metanoia*): the Greek signifies primarily a 'change of mind' or 'change of intellect': not only sorrow, contrition or regret, but more positively and fundamentally the conversion or turning of our whole life towards God."

69. Texts related to the Eucharist include: *QD* 40–818CD (priesthood); *QD* 41–820A (communion); *Ep.* 31–625A (priesthood); *Ep.* 21–604D (priesthood); *Amb.* 48–1361ff. (communion), 1364B (sacrifice); *Amb.* fin.–1417C (sacrifice); *Mystagogia* 21, 24–697A, 704D f. (communion); *QT* 35–377B (communion); *QT* 36–380Df. (communion); *Relatio motionis* 4–117B (priesthood); from Sherwood, *SMC*, 234n336.

my claim, show how Maximus's teaching flows out of his Trinitarian and christological vision.

Maximus, as noted in his introductory remarks to the *Mystagogy*, seeks to build on that which Denys left for others to explicate. Through his reworking and readjusting of the Dionysian (and Origenist) tradition, Maximus enhances and even transcends the work of his predecessors. This is illustrated in the way that Maximus situates the Dionysian Neoplatonism and symbolism of the liturgy and Eucharist within a more radical incarnational perspective, as Thunberg has argued.[70]

The beautiful elements and rhythms of the liturgy that culminate in the Eucharist, Maximus says, are placed before Christians to contemplate, so that "the beaming ray of [liturgical and eucharistic] ceremonies might lay hold participants, deliver them from an earthly life of idleness, graft them into the spiritual vine, and restore "the spiritual wage of the divine and very royal image which was snatched away from us in the beginning by the evil one."[71] Thus, from the outset, the *Mystagogy* is concerned with addressing issues of soteriological, redemptive, and anthropological importance. As Thunberg has indicated, for Maximus, the eucharistic liturgy is a contemplation and celebration of soteriological mysteries, and Maximus's speculation is rooted firmly in daily eucharistic reality.[72]

So how does the liturgy and eucharist, according to Maximus, draw believers into the redemptive Trinitarian life and deifying power of the incarnate Word? One way in which Maximus expresses this is how he asserts that the church celebrates who Christ is and what he has accomplished in his life, death, resurrection, and ascension. In his explication of the liturgical components (as symbolic realities[73]) Maximus says that

---

70. Thunberg, *MaC*, 172–73: "If my contention is correct, Maximus wants to say that eucharistic communion, through being in the perfect likeness with the Logos made man, effects in man, properly prepared, the likeness of man with God that goes beyond his natural qualities and deifies him according to the *tantum-quantum* principle . . . the perspective of Maximus is other than that of the Areopagite. If the latter is primarily interested in the reflecting quality of symbols, Maximus insists on an *incarnational* perspective, where the elevation of man is the direct fruit of the descent of the Logos, of his 'becoming thick,' in successive stages of the economy of salvation. . . . This is clearly in accord with his own incarnational vision, where the movements of descent and ascent are in a constant dialectical relationship. The Origenist monism and a Dionysian modified Neoplatonism are radically transcended."

71. Maximus, *Mystagogia*; in *CWS*, 184.

72. Thunberg, *MaC*, 114.

73. See Thunberg's informative discussion on symbol and mystery in Maximus, *MC*,

The Redemptive Goal of the Human Calling

> the first entrance of the bishop into the holy Church for the sacred synaxis is a figure and image of the first appearance in the flesh of Jesus Christ the son of God and our Savior in this world. By it he freed human nature which had been enslaved by corruption.... He redeemed all its debt as if he were liable even though he was not liable but sinless, and brought us back to the original grace of his kingdom by giving himself as a ransom for us.[74]

> [Again, the first entrance] signifies in general the first appearance of Christ our God, and in particular the conversion of those who are being led by him and with him from unbelief to faith and from vice to virtue and also from ignorance to knowledge.[75]

Here we see the dual emphasis of the coming of Christ and the redemption of the enslaved. This, according to Maximus, is the crux of the liturgical celebration: worshiping the Word made flesh who redeems and restores sinful humanity.

Furthermore, Maximus says that

> in exchange for our destructive passions he gives us his life-giving Passion as a salutary cure which saves the whole world. After his appearance, his ascension into heaven and return to the heavenly throne are symbolically figured in the bishop's entrance into the sanctuary and ascent to the priestly throne.[76]

In this way, both priest and community observe the playing out of the Christ-narrative. Christ appears, suffers, dies, redeems humanity and cures the whole world, then ascends to his heavenly throne. For Maximus, the liturgical celebration and is an engagement with and sharing in the Christian *kerygma*. It is the focal point of the spiritual life, the hub around which all the spokes revolve, and the place where the mystery of the deifying power of Christ's incarnation emanates into the heart of the church in the world.

Closely connected to this is Maximus's notion that *the church actually participates in and embodies the mysteries during the liturgical celebration.* It is not a matter of the church simply observing these realities being reenacted, but rather she actually enters into them, they enter into her, and she

---

149–73.

74. Maximus, *Mystagogia*, ch. 8; in *CWS*, 198.

75. Maximus, *Mystagogia*, ch. 24; in *CWS*, 208.

76. Maximus, *Mystagogia*, ch. 8; in *CWS*, 198.

undergoes deifying transformation. Maximus therefore, explains that every Christian should be exhorted

> to frequent God's holy church and never to abandon the holy synaxis accomplished therein because of the holy angels who remain there and who take note each time people enter and present themselves to God, and they make supplications for them; likewise because of the grace of the Holy Spirit which is always invisibly present, but in a special way at the time of the holy synaxis. This grace transforms and changes each person who is found there and in fact remolds him in proportion to what is more divine in him and leads him to what is revealed through the mysteries which are celebrated, even if he does not himself feel this because he is still among those who are children in Christ, unable to see either into the depths of the reality or the grace operating in it, which is revealed through each of the divine symbols of salvation being accomplished . . .[77]

According to Maximus, Christians are urged to regularly participate in the synaxis for several reasons. One is that the holy angels see and offer prayers for them. Another is that the grace of the Holy Spirit, which pervades all things at all times, is manifest in a more potent fashion during the Eucharistic celebration. As a result, the deifying grace of the Holy Spirit transforms each member of the church and refashions him or her into the *imago Christi*, whose potentiality resides within them.[78] Maximus notes, with a pastoral touch, that this occurs whether the Christian is aware of it or not. Because they are children of God through faith in Christ, and in spite of their immaturity, the power and grace which are revealed and operative in the liturgy accomplish God's salvific purposes in them.

Thunberg's comments on Maximus at this point reinforce my position. He says that for Maximus the church "is the place where the deifying grace of God is at work among men." For the Eucharist is conceived by Maximus "as a sacramental integration of the whole human person before and toward its final and ultimate goal, which is the Trinitarian God . . . the image and likeness of whom it carries and manifests." And regarding the symbolic and realistic perspectives of the sacraments, Maximus portrays them as "symbols, and as such they may be allegorically interpreted, but

---

77. Maximus, *Mystagogia*, ch. 24; in *CWS*, 206–7.

78. Keep this in mind, as we will see how Moltmann takes up the notion of *imago Christi* in ch. 5, where he spells out his theological anthropology in classic terms.

they are also a reality that transforms the life of Christians through divine grace."[79]

Because of the importance of Maximus's teaching on *theosis* in the construction of his theological anthropology, we have looked carefully at the church and its liturgy and sacraments as agents of deification. Throughout my analysis, I have sought to show how Maximus roots his theological anthropology and notions of redemption within his Trinitarian-christocentric vision. I have also pointed out ways that Maximus refines the spiritual tradition with which he works, as well as noting how Moltmann critically retrieves fertile themes from the patristic tradition (especially the Orthodox). Now I would like to consider another agent of deification in Maximus's Trinitarian and christologically based anthropology, that of asceticism.

Asceticism

For Maximus, asceticism[80] is integral to dogma and mysticism, to Christian thinking and Christian living. Like the other agents of deification we have considered thus far—the church and sacraments—Maximus entwines his teaching on asceticism with dogmatic theology. One text in particular demonstrates this, a passage from Maximus's exposition on the Lord's Prayer:

> The Logos bestows adoption on us when He grants us that birth and deification which, transcending nature, comes by grace from above through the Spirit. The guarding and preservation of this in God depends on the resolve of those thus born: on their sincere acceptance of the grace bestowed on them and, through the practice of the commandments, on their cultivation of the beauty given to them by grace. Moreover, by emptying themselves of the passions they lay hold of the divine to the same degree as that to which, deliberately emptying Himself of His own sublime glory, the Logos of God truly became man.[81]

---

79. Thunberg, *MaC*, 126–27.

80. Louth's exposition on Maximus's spiritual theology—with his attention to the themes of theological ascesis, asceticism for all Christians, the influence and transformation of Evagrius, and the primacy of love in Maximus's asceticism—has been particularly resourceful, *MTC*, 33ff. Sherwood's analysis of Maximus's teaching on asceticism is also illuminative, *SMC*, 81–87.

81. Maximus, *Lord's Prayer*, in *Philokalia*, 287.

This excerpt illustrates the way Maximus joins theological reflection and its outreach and outworking in the Christian ascetic life. It also further supports my claim that, for Maximus, theological anthropology emanates from Trinitarian and christological doctrine.

In the broader context from which the above passage is lifted, Maximus begins with a meditation on the Trinitarian source of true theologizing:

> Theology is taught us by the incarnate Logos of God, since He reveals in Himself the Father and the Holy Spirit. For the whole of the Father and the whole of the Holy Spirit were present essentially and perfectly in the whole of the incarnate Son. They themselves did not become incarnate, but the Father approved and the Spirit co-operated when the Son Himself effected His incarnation.[82]

Therefore, in these two brief passages, Maximus brings together crucial themes that pervade the body of his work. The Holy Trinity works cooperatively in the incarnation of the Son. Adoption, spiritual birth, and deification are gifts of grace granted by the Son and through the Spirit. Through the practice of the commandments, Christians are graciously transformed by divine beauty. And the goal of deification, which is worked out in the ascetic life, is made possible by and realized in imitation of Christ's *kenosis*. For both Maximus and Moltmann, the *kenosis* or self-emptying of Christ in his incarnation, life, and death, is foundational for the existence of the church, the life of Christian discipleship with all its rigors and sufferings, and for fulfilling the human calling in creation.[83]

Further, as one explores Maximus's Trinitarian and christologically-grounded ascetic theology, it becomes clear that asceticism is for all Christians, not just a select group of "elite spiritual athletes." For Maximus, baptism is the foundation of the Christian life, and growth into Christlikeness is built upon that identification with the death and resurrection of Christ. What's more, Maximus does not promote a kind of dutiful, joyless mortification in the face of a world that is evil to the core, ideas which are foreign to his work. Rather, Maximus emphasizes the intrinsic goodness of created things, as we have seen several times. He says that

---

82. Maximus, *Lord's Prayer*, in *Philokalia*, 287.

83. See *CoG*, 276ff., and 327, where Moltmann asserts that Christ's kenosis represents the authority of God and shapes the church's attitudes and actions: "The rule and the kingdom of God are no longer reflected in political rule and world kingdoms, but in the service of Christ, who humiliated himself to the point of death on the cross." Moltmann also speaks of the kenosis of the Spirit in the life and ministry of Jesus, *WJC*, 91ff.

it is not food which is evil but gluttony, not the begetting of children but fornication, not possessions but greed, not reputation but vainglory. And if this is so, there is nothing evil in creatures except misuse, which stems from the mind's negligence in its natural cultivation.[84]

Created things are not evil, but our misuse of them is. Moreover, it is not out of a sense of duty that believers refrain from certain things, but because of a desire to freely and gladly sacrifice for God, in response to God's loving, saving activity in Christ. Maximus explains that some "of the things we do for God are done because of the commandments, some not because of the commandments but through what one can call a free-will offering." To illustrate, "we are commanded to love God and our neighbor, to love our enemies, to refrain from adultery, murder, and so on. When we transgress these, we are subject to condemnation." He adds that, however, "there are other things which are not commanded, such as virginity, celibacy, poverty, the monastic life, and so forth." These willing sacrifices "have the nature of gifts, so that if from weakness we have been unable to observe some of the commandments we may propitiate our good Master with gifts."[85] Thus, it is important before launching into our discussion on mortification to reiterate that for Maximus mortification (and all its accompanying ascetic practices) is motivated by love for God, as a free-will offering, energized by God's grace, and with desire to use things rightly, as God intended.[86]

Asceticism, therefore, grounded as it is in Christology and the Son's *kenosis*, is an integral part of this discussion on the human calling. In order to realize one's created purpose as a human being, Maximus argues, she is to be baptized into Christ, to freely participate in self-emptying of the passions, and to cooperate with the grace and Spirit of God in the deifying, transformative process of the spiritual life.

---

84. Maximus, *CC* III, 4; in *CWS*, 62.

85. Maximus, *CC* IV, 67; in *CWS*, 82–83.

86. It would be interesting to juxtapose Augustine's *De Doctrina Christiana* (I. 27–30) with Maximus along these lines. Balthasar compares and contrasts Augustine and Maximus, along similar lines, dealing mainly with *Confessions* and *QT* (Balthasar, *Theological Anthropology*, 1–10).

The Influence of Evagrius

The influence of Evagrius on Maximus's ascetic theology is significant. One example is how he appropriates Evagrius's threefold pattern of the spiritual life: *praktike, physike,* and *theologia* (parallel to the threefold way of the western tradition, as mentioned above, the purgative, illuminative, and unitive). Moreover, Maximus entwines other threads from Denys, the Macarian Homilies (fourth century), and Diadochus of Photike (born c. 400) as he reworks and refines his sources into a deeply christological, incarnational ascetic theology. As Louth has indicated, for Maximus, "training in Christianity is a training in love" (*agape* and *eros*).[87] What I will show below is how Maximus reconfigures this ascetic tradition, based largely on Origen and Evagrius, by grounding it in his Chalcedonian Christology and painting it in the bright colors of Christ-like love.

Prayer and Contemplation

Having looked at ways that the church, sacraments, and asceticism inform and shape Maximus's teaching on *theosis* and the human vocation, I turn now to another agent of deification, prayer and contemplation. For Maximus, prayer and contemplation in their variegated forms, are indispensable in the church's quest for deification and the fulfillment of the human vocation. I am devoting more space to Maximus's teaching on prayer and contemplation because of the stress Maximus places on it. According to Maximus, pure prayer is most helpful "above all" in the mind's "pursuit of divine love."[88]

In the following, we will consider how Maximus takes up elements of Evagrius's teaching on prayer, contemplation, and the spiritual life. I will begin by looking briefly at Evagrius, then show how Maximus adapts and refines Evagrius's teaching. It will become increasingly clear, especially as

---

87. Louth, *MTC*, 38ff.

88. Maximus, *CC* I, 11–12. Moreover, Berthold highlights the primacy of contemplation in Maximus, where the word is found more than eight hundred times (as compared with forty-five times in Denys) (*CWS*, 216n21). See also Moltmann's reflection on the monastic triad employed in Luther's theology: *oratio; meditatio; tentatio* (prayer, meditation, trial/temptation). In his essay, "What Is a Theologian?" Moltmann examines these three themes in conversation with Anselm, Gregory of Nyssa, and others, stressing the importance of prayer and seeking to know "in wonder." He suggests that this prayerful posture before God is perhaps best illustrated by Mary, the mother of Jesus, when she "kept all these words and pondered them in her heart [Luke 2:19]" (51–52).

we move into the final chapter, why a closer look into Evagrius is important. According to Evagrius, the discernable pattern to the spiritual life involves three basic stages, as we covered earlier: *praktike*, *physike*, and *theologia*. To recap, *praktike* is the cultivation of the virtues, particularly through the activity of asceticism in pursuit of purifying the mind. *Physike* is the contemplation of created things, when the purified mind begins to discern their inner structures. And *theologia* is the goal, when contemplation ushers one into knowledge of and unity with God. This stage, as Louth says, "is a realm of prayer, which Evagrius regards as a state rather than an activity, not so much something you do as something you are," and is a realm in which the soul "recovers its true nature [as Evagrius explains]: 'the state of prayer is an impassible habit which snatches up the soul that loves wisdom to the intellectual heights by a most sublime love.'"[89] Consonant notions of the latter state are found in Maximus when he writes:

> It is said that the supreme state of prayer is when the mind passes outside the flesh and the world and while praying is completely without matter and form. The one who preserves this state without compromise really "prays without ceasing."[90]
>
> The one who truly loves God also prays completely undistracted, and the one who prays completely undistracted also truly loves God. But the one who has his mind fixed on any earthly thing does not pray undistracted; therefore the one who has his mind tied to any earthly thing does not love God.[91]

However, as I have been demonstrating, Maximus does not simply restate or recycle Evagrius's thoughts, but refashions some of the raw materials into his own conceptual work. Much of the scholarship on Maximus points this out, how he frequently synthesizes, builds on, and adapts the antecedent works of Evagrius, Denys, Macarius and others, typically placing extracted insights from their teaching into an incarnational context, where love for God and humanity are paramount.[92] This has profound implications for Maximus's conception of the human calling.

---

89. Evagrius, *On Prayer*, 53; as cited in Louth, *MC*, 37. Louth, 35–37, and Tugwell, "Evagrius and Macarius"; both provide excellent synopses of Evagrius's thought and his influence on Maximus.

90. Maximus, *CC* II, 61; in *CWS*, 55.

91. Maximus, *CC* II, 2, 1; in *CWS*, 46.

92. Balthasar, Louth, and Thunberg all provide detailed explications of this refining work in their studies of Maximus. See *CL*, 302–3; *MC*, 34–39; *MaC*, 97–101. Janet Williams also offers insightful comments regarding ways that Maximus integrates ideas from

Examples of this adaptation of Evagrius are: first, that Maximus removes the overly Origenistic metaphysic within the ascetic struggle of prayer; second, by discussing prayer, contemplation, and the spiritual life in terms permeated with love; and third, by stressing the centrality of Christ, his incarnation, and broader christlogical reflection as the basis for prayer and the spiritual life. An illustration of this is found in his *Commentary on the Our Father*, when Maximus explains that the

> aim of prayer should direct us to the mystery of deification so that we might know from what things the condescension through the flesh of the Only Son kept us away and whence and where he brought up by the strength of his gracious hand, those of us who had reached the lowest point of the universe where the weight of sin had confined us. Let us love more intensely the one who so wisely prepared for us such a salvation. By what we do let us show that the prayer is fulfilled, and manifest and proclaim that God is truly a Father through grace.[93]

In this passage we see a number of the elements discussed so far, and it demonstrates how each of them is viewed *in relation to the incarnation of Christ*—the aim of prayer, deification, grace, sin, love, and salvation. All are seen in light of the knowledge of "the condescension through the flesh of the Only Son." Christ's self-emptying incarnation, according to Maximus, is *the* basis for salvation and deification, and is the focus of the pray-er. The "aim" of prayer involves pondering the mysterious, deifying grace that the incarnate Son issues to those at the nadir of existence. His deifying salvation inspires a response of intense love and radical obedience.

In addition to the modification of Evagrius's work into a more christological focus, is another dimension in Maximus's teaching on prayer and contemplation. For Maximus, prayer and contemplation include finding God in the world, Scripture, and self (a division Maximus borrows from Origen).[94] We find this threefold reference in his *Mystagogy*, in which he discusses the world as "man" and man as the "world." We are only touching on it here, specifically in relation to prayer and contemplation. Maximus writes:

---

the Cappadocians, Evagrius, and the Macarian tradition, in "Pseudo-Dionysius," 199.

93. Maximus, *Lord's Prayer* 6; in *CWS*, 118.

94. Origen, *Commentary on John* 13, 42; cited in *CWS*, 220n71. For an illuminating exposition of prayer and Scripture in Origen, see Heine, *Origen*, 160–66, 207–9.

The Redemptive Goal of the Human Calling

> Thus if any one of these three men—the *world*, holy *Scripture*, and the one who is *ourselves*—wishes to have a life and condition that is pleasing and acceptable to God let him do what is best and noblest of all. And let him as best he can take care of the soul which is immortal, divine, and in process of deification through the virtues. . . . And let him be moved to do spiritual battle through knowledge against the incorporeal and intellectual powers and leave aside present and visible things. . . . And let him through an informed study of holy Scripture wisely get past its letter and rise up to the Holy Spirit in whom are found the fullness of all goodness and the treasures of knowledge and the secrets of wisdom. If anyone is shown to be interiorly worthy he will find God himself engraved on the tablets of his heart through the grace of the Spirit and with face unveiled will see as in a mirror the glory of God once he has removed the veil of the letter.[95]

It is in these three spheres—world, Scripture, and self—that Christians learn to participate in the process of deification, become worthy through development of the virtues, and behold the glory of God, as Maximus puts it. How this actually occurs, that is, how human beings in Christ experience God's deifying power as they pray and contemplate within these three realms, is the focus of the following section.

Before proceeding, however, it might be helpful to restate my broader purpose. At each step, I have sought to reiterate how Maximus's (and Moltmann's) conception of the human calling springs out of Trinitarian and christological reflection. Further, I have demonstrated how Maximus views all of creation in light of Christ, his incarnation, death, and resurrection. For Maximus, the reality of Christ's hypostatic union is found within the very fabric of the created order. Therefore, *theosis*, the practices of prayer and contemplation, and the outworking of the spiritual life, are all seen in vital connection to the incarnate Son, Jesus Christ. As I will show in the following, the church's practice of contemplative prayer leads human beings to the marrow of the universe, the person of Christ, through whom the Father and Spirit transform them into Christ's likeness.

Contemplation: The World

According to Maximus, contemplation in this first arena, the world, leads one to discern vestiges of the divine within nature and the created universe.

---

95. Maximus, *Mystagogia*, ch. 7; in *CWS*, 197 (italics mine).

As noted, *theoria physike* is the grace-empowered contemplation of what God has made so that one is led to the intimate knowledge of the One who made it. Maximus says: "When the mind is completely freed form the passions, it journeys straight ahead to the contemplation of created things and makes its way to the knowledge of the Holy Trinity."[96] In other words, the purified mind sees (in a limited but real manner), through contemplation, the Maker within the created, and moves toward knowing the triune God. He also says:

> For being all in all, the God who transcends all in infinite measure will be seen only by those who are pure in understanding when the mind in contemplative recollection of the principles of beings will end up with God as cause, principle, and end of all, the creation and beginning of all things and eternal ground of the circuit of things.[97]
>
> Gazing with a simple understanding on him who is not outside it but thoroughly in the whole of reality, it will itself understand the principles of beings and the causes why it was distracted by divisive pursuits before being espoused to the Word of God. It is by them that it is logically brought safe and sound to him who creates and embraces all principles and causes.[98]

Like Origen, Maximus understands the contemplation of nature as that which awakens one to recognize the *logoi* within creation. This, in effect, leads one to behold in new measure the glory of the supreme *Logos*. On this theme, Balthasar asserts that Maximus "can be considered the most world-affirming thinker of all the Greek Fathers; in his basically positive attitude toward nature he goes beyond Gregory of Nyssa." Further, where Origen regards "Scripture as alone supremely normative, Maximus accepts also the natural world, contemplated in the light of revelation, as a source of wisdom." The result is that perfect knowledge, "the knowledge of the believing Christian and even the knowledge of the mystic—is gleaned from both 'books' together." Hence, *theoria physike* (the contemplation of nature) and the *logoi* (the hidden structures of meaning within), "becomes for Maximus a necessary step, a kind of initiation, into the knowledge of God."[99] Maximus illustrates this when he says:

---

96. Maximus, *CC* I, 86; in *CWS*, 45.
97. Maximus, *Mystagogia*, ch. 1; in *CWS*, 186–87.
98. Maximus, *Mystagogia*, ch. 5; in *CWS*, 194–95.
99. Balthasar, *CL*, 61.

> Whether in the case of the written Holy Scripture, to the One revealed as the Word or, in the case of creation, to the One revealed as Creator and maker and fashioner . . . in both cases I think it necessarily follows that anyone who wishes may live an upright and blameless life with God, whether through scriptural understanding in the Spirit, or through the natural contemplation of reality in accordance with the Spirit. So the two laws—both the natural law and the written law—are of equal honour and teach the same things; neither is greater or less than the other, which shows, as is right, that the lover of perfect wisdom may become the one who desires wisdom perfectly.[100]

In Maximus there is no bifurcation between scriptural and natural contemplation. The distinction he does imply, though, is between those who seek to live a virtuous life with God, as lovers of perfect wisdom, and those who do not.

This, interestingly, is another area where Moltmann appropriates ideas from Maximus. At a recent lecture, Moltmann developed his argument for a Trinitarian understanding of creation's groaning and redemption, based on the two books teaching of Maximus and Bonaventure.[101] In ways that tend to be less common in Reformed theology, Moltmann argued that this contemplative approach to creation cultivates a deeper understanding of God's redemption, indwelling, and renewal of creation. He went on to speak about the implications of this perspective for Christian ethics, contemporary environmental issues, and other themes related to the human calling in creation.

Contemplation: Scripture

A second sphere where the Christian finds God through prayer and contemplation is that of *Scripture*. According to Maximus, Scripture is like a human being with body and soul, and must be understood as such if one is

---

100. Maximus, *Amb. 10*, 1128C–D; in Louth, *MC*, 109–10.

101. This was the plenary lecture at the Wesleyan Theological Society at Duke University, March 13, 2008. In this lecture, Moltmann considered the tradition of two books, looking at how nature is to be read along with and in light of God's scriptural revelation. He gave examples from the Syrian Fathers, the Cappadocians, Antony, Cassian, Scotus, and Maximus's teaching on the two robes of Christ (which deals with divine revelation in nature and Scripture).

going to engage in true contemplation. In the *Mystagogy* Maximus explains that

> the entire holy Scripture [is] taken as a whole man with the Old Testament as body and the New Testament as spirit and mind . . . the historical letter of the entire holy Scripture, Old Testament and New, is a body while the meaning of the letter and the purpose to which it is directed is the soul. . . . For as man who is ourselves is mortal [sic] in what is visible and immortal in the invisible, so also does holy Scripture, which contains a visible letter which is passing and a hidden spirit underneath the letter which never ceases to exist, organize the true meaning of contemplation.[102]

This "embodied" view of Scripture maintains that the contemplating Christian must approach Scripture in the same way that one approaches virtuous living in the body. By way of analogy, the Old Testament is seen as the material body, while the New Testament is the immaterial, that of spirit and mind. Maximus goes on to say that

> just as that man who is ourselves wastes the flesh in mastering by wisdom the desires and drives of the passions, so does holy Scripture spiritually understood circumcise its own letter. For, says the great Apostle, to the degree that "our exterior man perishes, the interior man is renewed day by day." This can also be thought and said of holy Scripture if we consider it morally as a man.[103]

When Scripture is "spiritually understood" in this manner, one gets past the exterior and in touch with the interior. The results are described as follows: To the extent that its letter withdraws, its spirit is enriched; and to the extent that the shadows of the temporal worship pass, so is there introduced the splendid, brilliant, and shadowless truth of faith. It is in accordance with and by virtue of this truth of faith that it principally is, is written, and is called Scripture, being engraved on the mind through spiritual grace.[104]

Genuine scriptural contemplation, as Maximus explains, is like the ascetic who drills down deep into the spiritual recesses, to find enrichment, and passes through transitory shadows into the effulgent brightness of

---

102. Maximus, *Mystagogia*, ch. 6; in *CWS*, 195–96.

103. Ibid., 196. Berthold notes that with this tropological understanding, "Maximus sees a threefold initiation into the Christian mystery represented in the liturgical, cosmic, and scriptural mystagogies: *Amb.* 66 (1409AB), 37 (1320), 27 (1285A), 42 (1360C)," in *CWS*, 219n65.

104. Maximus, *Mystagogia*, ch. 6; in *CWS*, 196.

The Redemptive Goal of the Human Calling

faith's light. When this occurs, the true meaning of Scripture is graciously etched on the mind.

Another image Maximus employs in his teaching on scriptural contemplation is that of Mt. Tabor, when Christ is transfigured before the apostles (Matt 17:1–13; Mark 9:2–8; Luke 9:28–36). Put succinctly, Maximus says that Christ takes the disciples with him up to the mountain "because of their diligence in virtue." There they behold Christ in his transfigured, unapproachable glory, and recognize "his great awesomeness." Moreover, they pass from a fleshly to a spiritual understanding of things, are "taught the spiritual meanings [*logoi*] of the mysteries that were shown to them," and instructed regarding the transcendent divinity of Christ, which is above "mind and sense and being and knowledge." Through their "theological denial that praises Him as being completely uncontained, they were led contemplatively to the glory as of the Only-begotten of the Father, full of grace and truth." Further, Christ's radiant garments convey "a symbol of the words of Holy Scripture," which become lucid and reveal "the meaning that lay hidden within them."[105]

In this brief section, we see a number of elements pertinent to our discussion of scriptural contemplation, which should help us recap before moving ahead. The first is the notion that the Christian is to engage in diligent cultivation of virtue. Another is that contemplation is the act of beholding the glory of God in the face of Christ, and a recognition that Christ's divinity is beyond human comprehension and objectification. Additionally, when contemplating the overflowing grace and truth of the Father in the Son, one comes to understand that Scripture, like Christ's garments, conceals his glorious person. Only those who move beyond a literal understanding of Scripture will lay hold of Christ through contemplation, and consequently worship the Creator. Maximus says that

> it is necessary that the one who seeks after God in a religious way never hold fast to the letter lest he mistakenly understand things said about God for God himself. In this case we unwisely are satisfied with the words of Scripture in place of the Word, and the Word slips out of the mind while we thought by holding on to his garment we could possess the incorporeal Word. In a similar way did the Egyptian woman lay hold not of Joseph but of his clothing, and the men of old who remained permanently in the beauty of

---

105. Maximus, *Amb.* 10, D17/1128A-B; Louth, *MC*, 108–9.

visible things and mistakenly worshiped the creature instead of the Creator.[106]

Authentic scriptural contemplation, therefore, does not settle for the written word alone, but seeks to move beyond in order to engage the living Word.[107] Thus, contemplating Scripture in search of Christ's indwelling presence, according to Maximus, is a crucial part of the human vocation. The various forms of contemplation are vital ways that human beings are transformed, enabling them to function as God's image in the world.

Contemplation: Self

To round out this discussion on prayer and contemplation, I need to touch on the third sphere where Christians find and encounter God, in the *self*. Thunberg's comment at this juncture is helpful:

> It is Maximus' conviction that the Logos always and in all "wants to effect the mystery of His embodiment." . . . Things belong together in Maximus' theological universe. The key to it is the doctrine of incarnation, the binding formula of which is that of the Council of Chalcedon. It is the Logos becoming man in Jesus Christ . . . that is the model and paradigm of the whole process of incarnation. This process is certainly interpreted in that perspective and from that starting point. This fact, however, does not exclude a high degree of parallelism between the three basic incarnations: in the *logoi* of things, the *logoi* of Scripture, and the *logos* in man.[108]

This reinforces what I have been seeking to demonstrate in Maximus's christologically grounded anthropology. That is, a significant part of realizing the human calling entails the ongoing incarnation of Christ in his followers, a reality that is structured by Maximus's Chalcedonian logic. It also underscores the three areas in which one engages in spiritual contemplation, where Christ is to be found hidden within each. We have considered contemplation of nature/world and Scripture; now we can turn our attention to the third, contemplation of humanity or the self.

---

106. Maximus, *Centuries on Theology* II, 73; in *CWS*, 163.

107. It would be interesting and provocative to place Maximus and Karl Barth in dialogue along these lines, particularly Barth's notions regarding the Word in its threefold form, its nature, and its knowability (*Church Dogmatics* I.1).

108. Thunberg, *MaC*, 159–60.

The Redemptive Goal of the Human Calling

On one level Maximus teaches that there is a discovery of spiritual riches, through asceticism and contemplation, within *ourselves*. He writes:

> The one who through asceticism and contemplation has known how to dig in himself the wells of virtue and knowledge as did the patriarchs will find Christ within as the spring of life. Wisdom bids us to drink from it, saying, "Drink waters from your own vessels and from your own springs" [Prov 5:15]. If we do this we shall discover that his treasures are present within us.[109]

By using these graphic verbs—dig, drink, discover—Maximus says that Christians who develop virtue and knowledge are like those who burrow into the ground in order to tap into the spiritual water table. Within them Christ bubbles forth as a life-giving spring, enabling them to drink from his subterranean supply.

Additionally, on a deeper level, which can be a bit more challenging to explain, as we saw earlier, Christians empowered by God's grace are able to discern vestiges of the divine within their own makeup, existence, and place within the cosmos. Yet they simultaneously recognize that the triune God most certainly (ultimately) transcends human constitution and situation. The following quote must be given in its entirety so we can catch the full meaning of Maximus's thought:

> Manifold is the relation between intellects and what they perceive and between the senses and what they experience. Thus the human being, consisting of both soul and sensible body, by means of its natural relationship of belonging to each division of creation, is both circumscribed and circumscribes: through being, it is circumscribed and through potency, it circumscribes. So in its two parts it is divided between these things, and it draws these things through their own parts into itself in unity. For the human being is circumscribed by both the intelligible and the sensible, since it is soul and body, and it has the natural capacity of circumscribing them, because it can both think and perceive through the senses.
>
> God is simply and indefinably beyond all beings. . . . So . . . the one who discerns with sagacity how he ought to love God, the transcendent nature . . . ineffably and unknowably attains the divine delight that is beyond reason and mind, in the form and fashion that God who gives such grace knows and those who are worthy of receiving this from God understand.[110]

---

109. Maximus, *Centuries on Theology* II, 40; in *CWS*, 156.
110. Maximus, *Amb.* 10, 1153A–C; Louth, *MC*, 124–25.

The gist of what Maximus is saying is that the human being is the fulcrum of God's universe and is interconnected with the wider creation. The human being, as body and soul, functions as the microcosm within the universal macrocosm. Once again, we see how Maximus paints this picture in terms of love for the transcendent God and dependence on him for wisdom and grace. Balthasar explains that Maximus sees the human being "as an intellectual and material microcosm" who "appears as the midpoint of a universe arranged in a polar pattern and as its final synthesis." As she is simultaneously "the subject of knowledge, through [her] intellect, and its object, through [her] body, [she] becomes both the world's axis and its system of coordinates." But this is not to be misconstrued, for [humanity] does not operate "as an independent lord," but "through [her] natural being, through [her] double essence, [she] is drawn into the internal mechanism of the macrocosm."[111]

Consequently, the contemplation of human nature and our position within the cosmos, leads us to a clearer understanding of the transcendent Creator. Further, through the spiritual contemplation of all visible things, besides human beings, one perceives reflections of invisible realities which point to the supreme Maker. Commenting on Paul's words in Romans, Maximus explains:

> And again, "The invisible realities from the creation of the world have been perceived and are recognized through the things he has made," [Rom 1:20] says the divine Apostle. And if we perceive what does not appear by means of what does, as the Scripture has it, then much more will visible things be understood by means of invisible by those who advance in spiritual contemplation. Indeed, the symbolic contemplation of intelligible things by means of visible realities is spiritual knowledge and understanding of visible things through the invisible. For it is necessary that things which manifest each other bear a mutual reflection in an altogether true and clear manner and keep their relationship intact.[112]

Balthasar goes so far as to say that Maximus's thoughts on this "may be the most astonishing thing he ever wrote—even if it is also the slowly ripened fruit of the whole Alexandrian metaphysical tradition."[113] What is intriguing here is the way Maximus elaborates, in an accretive, multilay-

---

111. Balthasar, *CL*, 175.
112. Maximus, *Mystagogia*, ch. 2; in *CWS*, 189.
113. Ibid., 176.

The Redemptive Goal of the Human Calling

ered fashion, on biblical tradition. In his estimation, those who spiritually contemplate the invisible within the visible (and vice versa) will grow in spiritual knowledge and understanding. This reciprocal reflection has far-reaching significance, especially for one's knowledge of the transcendent, invisible Father whom the Spirit reveals in the incarnate Son.

An Illustrative Text: Fourth Century on Love

Having considered these various agents of deification—the church, sacraments, asceticism, prayer and contemplation—I want to show how Maximus interlaces these various strands related to the human calling in a key text, his *Fourth Century on Love*. Rather than quoting large blocks of this text, I will simply point out the salient features within this particular text that demonstrate the validity of my overall claim. The organic structure of Maximus's *Fourth Century* shows the vital connections between the following themes: the end for which the Trinity created the world; human participation in the Holy Trinity (cf. 2 Pet 1:4); the deiform soul as rightly ordered in its desire for God and its love for God and neighbor; contemplation of the Trinity; the incarnation of one of the Trinity who brings divine grace to humanity; the believer's imitation of God and Christ; and the reinforcement of the primacy of love among the virtues (a central theme we will revisit in chapter 5).[114] For now, I simply highlight this text and these intrinsically connected themes, motifs that are essential in Maximus's teaching on the Trinitarian and christologically based human vocation.

Adumbrations of the Trinity in Human Beings

Being, Well-Being, Ever-Being

In addition to these important strands dealing with *theosis* and the redemptive goal of the human calling, is the notion of adumbrations of the Trinity within human beings an idea we considered earlier.[115] In my consideration

---

114. This sequential structure is seen in paragraphs 3, 8, 11, 15, 35, 36, 44, 47, 55, 77, 90, 100, the *Philokalia*, vol. 2; cf. Moltmann, "Response," 65.

115. In his analysis of natural theology, Moltmann discusses the notion of adumbrations of God in creation and human beings. He reflects: "The 'traces' of God in nature and human existence are a reflection of the coming new creation of all things." However, not "every soul is 'Christian by nature,' but every soul is by nature made and destined to be the image of God and to participate in his eternal kingdom." *ET*, 73.

of the Trinitarian matrix of the human vocation, I sketched Maximus's understanding of Trinitarian adumbrations in humanity and wider creation. Here I will look more closely at these traces of the Trinity in relation to certain triads that Maximus critically appropriates from Neoplatonic thought. Through his use of triads, Maximus again intertwines concepts that are crucial to understanding my overall claim, especially the notion of the redemptive goal of the human vocation. The first triad, *being—well-being—ever-being*, suggests that the constitution of human beings is a reflection of the Holy Trinity. Representative of Maximus scholarship on this point, Thunberg asserts that this triad is strictly anthropological in character and elucidates the Trinitarian structure of Maximus's understanding of the constitution and reconstitution of human beings.[116]

Carrying on the patristic tradition of distinguishing between the "image" and "likeness" of God in human beings (stemming from Gen 1:26), Maximus correlates this anthropological triad to the image and likeness distinction. Accordingly, being and ever-being correspond to the *image* of God in humanity. Well-being is related to the *likeness* of God that is restored in human beings through a life of active faith in Christ and worship in the church. Maximus ties this particular triad to a variety of other triads, with each one shedding more light on further aspects of redemption in Christ.[117]

What is particularly noteworthy here is how Maximus utilizes this triad, which is based on a combination of Aristotelian, biblical (Acts 17:28; Gen 1:26), Alexandrian, and Dionysian tradition, to show the deep-seated Trinitarian structure within the composition and redemption of human beings. According to Maximus, God communicates his proper being to the nature of humanity as an image (*eikon*) of Godself, and God communicates the divine goodness and wisdom to humanity's likeness (*homoiousios*).[118] As Thunberg has indicated, Maximus weaves together these related themes: that humanity is created in the image of God; that God's likeness is restored to human beings through a vital relationship of love and obedience to Christ; and that the very creation and existence of human beings and their

---

116. Other scholars—such as Balthasar, Sherwood, and Louth—agree that these adumbrations of the Trinity in creation are significant in order to understand Maximus's theological anthropology. See, e.g., Sherwood, *SMC*, 37ff.

117. See *QT* 60; *Amb.* 7; *Amb.* 42. This threefold schema of being, well-being, ever-being is also paralleled with a variety of other triads: three human births, the three redemptive births of Christ, the three days of creation (days 6–8), and the three laws: natural, written, and grace; cf. Thunberg, *MM*, 369–73; cf. Blowers, *CMJC*, 29, 39.

118. See Thunberg, *MaC*, 46ff.

The Redemptive Goal of the Human Calling

restoration signifies the goodness, wisdom, and life of the Holy Trinity. Thunberg argues that

> the anthropological triad of "Being," "Well-being," and "Ever-being" is another "adumbration" of God's Trinitarian life, and it stands in direct relation to the distinction in man between divine image and divine likeness. Consequently, one could expect to find in the very constitution of man—as an image of God, destined for likeness to Him—another "adumbration."[119]

Mind, Reason, and Spirit

There is another adumbration of the Trinity within human beings, as Maximus suggests in *Amb.* 7. In this text Maximus says that the *mind, reason*, and *spirit* of human beings are to be conformed to their divine archetypes: the Great Mind, Logos, and Spirit. Building on these reflections, Maximus adds in *Amb.* 10 that this triad of the human soul is an image of the Trinitarian Archetype. Thus, the soul's simplicity and unity reflects God's simplicity, while human goodness expressed in the virtuous life reflects God's goodness, and the way that humanity is liberated from everything that divides reflects the Holy Trinity's activity of unification in the cosmos.[120] Moreover, Thunberg posits that "it is not difficult to find in these references to three basic human activities, references to the three Persons of the divine Trinity." For the "Father is the principle of unity, the Son is the manifestation of the goodness of God, and the Spirit is the power of unification."[121]

Trinitarian Outlines and Apophaticism

However, as we have noticed in Maximus's theology, these outlines of the Trinity within human beings are just that—*outlines*, symbols, or foreshadowings of something, rather, someone who transcends human comprehension. While Maximus does present the notion of Trinitarian adumbrations

---

119. Ibid., 47.

120. Thunberg, *MaC*, 46–47; and *MM*, 129ff. Thunberg notes the intriguing similarities between Maximus and Augustine on the point of Trinitarian-psychological speculations, but adds that the historical evaluation of their relationship is difficult to deduce (*MaC*, 47). As mentioned previously, this is evidence against the oversimplification of de Régnon's Trinitarian typology, which bifurcates Latin and Greek theology. See also the argument proposed by LaCugna, *God for Us*, 11ff.

121. Thunberg, *MaC*, 47.

103

in human beings, he is careful to safeguard his teaching with an apophatic emphasis. Therefore, in Maximus's view, human beings bear the image of the triune God, and are conformed and restored to the divine likeness through intimate communion with the Trinity. This restoration of humanity, or redemptive goal as I have called it, is structured by Maximus's thoroughly Trinitarian theology and soteriology, and is based on his vision of Christ. To realize one's human potential through faith in God, union with Christ, and the transforming grace of the Spirit (*theosis*), is the gist of the redemptive goal of the human vocation. And, as I have sought to demonstrate in Maximus's work, this soteriological conception springs out of his Trinitarian and christological vision.[122] With Maximus's vision in mind and before us, I turn now to Moltmann's understanding of the redemptive goal of the human calling.

The Redemptive Goal of the Human Calling in Moltmann

In the previous section, I sought to demonstrate how Maximus integrates Trinitarian and christological reflection with an eschatologically oriented view of human redemption. This careful analysis further reinforced my overall claim: that Maximus's understanding of what it means to be fully human and to fulfill the human vocation, emerges from his Trinitarian and christological reflection.

What I aim to do now is show how Moltmann conceives of the redemptive goal of the human calling in creation. I will do this through an exploration of "the sabbath rest of all creation" in Moltmann's theology, while also noting parallels with Maximus on the Sabbath. I will start with a consideration of the background of this "Sabbath" metaphor, followed by a close look at the Trinitarian and christological patterns that structure Moltmann's teaching on the eschatological Sabbath. Finally, I will delineate the implications of the human vocation that arise from Moltmann's Trinitarian and christologically-based theology of the creation's Sabbath rest.

---

122. Again, Thunberg asserts that the Trinitarian dimension is evident throughout all of Maximus's theology, even though the apophatic safeguard is always present. He explains that the Trinitarian dimension "is fundamental, and it can be applied generally to all aspects of life: to creation, *to the constitution of man*, and *to soteriology* in all its phases and perspectives" (*MC*, 48, italics mine).

The Redemptive Goal of the Human Calling

Background of the Sabbath Rest of All Creation

As Moltmann does in his Christology (namely, within *The Way of Jesus Christ*), he also seeks to trace his teaching on the Sabbath rest of creation back to the biblical traditions. He asserts that the notion of the Sabbath rest of all creation is the goal of every Jewish and Christian doctrine of creation, and that the Sabbath opens up creation for its true future and full realization. Thus, every time the Sabbath is observed, the redemption of humanity and all of creation is celebrated in anticipation. "The sabbath is itself the presence of eternity in time," Moltmann argues, "and a foretaste of the world to come."[123] Moreover, it is the doctrine and practice of the Sabbath that reveals the true identity of the world as "creation," thereby sanctifying and blessing it.[124]

In *God in Creation*, where Moltmann develops his argument on the Sabbath rest in relation to Trinitarian and anthropological doctrine, he contends that the Christian traditions (especially in the Western church) have tended to neglect the notion of the "completion" of creation through "the seventh day." Whether or not his claim of the Western church's neglect of this element is verifiable is out of the scope of my own analysis. Yet I must say that I *do* find the notion of creation's completion through the seventh day represented in Augustine, Aquinas, Bonaventure, Barth, and Balthasar, to name a few key "Western" theologians.[125] On another note, I will demonstrate below some of the nexus between Moltmann and Maximus on the Sabbath rest of all creation, intriguing points of correlation that show the importance of this doctrine for conveying soteriological and eschatological facets of their theological anthropology.

Furthermore, Moltmann makes a curious observation concerning the way that certain modern theologians neglected the importance of the Sabbath based on their exegesis of the Gospels, where Jesus appears to set

---

123. Moltmann, *GC*, 276. Bauckham's overview of Moltmann's eschatology, which touches on key issues related to the human vocation, is particularly informative (*TJM*, 8–10).

124. Moltmann, *GC*, 276.

125. For example, we find teaching on the completion of creation through the seventh day in: Augustine, *Confessions*, bk. 13:36:51, p. 369ff.; Aquinas, *Summa Theologica*, vol. 1, 1a, quest. 73, pp. 352ff.; Bonaventure, *Breviloquium*, pt. 2, ch. 2, pp. 72ff.; Barth, *Church Dogmatics* 3.1, *Doctrine of Creation*, pp. 214ff.; regarding Balthasar, see Pitstick, *Light in Darkness*, 36ff.

aside the Sabbath commandment by healing the sick on that specific day.[126] Moltmann traces this understanding in theologians like Paul Tillich, who emphasizes that God in God's essential being is "the creative God," and that human beings created in God's image, see themselves as bearers of God's image if they become "creative human beings." Therefore, the God "who 'rests' on the sabbath," Moltmann argues, "the blessing and rejoicing God who delights in [God's] creation, and in [God's] exultation sanctifies it, recedes behind this different concept [as espoused by Tillich]." This view of God has significant anthropological ramifications. For "men and women . . . the meaning of their lives is identified with work and busy activity; and rest, the feast, and their joy in existence are pushed away, relegated to insignificance because they are non-utilitarian."[127]

Countering the utilitarian view of God and humanity, Moltmann proposes that creation and the Sabbath are rightly understood in relation to one another, as the biblical narrative suggests. The world is perceived as God's creation in light of the Sabbath, when women and men cease from their activities in creation and allow creation to be *God's* creation. "They recognize that as God's property creation is inviolable," Moltmann says, "and they sanctify the day through their joy in existence as God's creatures within the fellowship of creation."[128]

Moltmann argues, further, that the biblical traditions do not present the Sabbath as a day of rest following six days of work. Rather, God's entire work of creation was performed for the sake of the Sabbath. Citing Jewish theologian Franz Rosenzweig, Moltmann explains that the Sabbath is "the feast of creation," the purpose for which God created heaven, earth, and human beings.[129] This point is particularly important for what I seek to explain in this section, because for Moltmann the feast of creation is the feast or celebration of its completion, its consummation in God. "Because this consummation of creation in the sabbath also presents creation's redemption," says Moltmann, "the redemption enabling it to participate in God's manifested, eternal presence," it will "also be permissible for us to understand the sabbath as the feast of redemption." Again, Moltmann re-

---

126. See Mark 3:1–6; 2:23–28.

127. Moltmann, *GC*, 277.

128. Ibid.

129. Ibid. Müller-Fahrenholz reflects on Moltmann's engagement of Jewish theology, offering some intriguing insights into the teleological structure of Moltmann's thinking, in *KP*, 156–60.

The Redemptive Goal of the Human Calling

fers to Rosenzweig: "The sabbath is the feast of creation," but "a creation which took place for the sake of the redemption. It is manifested at the end of creation, and manifested as creation's meaning and destination."[130] These themes—of redemption, creaturely participation in God's presence, and creation's purpose and goal—are structured by Moltmann's Trinitarian and christological vision. As this section unfolds, I will demonstrate this, as well as show how Moltmann's Trinitarian and christological doctrine gives rise to and is interwoven with his anthropology.

Moltmann goes on to explore elements of the biblical vision of the Sabbath, with the Jewish understanding of how God's revelation embraces them, and uses these as vectors for developing his teaching on a messianic vision of creation, one that is permeated by the revelation and presence of the triune God. In his exposition, Moltmann explores the *completion of creation*, as described in the narrative of Genesis 1 and 2. In short, Moltmann says that creation is completed by God's rest, a rest *from* God's works and *in* God's works. The Sabbath of God's creation "already contains in itself the redemptive mystery of God's indwelling in his creation, although—and just because—he is wholly concentrated in himself and rests in himself."[131]

God's Transcendence and Immanence

As we saw in chapter 2, Moltmann is careful to balance the notion of God's transcendence and immanence in these reflections, something that Maximus also attends to carefully. He explains, "The works of creation display in God's acts the Creator's continual transcendence over his creation," but "the sabbath of creation points to the Creator's immanence in his creation."[132] Moreover, in some sense Moltmann posits that the Sabbath is a profounder mystery than creation. For creation is God's revelation of his works, while the Sabbath is the divine revelation of Godself. Consequently, the Sabbath

---

130. Moltmann, *GC*, 278.

131. Ibid., 279. See Müller-Fahrenholz's comments on Moltmann's understanding of the mystery of God's indwelling in creation, *KP*, 153–56.

132. Moltmann, *GC*, 279–80. Moltmann references Barth: "God . . . made himself temporal and human, i.e., He linked himself in a temporal act with the being and purpose and course of the world, with the history of man . . . His honour is compromised and at stake" (CD III/1, 214, in *GC*, 355n8). In the same note, he also cites Heschel, *Sabbath*, 60: "The Sabbath is the presence of God in the world."

of creation already signifies the beginning of the kingdom of God's glory, the hope and future of all created being.[133]

Moltmann and Maximus on 1 Kings 19

In his consideration of the biblical material regarding the profound mystery of God's presence in the Sabbath, Moltmann mentions the passage in 1 Kings 19,[134] where Elijah encounters God on Mount Horeb. In a rather mystical spirit,[135] Moltmann suggests that "God is present in the sabbath stillness, just as for Elijah on Horeb, the mount of God, God was in 'the voice of a hovering silence' (Buber's translation)."[136]

Maximus also develops a meditation on 1 Kings 19, one that accords with Moltmann's reflections on the mystery of God's presence in the Sabbath. Put succinctly, Maximus finds in 1 Kings 19 a spiritual teaching on the visionary intellect that encounters the inner principles (*logoi*) of Scripture as "a delicate breeze." Maximus interprets the ascent to Horeb as the cultivation of the virtues in the spirit of grace. The cave is the hidden sanctuary of wisdom within the intellect, where one encounters and mystically perceives spiritual knowledge that is beyond normal perception, in which God is said to dwell. Thus, everyone who diligently seeks God (through ascetic practice and attaining virtue) will enter the hidden sanctuary of wisdom (through contemplation), preparing them for mystical union with the Holy Trinity. Encountering God in this silence, therefore, is a rich metaphor for Moltmann and Maximus, one that expresses important ideas regarding redemption, sanctification, spiritual growth, and the mystery of God's presence in creation. In the following chapter, we will look further into Maximus's teaching on the three stages of the spiritual life in relation

---

133. Moltmann, *GC*, 280.

134. In this passage, Elijah returns to Horeb/Sinai, the place where Moses experienced a theophany, encountering the wind, earthquake, and fire, the same elements mentioned in 1 Kings 19. This time, however, God is experienced in the sheer silence, the barely audible whisper.

135. Müller-Fahrenholz explicates the mystical dimension in Moltmann's theology. He asserts that there is without a doubt a mystical filament running through Moltmann's theology, especially his theology of the Trinity (*KP*, 150–51). Bauckham develops an entire chapter on Moltmann's thinking about mysticism (*TJM*, 213–47). Moltmann acknowledges that there is a mystical element in his theology (*ET*, xxi).

136. Moltmann, *GC*, 280. He adds: "The works of creation show God exoterically and indirectly, as it were, as the Creator. But the sabbath, in its peace and its silence, manifest the eternal God who rests in his glory" (280).

The Redemptive Goal of the Human Calling

to his Trinitarian and christolgically based anthroplogy. I will show other examples below where Maximus brings together similar ideas in his meditations on the Sabbath, God's presence in creation and creatures, and the spiritual struggle for silence (*hesychia*) and stillness before God.

What I want to underline here is the way that Moltmann shows the connections between our vision of God and ourselves, as well as between creation, Sabbath, and redemption. It is this vision of the triune God, as the creative, redeeming, and resting God that lays the foundation for his theological anthropology. The Trinitarian and christological foundation and dimensions will become increasingly evident, especially as we move into the final chapter.

Human Rest in God's Rest

In addition to Moltmann's biblical reflections on the Sabbath as the completion of creation, he ruminates on the blessing and sanctification of creation, the feast of redemption, Jesus and the Sabbath, and Sunday as the feast of the beginning. Out of these biblical and theological reflections a few observations are particularly important in relation to my overall claim. The first deals with Moltmann's reflections on Hebrews 4:9–10, where the author says that "a sabbath rest still remains for the people of God; for those who enter God's rest cease from their labors as God did from his." Stemming from this passage and Revelation 14:13 (which speaks of the blessed dead who rest from their labors), Moltmann asserts that it is only in God's rest that created beings find their own rest. For God brought everything to being out of nothing, explains Moltmann, and all creatures are tormented by non-being and are restless in search of a haven where the menace of non-being cannot reach them. Moltmann draws insight from Augustine's famous dictum, that the human heart is restless until it finds rest in God, yet Moltmann adds that *all* of creation is suffused with this unrest, and seeks to transcend itself in the quest for the rest in which it might dwell.[137] He explains that it is only in God's Sabbath that humanity and all of creation find true rest. Moltmann says, "In the resting, and hence direct, unmedi-

---

137. Moltmann, *GC*, 282; Augustine, *Confessions* I.1, 43. See Moltmann's discussion of how humans, according to Augustine and Pascal, are related to and withdrawn from themselves, an "immanent transcendence," and how the restless heart finds rest in God alone (*SL*, 91). Likewise, in conversation with Pseudo-Dionysius, Maximus speaks of human desire and restlessness that is intended to drive us toward God, the only one who satisfies the hungers of the human heart and gives true rest. See Thunberg, *MM*, 199ff.

ated presence of God, all created beings find their dwelling." In "the resting presence of God all creatures find their sustaining foundation." Thus, the world that is created out of nothing, and for the Sabbath, finds repose in God and God's rest. It is this repose of the Sabbath, as Moltmann argues based on Hebrews 4, that prefigures the redemption of God's creatures.[138]

Sabbath Rest in Maximus

As mentioned above, this theme of Sabbath rest is also found in Maximus, and as we saw in Moltmann, Maximus also underscores the connections between the Sabbath, redemption, and mystical union with God. In pointing out some of the salient features of Maximus's teaching on the Sabbath, I will highlight some of these interconnections, as well as ways that his ideas emerge from Trinitarian and christological reflection.

Most of Maximus's theological meditations on the Sabbath are found in his *Centuries on Love*, where he suggests that Christians are to keep the Sabbath "spiritually," observing it in a threefold way.[139] Maximus explains, further, that the Sabbath is to be "prepared for" through the practice of the virtues (of body and soul), accompanied by works of righteousness.[140] Following his thoughts in the various *Centuries*, we find an interesting text in which Maximus links the Sabbath to the threefold perspective on the spiritual life. He says:

> In the Law and the prophets reference is made to the sabbath (cf. Is. 66:23), Sabbaths (cf. Ex. 31:13) and Sabbaths of Sabbaths (cf. Lev. 16:31, LXX); and to circumcision and circumcision of circumcision (cf. Gen. 17:1013); and to harvest (cf. Gen. 8:22) and harvest of harvest, as in the text, "when you harvest your harvest" (cf. Lev. 23:10). The texts about the sabbath surely refer to the full attainment of practical, natural and theological philosophy . . .[141]

138. Moltmann, *GC*, 282. Related to this theme of redemptive rest, Balthasar and Moltmann note the interweaving of Christian mysticism, Trinitarian theology, and salvation history in Joachim of Fiore; cf. Balthasar, *CL*, 310; and Moltmann, *CG*, 31, 42, 143ff.

139. Maximus, *CC* II, 86; in *Philokalia*, 80; cf. Blowers's remarks on the "ever moving repose" of which Maximus speaks in relation to the spiritual Sabbath (*CMJC*, 42); and Louth's illuminating comments regarding Maximus's teaching on the Sabbath (*MC*, 42–43). McDougall argues along the same lines regarding the grounding of Moltmann's theology and understanding of the Christian life in terms of the journey of love (*PL*, 143–44).

140. Maximus, *CC* II, 20; in *Philokalia*, 118.

141. Maximus, *Centuries on Theology* I, 36; in *Philokalia*, 121–22.

Maximus goes on to explain that the

> sabbath signifies the dispassion of the deiform soul that through practice of the virtues has utterly cast off the marks of sin. Sabbaths signify the freedom of the deiform soul that through the spiritual contemplation of created nature has quelled even the natural activity of sense-perception. Sabbath of Sabbaths signify the spiritual calm of the deiform soul that has withdrawn the intellect even from contemplation of all the divine principles in created beings, that through an ecstasy of love has clothed it entirely in God alone, and that through mystical theology has brought it together to rest in God.[142]

In these texts, Maximus weaves together a number of key threads I have been considering: the Evagrian schema of *praktike*, *physike*, and *theologia*; the deiform soul (*theosis* or deification); contemplation of the *logoi* in creatures; the ecstasy of love; mystical theology (union with God), and rest in God. In accord with Moltmann, these various threads related to Maximus's teaching on the Sabbath evince the eschatological orientation and soteriological emphasis within his theology.

Moreover, Maximus's teaching on the Sabbath is rooted in his vision of the Holy Trinity and his Christology. For Maximus, *theologia* (theological philosophy) means mystical union with the Holy Trinity. In his continued reflection on the Sabbath, Maximus explains that the Sabbath signifies "the complete reversion of created beings to God." As we saw in chapter 2, regarding the Trinitarian matrix of Maximus and Moltmann's theology, creatures are graced with the gift of being from their Maker, and are evoked to return to intimate union with the Holy Trinity. In addition to this reversion of creatures to God, Maximus says that the Sabbath is a "rest of the intellect" as one finds mystical repose in their Creator, a state of being in which the *nous* is freed from images and passions as it undergoes ecstatic union with God. In language that resonates with Moltmann's perichoretic theology, Maximus explains that the human intellect that experiences Sabbath rest in God becomes a temple mystically built by peace, a dwelling place of God in the Spirit, so that God and creature reciprocally dwell in one another.[143]

Maximus says, further, that the deeper meaning of the seventh and eighth days of the creation narrative is properly understood in light of

---

142. Maximus, *Centuries on Theology* I, 37–39; in *Philokalia*, 122.
143. Maximus, *Centuries on Theology* I, 47, 53; in *Philokalia*, 123, 124–25.

Christ. Accordingly, Christians who complete the spiritual preparation of the sixth day (with works of righteousness), cross over into the repose of the seventh day, when the intellect grasps the inner structures of creation, ceases from all movement, and rests in the Trinitarian God. For those Christians who journey from the sixth and seventh days to the eighth day, the grace of God enables them to participate in God's deifying energy, what Maximus calls the mystical resurrection. Here, in his typical christocentric fashion, Maximus brings together the ternary themes of the three Sabbath days, the threefold schema of Evagrian spirituality, and the three primary events of the Christ narrative. Intriguingly, Maximus begins from the end, with the resurrection, moves to the entombment, then recaps and discusses the resurrection in finer detail. What Maximus says, essentially, is that Christians participate with Christ in a mystical resurrection, leaving behind their linen clothes in the sepulcher (cf. John 20:6–7), convinced through their own experience of the reality that "the Lord has risen." The tomb, Maximus says, symbolizes this world or the heart of each faithful Christian, while the linen clothes and napkin represent the inner essences of things and the vision of God through which believers perceive the Logos in the structures of creation. Those who "bury the Lord with honor"—by embodying through the spiritual life the dynamics of his *kenosis*, crucifixion, and entombment—not only proclaim and exhibit the truth of Christ's resurrection, but actually participate in the Lord's rising to new life.[144]

What's more, these meditations on the spiritual Sabbath lead right to the two more prominent texts I referenced in earlier chapters: "The mystery of the incarnation of the Logos is the key to all the arcane symbolism and typology in the Scriptures . . ." and "All visible realities need the cross . . ."[145] Maximus, therefore, illustrates again that his theological anthropology springs out of his vision of the Trinity and the incarnate Word. In these selected texts, Maximus integrates themes related to the redemptive goal of the human calling: how Christians observe the Sabbath spiritually; preparing for it through the practice of the virtues and works of righteousness; by understanding the links between the Sabbath and practical, natural, and theological philosophy; how the Sabbath signifies the return of created beings to the Holy Trinity, so that their intellects find rest in God and participate in God's deifying energy; and how experiencing the spiritual Sabbath is directly tied to the believer's intimate sharing in the incarnation,

---

144. Maximus, *Centuries on Theology* I, 59–63; in *Philokalia*, 126–27.
145. Maximus, *Centuries on Theology* I, 66–67; in *Philokalia*, 127.

The Redemptive Goal of the Human Calling

death, and resurrection of Christ. Though Maximus articulates his teaching in different language and applies elements of the concepts in different ways, the God-centered quality of his theological anthropology is seen in his reflections on the Sabbath, as is the case with Moltmann.

The Sanctification of Creation through the Sabbath

Turning back to Moltmann, I want to consider another element of the biblical tradition on the Sabbath that he examines, the sanctification of creation through the Sabbath. Once again reflecting on Genesis 1 and 2, along with Jewish theology, Moltmann explains that in the Sabbath eternity and time touch.[146] Moreover, after demonstrating how the Sabbath belongs to the fundamental structure of creation, how some think that it is the longest and most important among the commandments (Exod 20:8–11), and how the Sabbath is to encompass all creatures, Moltmann speaks of how the faithful are to sanctify the Sabbath. He says that by abstaining from all productive work, humans acknowledge that the whole of reality is God's creation, the creation in which God is coming to rest. Through this abstinence, and celebration of all things as God's creation, human beings begin to fulfill their calling as God's image, as God's stewards over creation. Additionally, in celebrating the Sabbath one experiences an increased capacity for perceiving the beauty of all things (food, clothing, the body and soul), because existence itself is glorious.[147]

Moltmann's interpretive meditations on the Sabbath resonate with the spirit of Maximus's mystical theology. These last two elements—abstaining from work and the celebration of all creation—are harmonious with Maximus's teaching on asceticism and the contemplation of the inner beauty of all things as God's creation.[148]

---

146. Moltmann, *GC*, 286ff. Moltmann offers interesting insights regarding this interaction between eternity and time, in conversation with Abraham Heschel.

147. Moltmann, *GC*, 286; cf. Müller-Fahrenholz, *KP*, where he analyzes these connected ideas in Moltmann (*KP*, 184ff.). See also Sherrard's reflections on the sanctity and glory of all living things (*Human Image*, 10).

148. Moltmann, *GC*, 285ff. The mystical spirit of Moltmann's meditations on the Sabbath can be discerned as he considers the connections between abstaining from activity, recollecting oneself in God's presence, cultivating a eucharistic expression of existence, glorifying and enjoying God and God's creation, and remembering God and the Sabbath in the rhythms of life (*GC*, 287); cf. Bauckham, *TJM*, 213–21, 238ff.

The Sabbath as Feast of Redemption

In addition to these reflections on the sanctification of the Sabbath, is Moltmann's teaching on the Sabbath as the feast of redemption. The Sabbath, as we saw previously, is the consummation of creation, the completion of creation graciously given through the reposeful presence of the Creator in what has been created.[149] Moltmann elucidates this theme through a string of meditations on biblical images of redemption. Basically, he argues that the Sabbath as the completion of creation and the revelation of God's reposing existence in his creation, reaches out beyond itself to the time when God's creation and revelation are one. This is the essence of redemption, the eternal Sabbath and the new creation, when "the whole earth is full of God's glory" (Isa 6:3), when God is "all in all" (1 Cor 15:28), and when God dwells in the whole of his creation (Rev 21:3). "God is then manifest in the whole creation," Moltmann says, "and the whole creation is the manifestation and mirror of [God's] glory: that is the redeemed world."[150] Thus, the Sabbath opens up all of creation for the coming of God's glorious kingdom, and through its celebration, the messianic hope of God's people is kindled.

The Sabbath and Jesus Christ

One final aspect of the Sabbath and its relation to redemption concerns how the many biblical threads are brought together in the person of Jesus Christ. It is through his messianic mission that the Old Testament Year of Jubilee (Lev 25:8–55) is fully realized. As the promised Messiah, he ushers in the end-time Year of Jubilee, with its cosmic liberation, justice, righteousness, and peace, as the book of Isaiah envisioned (61:1–11). The Sabbath is to be understood, therefore, in the light of Jesus's messianic mission and in the context of his commandment of love and discipleship. Accordingly, Jesus did not abolish the Sabbath, rather he pointed to and embodied the liberty of the messianic era of which the Sabbath signifies.[151]

---

149. Moltmann, *GC*, 287.

150. Ibid., 288. Müller-Fahrenholz considers this theme in Moltmann, including some questions raised by critics of Moltmann's eschatological and soteriological vision (*KP*, 213ff.).

151. See Moltmann's further reflections on the relationship between Jesus, the early Christians, and the Sabbath, in *GC*, 292, 294.

The Redemptive Goal of the Human Calling

Trinitarian and Christological Patterns

According to Moltmann, the Sabbath rest of all creation is the redemptive goal of the human calling. This vision of comprehensive redemption, Moltmann says, emerges from biblical and creedal traditions. Moltmann is careful, moreover, to demonstrate the Trinitarian structure of this vision of the Sabbath and its relation to a "pneumatological doctrine of creation," that is based on the Trinitarian and pneumatological images of Scripture, as well as the Trinitarian framework of the Apostles' Creed.

For Maximus, the redemptive goal of the human calling is fleshed out in terms of *theosis*, while for Moltmann, the redemptive goal is the Sabbath rest of all creation. Where Maximus carefully nuances his vision of *theosis* in Chalcedonian terms (i.e., "unconfused"), Moltmann is careful to balance his perichoretic and eschatologically oriented vision of the reciprocal indwelling of God and creation in terms that preserve both the transcendence and immanence of God. Moreover, Moltmann's holistic vision of creation is understood in "ecological" terms, that is, as *oikos* theology, which speaks of creation as God's house, the place where God's Shekinah dwells. Accordingly, Moltmann asserts that the Creator, creation, and the goal of that creation are to be understood in a Trinitarian sense. Therefore, these three themes are explored together throughout many of Moltmann's works: the triune Creator and the Shekinah, the creation as the Trinity's dwelling place, and the goal of creation, to be transfigured into a new heaven and a new earth (Rev 21), where God and creation "rest" in one another.[152]

Incarnation, Tabernacle, Shekinah

Moltmann shows how this Trinitarian sense of creation—created out of nothing by the Father, recapitulated through the Son, and transfigured by the power of the Spirit—is intrinsically linked to the incarnation of the Word and his resurrection. The Old Testament doctrine of Shekinah, with its vision of the Creator-God dwelling among God's people, is fully realized in the New Testament portrayal of the incarnation of the Word,

---

152. It is intriguing to see further ways that Moltmann contemplates the Sabbath rest described in the biblical material, along with key passages in Augustine that speak of humanity and God resting in one another, as discussed earlier. For other examples, see Moltmann, "Homecoming," 280–81. Further, Moltmann shows in detail how this Sabbath vision addresses the contemporary ecological and religious crises, in "Reconciliation with Nature," 301–13.

who "tabernacles" (*eskenosen*) among humanity (John 1:14) and ushers in the new creation of all things through his life, death, and resurrection. In one place Moltmann explains, "The New Testament *incarnation theology* is *Christian Shekinah theology* . . . (Jn. 1:14; Col. 2:9) . . . The New Testament pneumatology is Christian Shekinah-theology . . . (1 Cor. 6:19)."[153] The interconnections between the Trinitarian understanding of creation, redemption, the incarnation, and the eschatological indwelling of God, are pervasive in Moltmann.

The notion of Christ the Word who tabernacles among human beings—based on Old Testament traditions and Johannine theology—is also taken up by Maximus and other patristic figures prior to him. For example, in a spiritual reading of Pentecost (Lev 23–25), Maximus explains how the Logos, as the trumpet, summons us with divine and hidden knowledge. As our propitiation, he expiates our sins in his own person by becoming like us and divinizing our sinful nature by the gift of grace through the Spirit. And as our tabernacle or booth, he "is the realization of that immutability with which our inner being, conformed to God, is concentrated on the divine, and also the securing bond of our transformation into an immortal state."[154] In other places, Maximus weaves together meditations on the Logos, who is the tabernacle and house of God, with ideas of his indwelling the virtuous souls of his followers. Thus, the holy tabernacle actually tabernacles within the Christian, making her a holy house of God where spiritual thanksgiving and feasting abounds.[155]

Implications for the Human Calling

The implications of this Trinitarian and christologically structured vision of redemption for the human calling are profound, especially for human

---

153. Raymond E. Brown affirms this understanding by explaining that the flesh of Jesus Christ is the new localization of God's presence on earth, that he is the replacement of the ancient tabernacle, and the One whom we behold (*etheasametha*) as one watches a person act out the play in a theater (*Gospel according to John I–XII*, 13, 502). See Moltmann's essay "Homecoming," 277–81. In it he explains, "The New Testament *incarnation theology* is *Christian shekinah theology* . . . (Jn. 1:14; Col. 2:9). . . . The New Testament pneumatology is Christian shekinah-theology . . . (1 Cor. 6:19)" (279).

154. Maximus, *Fifth Century of Various Texts* 49; *Philokalia*, 272–73; cf. McDermott, *Word Become Flesh*, 250ff., for his consideration of Theodore of Mopsuestia and other patristic figures who elaborate on the Logos theology of John 1.

155. Maximus, *Centuries on Theology* II, 78; in *Philokalia*, 157.

The Redemptive Goal of the Human Calling

beings as the image of God in creation. As we saw, this is another area where the parallels between Moltmann and Maximus are particularly interesting. According to Moltmann, the peace of the Sabbath

> is peace with God first of all. But this divine peace encompasses not merely the soul but the body too; not merely individuals but family and people; not only human beings but animals as well; not living things alone, but also, as the creation story tells us, the whole creation of heaven and earth.[156]

This vision of all-encompassing divine peace—that flows from the triune God through the incarnate Son—settles in all strata and corners of creation, in terms accordant to Maximus's description of the five cosmic syntheses wrought by Christ the divine-human Word, and carried on through divinely graced human beings. In a text that will be central in the next chapter (*Amb.* 41) Maximus explains that Christ, as the paradigmatic mediator

> unites man and woman . . . unites the earth by abolishing the division between the earthly paradise and the rest of the inhabited globe . . . unites earth and heaven . . . unites sensible and intelligible things . . . and ultimately—in an ineffable way—unites created and uncreated nature.[157]

These representative texts demonstrate how, according to Moltmann and Maximus, the presence of God brings peace, rest, and unity to all of creation. They also provide a segue into the next chapter, where I will analyze the Trinitarian-christocentric practice of the human calling in creation. Building on Maximus and Moltmann's eschatologically oriented visions of redemption, in which Maximus's understanding of *theosis* and Moltmann's conception of the Sabbath are structured by their Trinitarian-christocentric visions, I now turn to consider how they portray the communal praxis of the human vocation.

---

156. Moltmann, *GC*, 277. On this note, in *SL*, 94, Moltmann again quotes Maximus (as well as Gregory Palamas) regarding the way that human beings are transfigured body *and* soul through redemption in Christ: "By nature man remains wholly human in his soul and body, but by grace he becomes wholly God both in his soul and in his body."

157. Maximus, *Amb.* 41, 1305A–D, 1308A–C; Louth, *MC*, 158ff.

5

The Trinitarian-Christocentric Practice of the Human Calling

SO FAR I HAVE ATTEMPTED TO SHOW HOW MAXIMUS AND MOLTMANN'S understanding of the human vocation springs out of their Trinitarian and christological visions. I began by explaining how Maximus's refinement of his tradition, and Moltmann's retrieval of particular patristic themes, provide Trinitarian-christocentric visions that mutually illuminate one another, as well as offer constructive ways to move beyond some of the impasses of modern theology. Next, I showed how Maximus and Moltmann develop the human vocation within a Trinitarian matrix. I then looked at ways both Maximus and Moltmann base their understanding of the human calling upon their Christology. This was followed by an analysis of the redemptive goal of the human calling, in terms of *theosis* for Maximus, and the metaphor of the Sabbath rest for Moltmann.

These various stages of the study—exploring the Trinitarian structure, christological basis, eschatological and soteriological alignment—lead to this penultimate chapter. In this segment, my aim is to demonstrate how Maximus and Moltmann's Trinitarian and christological doctrine shapes their conception of the Christian community's praxis.

Transformative, Communal Praxis

McIntosh, based on his study of Maximus's mystical theology and John Henry Newman's insightful sermons, shows the relationship between Trinitarian and christological reflection and the transformative, communal praxis of Christ's followers. He contends, according to Newman's argument, that "a recovery of the ancient sense that beliefs, even when they exceed our understanding [such as Maximus' apophatic trinitarian theology or

The Trinitarian-Christocentric Practice of the Human Calling

Moltmann's perichoretic vision of the Trinity, Christ, and creation], can be measured in a practical sense by the shaping effect they have on the lives and consciousness of a believing community and its members."[1] Or, as Jaroslav Pelikan asserts, who himself bridged the Lutheran and Orthodox traditions, Maximus's theology illustrates how doctrine and spirituality are inseparable.[2] This organic connection between Trinitarian and christological reflection and the Christian understanding of what God intends for human beings (and how it is realized through the praxis of the spiritual life), twin themes in both Maximus and Moltmann, is the thrust of the following section.

I begin this chapter, accordingly, with an analysis of Trinitarian-christocentric praxis in Maximus, looking at his notion of the human being as an ordered microcosm, its disintegration through the passions, its reintegration through the virtues, and the double commandment of love. Further, I explore what Maximus intends by humanity's call to be a universal mediator, the three stages of the spiritual life, further threefold patterns of spiritual development, and the outworking of the human vocation in five cosmic syntheses or mediations.

Following this review of Maximus, I proceed to probe Moltmann's teaching on Trinitarian-christocentric praxis, with an in-depth look at his teaching on God's human image in creation, as *imago Dei*, *imago Christi*, and *gloria Dei*. Then I consider Moltmann's vision of the messianic fellowship of service for the kingdom of God, which further exemplifies the Trinitarian and christological structures of his anthropology, as worshipers of the triune God, disciples of the crucified Christ, and Spirit-empowered servants of the kingdom of God.

As noted, there are irreducible differences between Maximus and Moltmann and their respective theological visions. Yet there are certain striking points of correlation between them regarding the high calling on humanity, the graced role that is extended to human beings to cooperate with God in the redemption of creation, and the way this calling is based on and summed up in the twin commandments of love for God and love for neighbor. With these things in mind, I turn now to Maximus.

---

1. McIntosh, *MT*, 62; *DivT*, 54; cf. Janet Williams's comments on the practical ascetic activities in Maximus, personal transformation, and the christological structure of Maximus's thought, in "Pseudo-Dionysius," 195.

2. Pelikan, in the introduction to *CWS*, 4; cf. Lossky, *Mystical Theology*, 7–9.

Trinitarian-Christocentric Praxis in Maximus the Confessor

Human Being as Ordered Microcosm

According to Maximus's theological anthropology, human beings are created and called to become ordered microcosms. The concept of the human person as microcosm is one developed in Christian tradition to explain the dual composition of humanity, as body and soul or spirit.[3] This notion can be traced to Greek antiquity (probably under Oriental influence), with Democritus calling the human being a microcosm, and Plato's *Timaeus* describing the world as one large human being, though he never explicitly uses the term. Aristotle, however, does refer to the human being as microcosm, but the idea is not very prominent in his thinking. In Stoic philosophy, the concept becomes more widely used.

The Christian tradition takes up the earlier development of the concept, adding new strokes, linking the idea of microcosm to the image of God in human beings. Building on the thought of Greek philosophers and others like Philo of Alexandria, Christian theologians such as Basil of Caesarea, Gregory of Nazianzus, and Gregory of Nyssa employ the concept to convey such things as: the wisdom of the creator displayed through human beings; the task of human beings to bring body and soul into relationship with God; and their call to mediate between the intelligible and the sensible world.[4] As we will see, Maximus takes up these various elements related to the human as microcosm, synthesizing them within thoroughly Trinitarian, christological, and incarnational terms.

An essential part of Maximus's teaching on the human as microcosm is how, while created to reflect the created world and called to unify all that is separated and divided, the fall has prevented human beings from fulfilling their God-given task. Humanity, rather than staying centered upon the triune God through communion with Christ, has succumbed to the disintegrating effects of the passions. Now human beings, because of the fragmenting consequences of sin, continue to reflect the created world,

---

3. See Thunberg's analysis of the human as microcosm where he traces this concept back to its presence in Greek antiquity (under Oriental influence), in Democritus, Plato's *Timaeus*, Aristotle, Stoic philosophy, and its development in Christian tradition ("Human Person," 291–97); cf. Müller-Fahrenholz, *KP*, 108ff., where he considers the micro and macrocosmic features of Moltmann's anthropology.

4. Thunberg, "Human Person," 295–97.

The Trinitarian-Christocentric Practice of the Human Calling

but in a disordered fashion, and are unable to fulfill their divine calling of mediating in the universe. According to Maximus, the chief culprit for the disintegration of the human as microcosm is self-love (*philautia*). In order to better understand the human calling in creation to serve as an ordered microcosm, I want to briefly point out a few key features of Maximus's teaching on the disintegrating effects of the passions.

Self-Love: Background

The first feature concerns the background from which Maximus's teaching on self-love emerges. As we have seen in other places, Maximus draws from Evagrius and the Evagrian tradition. According to Evagrius and the Evagrian tradition, self-love is the basis of all the vices and the foundation of the eight vices of the Evagrian hierarchy.[5] Linked with his appropriation of Evagrius, are elements of ideas on self-love taken from a host of figures, such as Plato, Philo, Clement, Basil, Gregory of Nazianzus, Denys, and Thalassius. A full consideration of the elements appropriated from these thinkers would take us off course. However, I must mention the striking parallels between Maximus and Augustine, noted by Balthasar and Thunberg. Both these scholars have pointed out the remarkable similarities between Augustine's teaching on *concupiscentia* and Maximus's teaching on *philautia*.

Put briefly, both Maximus and Augustine conceive of this vice of self-love and lust as a movement away from God to an unhealthy preoccupation with matter.[6] While Balthasar and Thunberg entertain the possibility of the idea that Maximus may have been familiar with Augustine's writings, they both agree that it is difficult to prove.[7]

---

5. Thunberg, *MM*, 233ff., directs readers to representative texts in Evagrius: *Par. Gr.* 913 (no. 53) and *Par. Gr.* 3098 (no. 10), in Muyldermans, note additionelle à: Evagriana, Mus 44 (1931), pp. 379, 382. For informative scholarship on Evagrius, see Konstantinovsky, *Evagrius Ponticus*, and Corrigan, *Evagrius and Gregory*.

6. As explained earlier, this does not imply a negative view of material things. Balthasar cites and clarifies Maximus's view on this: "The perfect soul is one whose whole emotional capability is perfectly oriented toward God" (*CC* III, 98; *PG* 90, 1048A). "If this soul regards the world 'indifferently' from now on, it is not out of contempt for earthly things, but because God is endlessly more beautiful than any of them" (*CL*, 342). One finds similar thoughts in Moltmann, *GC*, 233–34. McDougall's comments on Moltmann's related ideas in *Spirit of Life* are helpful (*PL*, 148).

7. Balthasar, *CL*, 13ff.; Thunberg, *MM*, 237ff.; Thunberg also references Berthold, "Did Maximus the Confessor," 14–17.

Another feature is the notion that self-love is, in Maximus's estimation, the propagator of the other vices. He asserts that self-love is "the mother of the passions," the mother of the vices," "the origin of all the passions," and that the person who "is dominated by self-love is dominated by all the passions."[8]

Additionally, Maximus explains that self-love, as the mother of the passions, is understood as a preoccupation with the body, an inner fixation on bodily sensations and the sensible world. It is important to know, however, that this in no way implies a negative evaluation of the physical body and the sensible world. Maximus is emphatic about the goodness of all created things.[9] To illustrate, Maximus says, "For certainly God created these things and gave them to the human race for their use (*kresis*). And everything that God made is good and was intended for us to use well." Yet "in our own weakness and fleshly attitudes, we have preferred material things to the commandment of love."[10]

According to Maximus, while the body and the material world are good creations of God, the fall brought to light humanity's misuse of the natural capacity for spiritual pleasure and the preference for sensual pleasure. While human beings seek to fulfill the inner aching with sensual pleasure, they remain unfulfilled and restless.[11] For it is only in the triune God that human beings can begin to find the satisfaction for which they hunger and thirst.[12]

---

8. Maximus, *CC* II, 8, 59, 8; in *Philokalia*, 66, 75, 84; cf. Thunberg's comments regarding how Maximus reworks the Evagrian tradition on the vices (*MM*, 248ff.).

9. Balthasar, *CL*, 61. Of course, for both Maximus and Augustine, created matter is good, as God declared in the creation narrative (Gen 1:18ff.). What is problematic, in their estimation, is a disordered perspective on created matter, when humans focus on and prefer created things over the Creator. See Augustine, *Teaching Christianity*, bk. 1:2, 107ff.; *Trinity*, bk. 13:6, 362ff.; *Confessions*, bk. 10:22–27, 249–54.

10. Maximus, *AL*, PG 90, 916D–917A; in Balthasar, *CL*, 184. As noted above, I point out Balthasar's critique of Maximus regarding elements of his soteriology (*Theological Anthropology*, 9ff.).

11. In a key text that speaks to the proper functioning of human desire, Maximus says: "Our reason also should be moved to seek God, the force of desire should struggle to possess him and that of anger to hold on to him, or rather, to speak more properly, the whole mind should tend to God, stretched out as a sinew by the temper of anger, and burning with longing for the highest reaches of desire" (*On the Lord's Prayer* 4, in *CWS*, 112–13). The wording here is reminiscent of Denys, where in *The Divine Names* he says, "So let us stretch ourselves prayerfully upward to the more lofty elevation of the kindly rays of God" (680C).

12. In Maximus we find thoughts on desire and the inward motion it produces,

The Trinitarian-Christocentric Practice of the Human Calling

Finally, as Thunberg has pointed out, self-love and the passions and vices it engenders, cause a twofold separation: from God and the divine purpose for humanity, as well as from one's neighbor and the whole of humanity. It is the double commandment of love (as described in Israel's *Shema*)[13] that counters and heals this debilitating separation. Through love for God *concupiscence* is overcome, and through love for neighbor anger is defeated.[14] The emphasis on love as the antidote to and victory over the fragmenting effects of the vices, is also found in Moltmann, as I will show in his teaching on the image of God in human beings and their fulfillment of the divine calling in creation.

Reintegration through the Virtues

If the human person as microcosm is disintegrated through the passions, self-love, and vices that stem from the misuse of the three faculties of the soul, then they are to be reintegrated through growth in the virtues. The disordered nature of the human being as microcosm is properly reordered through life in intimate connection to Christ, which involves following and imitating Christ, the one who embodies and emanates the fullness of virtue. Here I will look briefly at the active assimilation to Christ that takes place through the cultivation of the virtues, detachment, love, and Christ's ongoing incarnation in the virtues of his followers.

Virtues, Detachment, and Love

Where self-love is the vice that gives birth to other vices, Maximus says that humility (*tapeinosis*) is the foundation of all virtue. For example, in *Letter 2: On Love*, Maximus says that "humility [is] the first foundation of the

---

notions consonant to Denys and Gregory of Nyssa, whose ideas he uses to correct Origen and Evagrius who held that desire for God would eventually be sated. However, Maximus does enhance Gregory's perspective on yearning, motion, and rest, as Balthasar points out: "In Maximus' thought, the bowshot of yearning [as seen in Gregory's arrow parable] is tamed into a metaphor of perfectly measured beauty, which brings both motion and rest together in the perfection: the archetypally Greek image of the 'sacred dance'" (cf. *Amb.*; *PG* 91, 1292C; *Centuries on Theology* II, 77–78; *CWS*, 164–65).

13. "Hear, O Israel: The Lord is our God, the Lord alone. You shall love the Lord your God with all your heart, and with all your soul, and with all your might" (Deut 6:4–5). See Moltmann's reflection on this passage, love for God and others, and *sapientia*, in "What Is a Theologian?" 49–50.

14. Thunberg, *MM*, 281ff.; Maximus, *CC* IV, 36; *CWS*, 40.

virtues, by which we come to know ourselves, and are able to throw off the main tumor of pride."[15]

Further, is the role that detachment (*apatheia*) plays in the reintegration of the human microcosm. The notion of detachment developed by Maximus flows out of earlier Christian teaching on spiritual perfection, including the work of Clement of Alexandria, Origen, and Gregory of Nyssa. But, as in other areas, the chief influence on his understanding of detachment is Evagrius. As is often the case, Maximus appropriates a theme like detachment from Evagrian tradition, situates it within a thoroughly incarnational and christological context, and reconfigures it. In this regard, McIntosh says that Maximus's great achievement is to set mystical theology (including his teaching on detachment) within the framework of incarnational thought.[16]

In the case of *apatheia*, Maximus not only roots his ideas on detachment within christological reflection, but he also intertwines detachment with the active element of love, so that detachment is an imitation of God's goodness and equal love for all creatures, a state of being that is attained in cooperation with divine grace and in communion with Christ. These elements can be seen in the following illustrative text, where Maximus says:

> [The one] who loves Christ is bound to imitate him to the best of his ability. . . . The whole purpose of the Savior's commandments is to free the intellect from dissipations and hatred, and to lead it to the love of Him and one's neighbor. From this love springs the light of active holy knowledge.[17]

For Maximus, detachment is not merely an inner equilibrium one realizes as a kind of emptiness, in a negative sense, as is often the case in Evagrius. Rather, detachment is experienced and evidenced in one's positive use of his or her faculties in the service of love for God and neighbor. Thunberg's comments on this are helpful:

> Thus detachment cannot be just a kind of emptiness. In its "negative" aspect it is an emptiness from passions, but in its positive aspect it is related to a good use of all man's faculties with a view to his divine goal and in the service of love. Maximus . . . says that the *habitus* of detachment is not only a negative condition for contemplation and true knowledge, a peaceful state as such, but also

---

15. See Maximus, *Letter 2: On Love*, 396A; in Louth, *MC*, 86.
16. *MT*, 61.
17. Maximus, *CC* IV, 56–58; *Philokalia*, 107.

The Trinitarian-Christocentric Practice of the Human Calling

a state in which "the face" of man's psychic disposition (διάθεσις) is elevated in praise of God, a face which is formed by many and varying virtues. It is thus not in emptiness that man has to praise God, but in the fullness of his virtues, which are of his nature, and these virtues are manifold, i.e. they vary according to the variety of man's own make-up, the differentiation of his natural faculties.[18]

Through his adaptation of the Evagrian teaching on *apatheia*, and the way he constructs his own understanding upon a christological basis, Maximus develops his christocentric vision of the human being as microcosm. Moreover, as we saw in previous sections, Maximus's teaching on *apatheia* is rooted in his understanding of the *kenosis* of Christ. As believers follow Christ in lives of discipleship, engaging in the pursuit of God and spiritual growth through ascetic exercises, they are graced with *apatheia*, that peace, freedom, and stillness that comes from union with the Trinity. If you recall, the way that Maximus and Moltmann's teaching on the redemptive goal of the human calling (in terms of *theosis* and Sabbath rest) ties in here. Union with the triune God through Christ, and true rest for the soul that results from the life, death, and resurrection of Christ, are deeply connected to Maximus's thinking on *apatheia* and the role it plays in reintegrating the human microcosm through the virtues.

Further, according to Maximus, love is the culmination of all the virtues. The reintegration of human beings, both individually and collectively, occurs within the context of love, as one imitates the divine love of the Father and Son in his or her love for God and others. Another text illustrates this, when Maximus reflects on Christ's words in the Gospel:

> "But I say to you," says the Lord, "love your enemies . . . do good to those who hate you, and pray for those who mistreat you" (Matthew 5:44). Why did He command this? To free you from hatred, irritation, anger and rancor, and to make you worthy of the supreme gift of perfect love. And you cannot attain such love if you do not imitate God and love all [people] equally. For God loves all [people] equally and wishes them "to be saved and to come to the knowledge of the truth" (1 Timothy 2:4).[19]

For Maximus, whose work is seeded with meditations on love—the love of Christ for those who oppose him, the love of God for all people, the love of God as the culmination of the spiritual life and growth in virtue—the

---

18. Maximus, *QT* 54; cf. Thunberg, *MM*, 308.
19. Maximus, *CC* I, 61; in *Philokalia*, 59.

human calling is realized as women and men imitate God and follow Christ in active love for all God's creatures.

What's more, where self-love and the horde of vices it engenders disintegrate the human person, causing fissures and divisions within humanity and all of creation, it is love, argues Maximus, that reintegrates and reunifies God's good creation. In his teaching on the five syntheses that human beings facilitate as mediators in the cosmos, it is the love that flows between the Father, Son, and Spirit, through the incarnate Word, and into the church, that makes these synthesizing, healing mediations possible. Thus, for Maximus, love is spoken of as "the supreme gift of perfect love," and it is this love that brings together all things in Christ.[20]

The Ongoing Incarnation of Christ in the Virtues

In grace-empowered obedience to the twin commandment of love, Maximus explains, Christians experience the ongoing and multiform incarnation of the Logos in their own virtues, as we saw in his teaching on *theosis*. Regarding this incarnation that occurs in the virtues, I would like to make several points. First, and linked with the above thread, is the notion that love is the essence of the incarnation of the Logos in the virtues. Moreover, in yet another way that Maximus distinguishes his thinking from Evagrius, he constructs his version of the virtues so that "love is the absolute terminus," as Aidan Nichols argues.[21]

Second, is the rich tradition from which Maximus draws as he constructs his own teaching on the incarnation of the Logos in the virtues.[22] One key New Testament text upon which a number of patristic authors build is Galatians 4:19 where Paul speaks of Christ being formed in the believers at Galatia. Origen, in his reflections on this passage, asserts that

---

20. Thunberg asserts that we should "be prepared to conclude that it is the idea of man as a created microcosm, clothed with a task of mediation, which serves best to describe Maximus' attitude to the positive function of virtues in relation to the different faculties of man. He is not, like Evagrius, interested in a departure from the lower elements in man, but in a restoration and re-integration of man as a whole. This reintegration however must take place in love . . . the summit of virtues—not as their abolition as we found in Evagrius" (*MM*, 308–9).

21. Nichols, *Byzantine Gospel*, 181.

22. Nichols offers a concise and helpful summary of key figures and themes related to the idea of an incarnation of Christ in the virtues, particularly in Origen, Gregory of Nyssa, and Karl Rahner (*Byzantine Gospel*, 186, 187).

The Trinitarian-Christocentric Practice of the Human Calling

Christ is born and formed in Christians, and that the presence of the Logos *is* the virtues. Further, Gregory of Nyssa emphasizes that as the Christian grows in the virtues, she participates in the Logos, and through detachment, the beautiful virtues of the Logos emanate from her life. Finally, Evagrius, like Gregory of Nyssa, underscores the role of detachment in the cultivation of the virtues, particularly the practical virtues, which he says are the "fleshes of Christ" taken on by the believer.[23]

Using his predecessors' ideas, Maximus develops his own distinctive understanding of the incarnation of the Logos in the virtues. Accordingly, Maximus adjusts, refines, and synthesizes some of these key elements on the relationship between the incarnation and the virtues. In *Questions to Thalassius* 22, Maximus explains how Christ becomes incarnate in his followers as they cultivate the virtues. The way in which he does this brings us to a third point, and that is the christological structure of his teaching on the incarnation of the Logos in the virtues. In this multilayered text—*Questions to Thalassius* 22—Maximus offers a substantial meditation on a number of biblical texts as he seeks to answer and illumine the question of how God will show his riches (Eph 2:7) at the end of the ages, which has already come upon us (1 Cor 10:11). Radiating from one of his key assertions—that the Logos seeks to realize his embodiment in those who are worthy—Maximus interweaves a number of threads we have seen throughout his work. Two of these demonstrate how he reworks the Evagrian teaching on the virtues. First, Maximus explains that God

> who, by the sheer inclination on his will, established the beginning of all creation, seen and unseen, before all the ages and before that beginning of created beings, had and ineffably good plan for those creatures. The plan was for him to mingle, without change on his part, with human nature by true hypostatic union, to unite human nature to himself while remaining immutable, so that he might become a man, as he alone knew how, and so that he might deify humanity in union with himself. Also, according to this plan, it is clear that God wisely divided "the ages" (αἰῶνες) between those

---

23. Thunberg's analysis in *MM*, 324–25, of these patristic sources is helpful, yet I am not fully convinced by certain points of his interpretation of Evagrius (e.g., contrasting Maximus and Evagrius, as starkly as he does, on moral perfection). Thunberg also discusses Methodius of Philippi's perspective (ca. 260–312), how Gal 4:19 also inspired his teaching on the virtues, and how he linked knowledge and virtue to a birth of the *logoi* in the heart of Christians (*MM*, 325).

intended for God to become human, and those intended for humanity to become divine.[24]

Once again, the extensive christological structure of Maximus's thinking is seen, in God's plan to mingle with, unite, and deify humanity in union with Godself, something that distinguishes him from Evagrius in this area. Regarding the way Maximus brings together the notion of how Christ indwells believers and this relates to the life of the virtues, Thunberg comments:

> Maximus obviously emphasizes the idea of Christ's presence, birth and embodiment in the virtues in order to demonstrate that the work of human perfection has two sides. From one point of view it means restoration, integration, unification and deification; from another point of view it means divine inhabitation in human multiplicity. This double character is manifest almost everywhere when Maximus dwells on this theme, and the explanation can hardly be other than that Maximus' late Chalcedonian theology with its stress on *communicatio idiomatum* and *perichoresis* also brought him to the conviction that Incarnation and deification are two sides of the same mystery. . . . Deification and Incarnation differ from each other in so far as deification is fulfilled only after death, while Incarnation is established in a historical event, to which all other forms of incarnation have to be related; but it is Maximus' conviction that both are equally based on the fact that "God ever wills to become man in the worthy."[25]

Therefore, his teaching on the incarnation of the Logos in the Christian virtues, which stems from the Evagrian tradition, stresses the christological elements of this reality, in ways that are unique to Maximus. As Christians cultivate the virtues, with love as the essence and terminus of them all, Christ comes to indwell the believer. His incarnation opens up and paves the way for the deification of human beings, and there is interconnection and interplay between these dynamic realities of Christ's inhabitation of the believers, Christ's incarnation, humanity's deification, with Chalcedonian logic spelling things out in a very nuanced fashion.

Connected to the above point regarding the christological structure of Maximus's teaching on the indwelling of Christ in the virtues, is another

---

24. Maximus, *QT* 22, Q. 137; CCSG 7:137–43; from Blowers, *CMJC*, 115.

25. Thunberg, *MM*, 325, 326. See Sherrard's comments regarding the ongoing incarnation of Christ: This "does not imply any incompletion in Christ, [but] implies incompletion in the present state of creation" (*Human Image*, 124).

The Trinitarian-Christocentric Practice of the Human Calling

aspect that Thunberg and Nichols note: that of reciprocity in relation to Christ's presence in the Christian virtues.[26] In the relationship between spiritual knowledge, Christian virtues, and deification, there is a reciprocity between "the aspect of divine 'economic' differentiation and Incarnation on the one hand, and human integration, unification and deification on the other."[27] According to Maximus, there is a correspondence between the divine attributes and the human virtues, in the same way the incarnation of the Word and the deification of human beings correlate with one another. In his *Epistle* 2, Maximus speaks of this reciprocity, so that in the blossoming of humanity's natural capacities there is a moral expression of the divine attributes, something that occurs as believers are united to God through desiring love. As Nichols says, Maximus "allows that deifying love, uniting both God with the man and individual human beings among themselves, justifies a communication of idioms—what he calls in [the context of *Epistle* 2] a 'relational exchange,' *antidosis schetike* . . . ,' " something "comparable to that which takes place through the hypostatic union between the divinity and humanity of the Word incarnate." Therefore, in "his great love God allows himself to be differentiated in terms of the amount of practical virtue found in each person, so that human virtue in all its variations can find its true significance in him."[28] Maximus finds evidence of this correspondence and reciprocity in an intriguing interpretation of Hosea 12:10 (12:11 based on the LXX reading: ἐν χερσὶν προφητῶν ὡμοιώθην), which he takes to mean that in God's great love, God conforms Godself to everyone based on the amount of practical virtue which is found in each person.[29]

---

26. See Thunberg, *MM*, 329ff. and Nichols, *Byzantine Gospel*, 186ff.

27. Thunberg, *MM*, 329.

28. Nichols, *Byzantine Gospel*, 188. Thunberg posits that God is "as it were, differentiated according to human differentiations, which thereby gain their proper place and true meaning. God accepts likeness to men. But this implies on the other hand, from the point of view of man, that man is at the same time deified, developing his *likeness* unto God, which is in Maximus always of a moral and volitional character" (*MM*, 330).

29. As Sherwood outlines the *agents of deification* in Maximus, Thunberg speaks of *agents and forms of divine incarnation in the virtues* of each Christian. He highlights in Maximus the grace of baptism, faith (which is the basis of Maximus's hierarchy of the virtues), how purification from passions prepares for the experience of the indwelling of Christ, how the presence of the Logos comes to believers through both virtue and knowledge, and how a divine incarnation in human virtuous living occurs by means of knowledge and contemplation by means of reason and intellect (327–28).

Human Being as Universal Mediator

So far, in this section, I have sought to demonstrate how Maximus conceives of the human being as ordered microcosm, a reality that has been disrupted by the fall and the subsequent disintegration through the passions, namely self-love that gives birth to the other vices. Maximus speaks, further, of the reintegration of the human microcosm through the virtues, so that through the cultivation of the virtues, detachment from created things, growth in love for God and neighbor, and Christ's ongoing incarnation in the virtues, human beings begin to realize their God-given potential. This leads to a further theme in Maximus's understanding of the human calling in creation—that of the human being as universal mediator. In the following section, I consider the three stages of the spiritual life, a further threefold pattern of spiritual development, and the five syntheses in which human beings are called to cooperate with Christ, who is the ultimate and archetypal mediator in the universe.

THREE STAGES OF THE SPIRITUAL LIFE

Previously, we looked at Maximus's use of the Evagrian schema of the spiritual life: *praktike*, *physike*, and *theologia*, noting how Maximus frequently takes up the raw materials of his predecessors, adjusts, refines, and reshapes them. This, again, is the case with the threefold model of the spiritual life.

In brief, Maximus draws from the tradition stemming from Clement of Alexandria, Origen, Gregory of Nyssa, and Evagrius.[30] With Clement, a general threefold pattern is found, with each element focusing on humanity's spiritual operations. The first deals with the ascetic struggle against the passions and for growth in the virtues, while the second concerns the contemplative life and growth in knowledge (*gnosis*), and the third speaks of the consummation of *gnosis* when one experiences continuous vision of God. Origen adds further strokes, distinguishing between *ethicum*, *physicum*, and *enoptice*, as well as seeking to show how each of these stages is related to the Old Testament books of Proverbs (which deals with freedom from passions and the cultivation of virtues), Ecclesiastes (focuses on contemplation and insight into creation), and the Song of Songs (speaking of contemplation of God and union with the Trinity).[31] Gregory of Nyssa

---

30. See Thunberg, *MM*, 333.
31. See Rahner, "Spiritual Senses," 88ff.

The Trinitarian-Christocentric Practice of the Human Calling

builds on Origen's teaching, developing his own threefold perspective based on the life of Moses. Moses's spiritual odyssey becomes paradigmatic for Christian growth, with his experience of the light as the first stage, passing through the cloud in the second, and entering the darkness as the third. Evagrius builds on this tradition, elaborating further and systematizing the threefold perspective of the spiritual life.[32] What is particularly important is how Maximus synthesizes and refines the tradition, shaping it on the anvil of his Christology, so that its christological contours and Trinitarian elements are brought out.

One way in which Maximus demonstrates how his christological vision structures his teaching on the three stages of the spiritual life is seen in how he ties it to the person and physical body of Christ. For example, based on the ideas of Evagrius, Maximus correlates the three stages of the spiritual life with christological realities. In the first stage, we saw previously that Maximus does not restrict *praktike* to the ascetic struggle against the passions, or to the establishment of an equilibrium in the soul, as Evagrius tends to do. Rather, the *vita practica* suggests an acquisition of positive virtues as well, virtues which demonstrate the two aspects of the commandment of love, so that the various operations of *praktike* are incarnations of Christ.[33]

Furthermore, Maximus suggests that the first stage (*praktike*) is the *flesh* of Christ; the second stage (*physike*) is the *blood* of Christ; and the third (*theologia*) is the *bones* of Christ, which holds everything (within the spiritual life and the wider cosmos).[34] We will see (below) how Maximus's use of this eucharistic language is developed in other ways, especially within his *Mystagogy*, where Maximus details ways that the spiritual life is worked out within the context of the church's liturgical and sacramental activity.

---

32. See Louth's helpful review of Evagrius on the three stages, *Origins of the Christian Mystical Tradition*, 99–110.

33. See Thunberg, *MM*, 309–30; cf. Cooper, "Maximus the Confessor," 163ff.

34. Maximus, *QT* 35; cf. Thunberg, *MM*, 352; Blowers, *Exegesis and Spiritual*, 75n44. Thunberg remarks about the important modifications Maximus makes to Evagrius's thoughts: "Already Evagrius calls the virtues 'fleshes of Christ,' and 'natural contemplation' 'blood of Christ,' and finally knowledge of God the 'breast,' i.e. the heart, of Christ. Now Maximus follows him in this tradition, but, as it seems, with some significant changes" (*MM*, 352). These modifications of Evagrius, once again, demonstrate the primacy and pervasiveness of christological thinking in Maximus. Every facet, every stage, every movement of the spiritual life is vitally connected to Christ and portrayed in christologically rooted language.

A further way that Maximus demonstrates how his christological thinking shapes and informs his teaching on the stages of the spiritual is seen in yet another way that he links the above eucharistic symbolism with three kinds of spiritual death and resurrection. As we saw in chapter 3 (on the christological basis of the human calling), Maximus says (in terms consonant with Moltmann and the "Western tradition"):

> Every individual who believes in Christ is nailed to the Cross with Christ, according to the measure of his own strength and the type and condition of his virtue; at the same time, he nails Christ to the Cross with himself, precisely in that he is crucified with Christ in a spiritual way.[35]

This cross-centered thinking is worked into Maximus's own version of the three stages of the spiritual life, so that Christians experience an ongoing crucifixion and resurrection as they mature in Christ. Accordingly, Maximus explains that in the practical stage, where one dies to the temptations of the sensible world, the believer experiences the crucifixion of the *flesh* of Christ. This leads to natural contemplation, when one learns to abandon symbolical contemplation of things, so that one participates in the crucifixion of the *soul* of Christ.[36] Finally, the Christian advances to the *mystagogia* of theology, where one learns to deny all the explicit qualities of God in relation to what God is in himself, so that one experiences the crucifixion of the *mind* of Christ and advances to the very divinity of Christ.[37]

Therefore, we see once again how Maximus weds his teaching on spiritual development with christological language, adjusting the Evagrian tradition so that its incarnational and cruciform features are more clearly discerned. According to Maximus, these three kinds of crucifixion bring about new life and spiritual growth, so that believers are drawn into the

---

35. Maximus, *Amb.*; *PG* 91, 1360AB; Balthasar, *CL*, 278. As noted previously, Balthasar proposes: "Outside of Origen . . . and Pseudo-Macarius . . . this kind of mysticism of suffering, which reminds us of Pascal, does not exist in the East" (278n5).

36. Based on the above text, *Amb.* 47; *PG* 91, 1360CD; cf. Thunberg's comments on what distinguishes Maximus from Evagrius on this point: "Thus Maximus balances the more or less Evagrian idea of a continuing resurrection with Christ with the corresponding idea of a crucifixion, which does not stop short even of the last stage of spiritual development. By doing so, he excludes the Evagrian idea of a simple return of the mind from an existence which has been only accidentally bodily and limited" (*MM*, 353–54).

37. Thunberg adds, "To Maximus θεολογία is not only the supreme form of knowledge, as it is to Evagrius; it is a relationship, above *all* knowledge that human beings can imagine, with a God who is himself above knowledge" (*MM*, 357).

dynamic reality of Christ's death and resurrection. Thus, it is not difficult to see here now Maximus's theological anthropology and portrayal of spiritual development spring out of his christological vision.

FURTHER THREEFOLD PATTERNS

A further threefold pattern of spiritual development concerns Maximus's use of the terms *being*, *well-being*, and *ever-being*. Without repeating all that was stated earlier or going into too much detail on this triad, I simply want to point out a few things that reinforce what I have been showing in Maximus, that is, how his Trinitarian and christological teaching structures his notion of human being as universal mediator.

First, in texts like *Amb.* 10, Maximus depicts spiritual development through the triad *being*, *well-being*, and *ever-being*.[38] As is often the case with Maximus, each of these terms evinces new meaning as one peels back its layers. As Balthasar, Thunberg, and Louth have indicated, these terms are best understood in relation to the network of associated words, much like knots tied together in the wider web of Maximus's thought. Maximus appropriates these three terms—stemming from Aristotelian thought, biblical material (cf. Acts 17:28),[39] Clement of Alexandria, Proclus, and Pseudo-Dionysius's Neoplatonic theology—and links them with a number of Trinitarian and christological terms and concepts.[40]

For example, Maximus joins these three terms to three other triads, including the three human births, the three redemptive births of Christ, the three days of creation and Sabbath, and the three laws.[41] Thus, the notion of *being*, which refers to humanity's origin—God, is tied to Christ's birth in body and soul, the sixth day of creation, and the natural law. Second, the idea of *well-being*, which refers to humanity's motion toward God, is joined to Christ's birth at baptism, the seventh day of creation, and the written law. Finally, the notion of *ever-being*, which refers to the Christian reaching their goal through union with the Trinity, is linked to Christ's birth at the

38. See Louth, *MC*, 102ff.

39. "For 'In him we live and move and have our being'; as even some of your own poets have said" (Acts 17:28).

40. See Louth, *MC*, 94–96.

41. See Balthasar, *CL*, 143ff.; Thunberg, *MM*, 369–70; and Louth, *MC*, 30. Also noteworthy are Balthasar's comments regarding the way Maximus connects this "pattern of individual asceticism" with "his own schema of the 'three laws' of salvation history" (*CL*, 302).

resurrection, the eighth day of creation (the "Sabbath of Sabbaths," where one ultimately rests in the Trinity, as we saw earlier), and the law of grace.[42]

What I want to highlight here is how Maximus takes up these concepts, with their nuanced meanings from philosophical and theological sources, and remolds them based on his Trinitarian-christocentric outlook. Thus, his penchant for triads (in the spirit of Pseudo-Dionysius), his perspective on the movement of procession, return, and rest, and his ternary understanding of spiritual development, is based on his Trinitarian reflection (with the Holy Trinity as beginning, middle, and end), and his Christology (anchoring it to Christ's incarnation, baptism, and resurrection). Like Denys, Maximus delights in discerning triadic structures throughout the universe (and the church's liturgy), as he develops ideas related to the spiritual stages of purification, illumination, and unification, and discloses how all of creation is rooted in and restored by the incarnation, crucifixion, and resurrection of Christ.[43]

The Five Syntheses or Mediations

It is important to understand that the above three stages of the spiritual life and other related threefold patterns of spiritual development—which arise from and are shot through with Trinitarian and christological reflection—are to be viewed in relation to humanity's call to participate in five great syntheses in the cosmos. Therefore, restoration of the human microcosm through life in Christ and union with the Trinity, enables human beings to participate with God in the bringing together of all things in Christ.

---

42. See *Amb.* 42; *PG* 91, 1348 D; *Centuries on Theology* 1. 56; *PG* 90, 1104 C (cf. *Amb.* 65; *PG* 91, 1392 B–D) and *QT* 64; cf. Blowers, *CMJC*, 166; Thunberg, *MM*, 369. It is crucial to recognize the prominence of *grace* in Maximus's mystical theology. As Thunberg posits, with the eighth day and the mystery of ever-well-being, we are "at the fulfillment of spiritual perfection, and as in the case of the stage of θεολογία or μυσταγωγία, *it is entirely above natural human capacities and human efforts to attain. Both are freely given by God, and are received from him in burning love*" (*MM*, 372, italics mine).

43. See Louth, *MC*, 30ff., where he speaks rather beautifully of Denys's influence on Maximus. He says that Denys "took over as well the Neoplatonic fascination with triads (not at all unwelcome to Trinitarian Christians), finding a triadic structure throughout the cosmos and the Christian liturgy, and introducing the triadic rhythm of purification, illumination, and union (perfection) to attempts to understand the transforming action of divine grace. He also introduced—or gave wider currency to—philosophical terminology such as being-potentiality-activity (or being—power—energy) and *being—well being—eternal being*, and developed along Neoplatonic lines the doctrine of providence (*pronia*)" (italics mine).

The Trinitarian-Christocentric Practice of the Human Calling

The mediation which Christ fulfilled on humanity's behalf (through his incarnation, life, death, and resurrection), enables and exemplifies the task of mediation extended to redeemed humanity. In the following, I explore what Maximus intends by these five cosmic syntheses[44] that pertain to the human calling in creation, how they arise from and are shaped by his Trinitarian and christological thinking, and how these mediations are performed through the church's liturgical and sacramental life.

In *Amb.* 41, the main text where Maximus speaks of these syntheses, he offers a concise, multifaceted summary of the five-fold work of mediation accomplished by Christ which Christians are to realize in imitation of the supreme Mediator.[45] In these dense texts where he discusses excerpts from Gregory of Nazianzus, Gregory of Nyssa, and Denys, Maximus introduces the notion of the division of being, how humans are created to hold together these divisions of being, functioning as microcosms the mediate the divisions. Next, Maximus speaks of the fall and how it impeded humanity's fulfillment of its role as mediator, then reflects on how through Christ's incarnation God recapitulated and restored humanity's primordial function as microcosm and bond of creation.[46] Throughout this text, moreover, Maximus articulates the human calling within a Trinitarian and christological framework, describing this unifying task in Trinitarian (e.g., *perichoresis*) and christological terms (e.g., *syndesmos*, union, recapitulation).[47]

Also, something that ties these five mediations to the previous section is the way that Maximus correlates the mediations with the threefold

---

44. See Thunberg, "Human Person," 306–9, where he suggests that Maximus was the most explicit on the point of humans as microcosms. He also summarizes the five mediations: "between the sexes (since disastrous antagonism is overcome), between paradise and the inhabited earth, between heaven and earth, between sensible and intelligible creation (so that all is held together by the universal principle, *logos*, intended by God at the creation), and, finally, between God and the whole creation through ecstasy and mystical union, so that God becomes all in all, without destroying any created differentiations or anything of humanity's instituted free will, yet bringing all to its fulfillment, gathered around humanity in perfect likeness to God" (309).

45. On this theme, Balthasar says: "The syntheses realized by Christ are the plan for those others that the world and every individual, by the grace of Christ, must realize in themselves. . . . [These] syntheses that Christ brings to fulfillment in and with us, his members . . . include what one might call Maximus' 'spirituality': his ascetical and mystical theology" (*CL*, 275).

46. See Louth, *MC*, 155ff. Louth suggests that *Amb.* 41 unites two of Maximus's favorite themes: the incarnation of Christ and the division of being.

47. *Amb.* 41, 1308B; 1305B, C, D. As I discussed in ch. 2, Moltmann's perichoretic thinking accords with certain elements of Maximus's use of *perichoresis*.

approach to the spiritual life. Thus, the first two mediations fall under *praktike*, with particular attention to detachment. The third and fourth mediations are part of *physike*, where natural contemplation, imitation of the heavenly virtues, and contemplation of intelligible things are the foci. Finally, the fifth mediation is related to *theologia*, where Maximus discusses mystical union with God in apophatic, Trinitarian terms.

As mediator in the cosmos, humanity is divinely called and graced to participate with God in the unification and restoration of all things. As Maximus suggests in *Amb*. 41, this bringing together of all things in Christ unfolds in a series of cosmic syntheses. Looking at each of these is important in order to properly understand Maximus's teaching on the human vocation, and to demonstrate how this teaching is shaped by his Trinitarian-christocentric vision.

The First Mediation: Between Male and Female

The first of the cosmic syntheses is between male and female. In order to stay focused, I will touch on a few essential points regarding this synthesis. Combining elements from Galatians 3:28,[48] Clement of Alexandria, Gregory of Nazianzus, Gregory of Nyssa, and Evagrius, Maximus posits that procreation through sexual intercourse was introduced into human life after the fall. What's more, sexual differentiation is due to the fall.[49] Thus, it was through the incarnation of the Word that humanity was rescued, and their mode of living as male and female was renewed. Christ's life, accordingly, becomes the model for his followers. As he lived a life of obedience to God—abstaining from the misuse of the human faculties, rightly using them through devotion to God, self-discipline, and love to God and neighbor—his disciples are to overcome the effects of the fall that divide and fracture men and women. It is, therefore, through chaste living and sexual purity that men and women are integrated in Christ.[50]

---

48. "There is no longer Jew or Greek, there is no longer slave or free, there is no longer male and female; for all of you are one in Christ Jesus" (Gal 3:28).

49. Admittedly, this mediation between male and female, which touches on a number of critical issues related to gender and sexuality, requires more attention than I can give here. Valerie Karras has devoted careful attention to the complex of issues in Gregory of Nyssa, whose ideas Maximus appropriates, as well other figures related to Maximus: Karras, "Sex/Gender"; "Re-evaluation of Marriage"; "Patristic Views."

50. Lossky reflects: Men and women "must first overcome the sexual separation by a chaste life, by a union more total than the external union of the sexes, by an 'integrity'

The Trinitarian-Christocentric Practice of the Human Calling

Through spiritual rebirth, moreover, men and women are introduced to new life, life as God intended for humanity, where the corruptive power of self-love and the passions are overcome. Based on their relationship to Christ, man and woman transcend the differentiation between male and female.[51] This does not mean, however, that male and female lose their distinct qualities, for, as we have seen elsewhere, Maximus's Chalcedonian logic prevents dissolving, blending, or mixing things so that they lose their distinctness. As Thunberg comments, "Again we have found that an overcoming of differences, as presented by Maximus, does not imply an elimination of them as such, but rather their proper use."[52]

Related to this first synthesis between male and female is, I think, something that coincides with the egalitarian impulses found within Moltmann's theological anthropology. According to Maximus, as men and women commune with Christ, properly using their God-given desires and faculties, they transcend the differentiation between male and female (Gal 3:28), and become one in Christ, equally called and empowered to function as mediators in the cosmos. Thus, through their communion with Christ, the universal Logos, they are enabled to realize their common principle of human nature and fulfill their vocation in creation. Likewise, in Moltmann's perspective, men and women who are baptized into Christ (Gal 3:27–28), who commune with Christ and one another in the fellowship of the Spirit, transcend themselves, forming a higher unity, and are equally empowered to function as servants of the messianic kingdom.[53]

---

which would be integration" (*OT*, 74).

51. In another passage from *Amb.* 41, Maximus reflects on the unity between male and female as they live before God as human beings, those who equally bear the divine image: "First he united us in himself by removing the difference between male and female, and instead of men and women, in whom above all this manner of division is beheld, he showed us as properly and truly to be simply human beings, thoroughly transfigured in accordance with him, and bearing his intact and completely unadulterated image, touched by no trace at all of corruption" (in Louth, *MC*, 1312A, 160).

52. Thunberg, *MM*, 381. Thunberg also comments on the interesting images Maximus employs regarding this first synthesis; *Amb.* 48, *PG* 91, 1364 B, D.

53. See Moltmann, *SL*, 117ff., and *GC*, 222ff.; cf. Müller-Fahrenholz's commentary on the egalitarian dynamic in Moltmann's theology, *KP*, 223ff.

Second Mediation: Between Paradise and the Inhabited Earth

In addition to the first mediation between male and female is the second synthesis, between paradise and the inhabited earth. Maximus explains, "Then, by a way of life proper and fitting to saints, the human person unites paradise and the inhabited world to make one earth, no longer is it experienced as divided according to the difference of its parts, but rather as gathered together, since no introduction at all of partition is allowed."[54] Essentially, what Maximus argues concerning this second mediation, is that in the fall, humanity chose the sensual pleasures of the created world over the Creator. This fatal choice, and misuse of free will, introduced further divisions or obstacles into the universe, namely between the fullness of God's heavenly presence and the earth. Therefore, through Christ's incarnation, his God-honoring *human* behavior as an ongoing act of love, and his resurrection, the disunity caused by human sin is overcome. Based on his understanding of Luke 23:43,[55] Maximus explains that through his crucifixion and resurrection, Christ opens the door and paves the way for human beings to follow him into paradise.[56] With the attitude of the penitent criminal hanging next to Christ, Christians are to actively imitate Christ, by identifying with his crucifixion (through mortification), by cultivating virtues, attitudes, and actions rooted in love for God and neighbor. As Lossky says, "At [the] second stage, man must reunite Paradise to the rest of the terrestrial cosmos, by a love of God which would at once detach him from everything and allow him to embrace everything," always "carrying Paradise in himself, he would have transformed the whole earth into Paradise."[57] This mediation between paradise and the inhabited earth leads to the third.

---

54. *Amb.* 41, 1305A; in Louth, *MC*, 157.

55. Luke 24:42–43: "Then he [the criminal hanging next to Christ] said, 'Jesus, remember me when you come into your kingdom.' He replied, 'Truly I tell you, today you will be with me in Paradise.'"

56. "On the cross," Lossky adds, "Christ reunited the whole of the terrestrial cosmos to Paradise: for when he allowed death to enter Him to consume it by contact with His divinity, the darkest place on earth becomes radiant; there is no longer any accursed place" (*OT*, 75). This is yet another place where Maximus demonstrates a staurocentric, kenotic understanding of the human calling and spiritual development.

57. Lossky, *OT*, 74.

The Trinitarian-Christocentric Practice of the Human Calling

Third Mediation: Between Heaven and Earth

The third mediation, according to Maximus, addresses the division that "in accordance with which the nature perceived by the senses is divided into heaven and earth."[58] What Christ has done to enable and exemplify this mediation, Maximus explains, is "by his ascension into heaven, he clearly united heaven and earth, and with his earthly body that is of the same nature and consubstantial with ours," Christ entered into heaven and showed that the whole nature that can be perceived through the senses is, by the most universal *logos* of its being, one, thus obscuring the peculiar nature of the division which cuts it into two."[59] Again, Lossky's comments are helpful: "After the Resurrection, the very body of Christ mocks spatial limitations, and in an integration of all that is sensible, unifies earth and heaven." In imitation of Christ, he adds, the human vocation means that in "the third place, his spirit, and his body itself, would triumph over space by unifying all of the sensible world, the earth and its firmament."[60]

As the previous mediation was anchored in Maximus's understanding of Luke 23:43, this one is based on his interpretation of Colossians 3:1–3.[61] In view of this biblical text, Maximus says that human beings in Christ are restored to their original vocation as mediators in the cosmos. As they are raised with Christ, participating with him in his ascent to heaven through growth in the spiritual life, Christians reflect the virtues of the angels, rising above earthly concerns, thereby bridging heaven and earth, as Christ himself does.[62]

In each of these mediations, Maximus's teaching on what it means to be authentically human, realizing the divine purpose for humanity, emerges from his vision of the cosmic Christ, who recapitulates the universe in himself, and models the microcosmic function that human beings are to learn from him. Maximus ties this imitation of Christ to his threefold approach

---

58. Maximus, *Amb.* 41, 1305A; in Louth, *MC*, 157.

59. Maximus, *Amb.* 41, 1309B, C; in Louth, *MC*, 159.

60. Lossky, *OT*, 75, 74.

61. "So if you have been raised with Christ, seek the things that are above, where Christ is, seated at the right hand of God. Set your minds on things that are above, not on things that are on earth, for you have died, and your life is hidden with Christ in God" (Col 3:1–3).

62. Maximus, *Amb.* 41; *PG* 91, 1305 D–1308 A; cf. Thunberg, who speaks of the restoration of humans to their original vocation, their resemblance to angels through the virtues, and spiritual ascent to God through the Logos (*MM*, 391–92).

to the spiritual life, so that through *praktike*, *physike*, and *theologia*, Christians play their part in reuniting and restoring all of creation through active cooperation with the grace of the Holy Trinity. Maximus's teaching on the human calling in creation, as I am seeking to highlight, is deeply rooted in his Trinitarian and christological vision. We can only understand what it means to be human, Maximus suggests, as we view humanity (and all of creation) in relation to the Trinity and the divine-human Logos who restored creation and exemplified the human vocation in his earthly life.

Fourth Mediation: Between Intelligible and Sensible Creation

The fourth mediation is between intelligible and sensible creation. Maximus says that Christ performed this mediation by "passing with his soul and body, that is, with the whole of our nature, through all the divine and intelligible ranks of heaven," so that "he united the sensible and the intelligible and showed the convergence of the whole of creation with the One according to its most original and universal *logos*, which is completely undivided and at rest in itself."[63] The mediation of Christ prepares the way for the mediation of humanity, as Maximus explains: "And then the human person unites what is perceived by the mind and what is perceived by the senses with each other by achieving equality with the angels in its matter knowing, and thus makes the whole creation one single creation," so that it is "no longer divided by what it can know and what it cannot know, through its equality to the angels lacking nothing in their knowledge and understanding of the *logoi* in the things that exist." This occurs according to "the infinite pouring out of the gift of true wisdom inviolably and without intermediary furnishes, so far as is permitted, to those who are worthy a concept of God beyond understanding or explanation."[64] The fourth mediation, which stresses Maximus's holistic understanding of humanity as body and soul, as well as the deep connection between humanity and all of creation, leads to the final mediation.

---

63. Maximus, *Amb.* 41, 1309C; in Louth, *MC*, 159–60. Regarding this mediation, Lossky says that by the Ascension, "Christ reunites the celestial and terrestrial worlds, the angelic choirs to the human race." Therefore, following Christ's example, men and women "must penetrate into the celestial cosmos, live like the angels, assimilate their intelligence and reunite in [themselves] the intelligible world to the sensible world" (*OT*, 75, 74).

64. Maximus, *Amb.* 41, 1308A; in Louth, *MC*, 158.

The Trinitarian-Christocentric Practice of the Human Calling

THE FIFTH MEDIATION: BETWEEN GOD AND GOD'S CREATION

The fifth and final mediation[65]—between God and God's creation—is effected by Christ, as Maximus says, so that

> in his humanity, he goes to God himself, having clearly *appeared*, as it is written, *in the presence of God* the Father *on our behalf* (Heb. 9:24), as a human being. As Word, he cannot be separated in any way at all from the Father; as man, he has fulfilled, in word and truth, with unchangeable obedience, everything that, as God, he has predetermined is to take place, and has accomplished the whole will of God the Father on our behalf.[66]

As we have seen in the previous mediations, Christ's mediatory work enables the rest of humanity to fulfill the fifth synthesis, in which

> the human person unites the created nature with the uncreated through love (O the wonder of God's love for us human beings!), showing them to be one and the same through the possession of grace, the whole [creation] wholly interpenetrated (*perichoresis*) by God, and become completely whatever God is, save at the level of being, and receiving to itself the whole of God himself, and acquiring as a kind of prize for its ascent to God the most unique God himself, as the end of the movement of everything that moves towards it, and the firm and unmoved rest of everything that is carried towards it, being the undetermined and infinite limit and definition of every definition and law and ordinance, or reason and mind and nature.[67]

---

65. "This vision is a kind of culmination of all that the early church envisaged in its painful struggle to find *a true anthropology*, worthy of beings created in the image and likeness of God, beings who, in their relationship to God and in developing their spiritual capacities, are also able to transcend their own limits" (from Thunberg, "Human Person," 309, italics mine).

66. Maximus, *Amb.* 41, 1311C, D; in Louth, *MC*, 160. Concerning Christ's work in the fifth mediation, Lossky says: "He who sits at the right hand of the Father introduces humanity above the angelic orders and into the Trinity Itself; and these are the firstfruits of cosmic deification" (*OT*, 75). Believers, inspired by and in imitation of Christ's unswerving obedience to the Father, are progressively brought into vital communion with the Holy Trinity. Each of the five cosmic mediations, therefore, is shot through with christological reflection, and leads to union with the triune God.

67. Maximus, *Amb.* 41, 1308B; in Louth, *MC*, 158. Based on the mediation of the New Adam, Lossky explains, "The cosmic Adam [redeemed humanity], by giving himself without return to God, would give Him back all His creation, and would receive from Him, by the mutuality of love, that is to say by grace, all that God possesses by virtue of His nature." Therefore, "in the overcoming of the primordial separation of the created

In this passage, Maximus interweaves a number of the key themes we have considered in previous sections. In this final mediation, it is *love* that joins creatures to the Creator in mystical union (*theologia*), the love that flows between the Trinitarian persons and into creation, drawing all of creation back into the very life of God. Moreover, because of the descent of the Logos, human beings can ascend to God, finding that ultimate Sabbath rest for which they have been created and for which they long. As they come to rest in God, a divine-human exchange takes place (*communicatio idiomatum*), humanity is graced to become what God is (cf. 2 Pet 1:4), a dynamic that Maximus describes in *perichoretic* terms. Thunberg's comments underscore the Trinitarian and christological features of this fifth mediation:

> Through this mediation in Christ man should *penetrate* (περιχωρεῖν) *entirely into God*—and become all that God possibly is, though *without ontological identity*—and receive Him instead of himself and be awarded God alone as the reward of his ascension.... The fifth mediation thus implies a full realization of the human consequences of the hypostatic union in Christ. God and man are not only no longer separated and divided but are united without confusion or change, and their union also implies a true communication and inter-penetration, so that Christ brings man into heaven, and man enters entirely in God. The Chalcedonian theology, such as Maximus understood it, thus remains the core even of his presentation of the fifth mediation, which results in mystical union.[68]

Therefore, in his portrayal of the five cosmic mediations, we find repeated examples of how Maximus's anthropology springs out of his Trinitarian-christocentric vision. According to Maximus, men and women fulfill the human calling as they follow and participate with Christ in his mediatory work. Within themselves, as microcosms of the universe,[69] hu-

---

and uncreated, there would be accomplished man's deification, and by him, of the whole universe" (*OT*, 74).

68. Thunberg, *MM*, 406. Thunberg traces, additionally, a handful of crucial elements concerning this fifth mediation, including the distinction between created and uncreated nature, the principle and mode through which humans are united with God, the hypostatic union of Christ, and participation in divine love through grace, 405–6.

69. In addition to his teaching on the human microcosm, Maximus explains that the illumined intellect and the refulgent body (through experiencing God's radiant glory in Christ), become "a workshop of virtue" (*Third Century of Various Texts* 21, the *Philokalia*, 214).

The Trinitarian-Christocentric Practice of the Human Calling

man beings are empowered by grace to mediate God's unifying love in the world. While this mediatory work entails the rigorous engagement of spiritual practice by individuals, Maximus is careful to depict the communal nature of this endeavor. In the following section, I show how Maximus represents the human calling within an ecclesial framework.

The Ecclesial Context

Having considered these five cosmic mediations that Maximus uses to describe the human vocation, it would be remiss to not explain briefly how they are worked out within an ecclesial context. Consequently, I want to point out a few elements regarding the interconnection between the vocation of humanity as mediator and the life of the church.

The "Churching" of the World

The first is what Anestis Keselopoulos calls the "churching" of the world, in his study, *Man and the Environment*.[70] In his analysis of Maximus, Keselopoulos speaks of the ecclesial-eucharistic realm in which humanity works out its divine calling. Building on his Trinitarian and christological framework, Maximus describes humanity's calling to renew creation by restoring its proper orientation and authentic mode of functioning, so that it might realize its divine end.[71] By "the churching of creation," Keselopoulos means that Maximus's theology describes how the church is called and commissioned to make humanity and all of creation part of the kingdom of God.[72] He points to Maximus's *Mystagogy* for the encapsulation of these ideas. As indicated in previous sections, the church is the symbol of God in the world, the divine archetype that is called to hold together and unify the cosmos. All of creation, both intelligible and sensible, is destined to participate in the divine energies, to become a beautiful temple in which praise and glory are rendered to the Creator.[73]

---

70. This illuminative study focuses on St. Symeon the New Theologian, yet includes insightful commentary on Maximus whose theology informed and shaped Symeon's. Interestingly, Keselopoulos engages Moltmann's theology at several points, noting its resonance with Greek Patristic thought, especially that of Maximus and Symeon the New Theologian (cf., *ME*, 54n44 and 93n79).

71. Keselopoulos, *ME*, 144.

72. Ibid., 151–52.

73. Ibid., 153.

Keselopoulos highlights in Maximus's *Mystagogy* that humanity and the world are not self-existent, isolated entities, but are organically connected. Moreover, human beings, in their created structure, are to function as priests who bring all of creation into intimate communion with the Holy Trinity. Accordingly, the churching of the world

> is to be understood as a gathering of all things that exist into one unity, so that none of them is in opposition or conflict or at enmity with any other, and so as to secure the one nature of sensible things and the "one nature of things created." In this case, man freely participates and becomes a co-worker in the unifying work of God's energies. This cooperation in the unity of beings is manifested in the mysteries of the Church, which are the means whereby rational beings are led up and brought together into the unity of things sensible and intelligible in relation to their unity with the uncreated God.[74]

What's more, through humanity's eucharistic approach to the world, men and women cooperate with God in the transfiguration of the world so that it reflects the beauty of the Creator. The church, made up of human beings made in the image and likeness of the triune God, does the work of God in the heart of the world. And at the heart of the church, is the mystery of the Eucharist, so that

> at every Divine Liturgy, the eucharistic change of the bread and wine into [the] Body and Blood of Christ is both the firstfruits and the goal of the ultimate transfiguration and renewal of the world. . . . With this prospect and this reality before him, the Christian . . . seeks material goods in order to secure his biological existence, but he also has a "mystagogical" attitude which discerns within material things the uncreated Grace, thus making his use of material things into Liturgy and Eucharist.[75]

Therefore, the human calling to serve as microcosms and mediators in creation, is fulfilled within the ecclesial-eucharistic realm, where Christ's reconciling activity operates in and through God's people.

---

74. Ibid., 155.
75. Ibid., 167–68.

The Trinitarian-Christocentric Practice of the Human Calling

The Church's Liturgy and Chalcedonian Christology

A second element deals with the way Maximus links the human vocation to the church's liturgy and Chalcedonian Christology. As Balthasar has suggested, Maximus takes the monastic theology of Evagrius (including the threefold schema of the spiritual life), and transplants it into an ecclesial context, basing it on Chalcedonian Christology.[76] This notion of mystical ecclesiology balances the aspects of individual and collective spiritual life. Furthermore, for Maximus, the church's liturgy is "the act that makes real the universal presence of the hypostatic Christ . . . the midpoint between God and creation, heaven and earth, new age and old, Church and world."[77] While the liturgy signifies many spiritual realities related to the salvation and deification of humanity and creation, it is more than "a mere symbol; it is, in modern terms, an *opus operatum*, an effective transformation of the world into transfigured, divinized existence." Thus, for this reason, in Maximus' view "the liturgy is ultimately always 'cosmic liturgy': a way of drawing the entire world into the hypostatic union, because both world and liturgy share a christological foundation."[78]

A careful reading of Maximus's *Mystagogy* reveals this christological foundation—of the world, the church, the liturgy, salvation and deification, the spiritual life, and humanity's mediatory role in the cosmos. As Maximus linked the five mediations with the Evagrian threefold schema, he does the same with his ecclesiology, fusing anthropology, ecclesiology, and mystical theology. We see elements of this when he says that

> man is a mystical church, because through the nave, representing the body, it proposes moral wisdom [*praktike*], while by means of the sanctuary, representing the soul, it spiritually interprets natural contemplation [*physike*], and by means of the mind of the divine altar it manifest mystical theology [*theologia*].[79]

As a mystical church, microcosm, universal mediator, and image of the triune God, humanity is divinely called to gather all of creation, through the liturgical celebration, "for the mystery accomplished on the

---

76. Balthasar, *CL*, 321ff.

77. Ibid., 316.

78. Balthasar adds: "This is something new and original and must be regarded as Maximus' own achievement" (ibid., 322).

79. Maximus, *Mystagogia*, ch. 4; in *CWS*, 190.

divine altar."[80] And through this mystery, humanity and all of creation are transfigured through union with the Trinity, a union that is guided by Maximus's rigorous Chalcedonian logic (i.e., unchanged, unmixed).

Therefore, as we have seen in this section, the human calling is realized in an ecclesial context. Through bringing out the connections between the church's liturgy and Chalcedonian Christology, Maximus envisions the renewal of humanity and the cosmos through union with the Trinity. In the next part, I turn to the Trinitarian-christological praxis in Moltmann.

Trinitarian-Christocentric Praxis in Jürgen Moltmann

Where Maximus articulates the human vocation through the images of human being as ordered microcosm and universal mediator, Moltmann discusses God's human image in creation and the messianic fellowship of service for the kingdom of God. In this section, I consider Moltmann's analysis of God's human image in creation, as *imago Dei, imago Christi*, and *gloria Dei*. Next, I look at how his understanding of the human calling, as bearers of the divine image, is spelled out in the context of the church as the eschatological community of God's kingdom.

God's Human Image in Creation

In *God in Creation*, Moltmann explores the fundamental concept of theological anthropology,[81] the *imago Dei*, looking into key biblical passages and the works of Eastern and Western theologians such as Augustine, Aquinas, Gregory of Nazianzus, Lossky, and Stăniloae. His analysis has, consequently, led some of his students and readers to revisit these fundamental concepts within theological anthropology.[82]

Moltmann outlines his discussion on the image of God in creation based on a Trinitarian structure, asserting that "anthropology and theology are always mutually related," and that "human beings are *imago trinitatis*

80. Maximus, *Mystagogia*, ch. 5; in *CWS*, 195.

81. Cf. Burns, *Theological Anthropology*. Burns offers a concise, helpful overview of many key themes in theological anthropology, including figures from the Eastern and Western traditions.

82. Examples of this include: Bauckham's commentary on Moltmann, *TJM*, 176ff., 199ff.; McDougall, *PL*, 59ff., 101ff.; Müller-Fahrenholz, *KP*, 80ff., 107ff., 160ff.; van Prooijen, *Limping but Blessed*—the entire work focuses on Moltmann's quest for a liberating theological anthroplogy.

The Trinitarian-Christocentric Practice of the Human Calling

and only correspond to the triune God when they are united with one another."[83] Within this biblical and patristic context, Moltmann considers the image of God in human beings, according to their messianic alignment.[84] So, from the outset of his study on the divine image in humanity, one can see how Moltmann is committed to discerning the Trinitarian structure of theological anthropology, and to bringing out the Trinitarian and christological features.

Imago Dei

In the first part of Moltmann's discussion, he considers the original designation of human beings, that is, *imago Dei*. In the flow of an ongoing exposition of Genesis 1:26–30—a central passage in the history of Christian anthropology, as we saw in Maximus and his interlocutors—Moltmann speaks of God implanting the divine image and glory in the earthly creation and how this draws God into the very history of God's creatures. If you recall, we also saw this in Maximus, when he portrays the church as the image of God and explains how the triune God, through the incarnation of the Word, is drawn into human history, in order to recapitulate all of creation.

In addition to his exposition of Genesis 1, Moltmann also reflects on the notion of archetype or pattern found in the Platonic thinking of patristic theology and in New Testament passages that speak of Christ as the image of God through whom everything is created (e.g. Col 1:15ff.; Heb 1:3),[85] and to whom believers are to become like in form (Rom 8:29).[86] As

---

83. Moltmann, *GC*, 215–16; cf. Bauckham's comments regarding Moltmann's view on how the "trinitarian perichoresis, in which the divine Persons are themselves in their distinction from and (equally) at-oneness with each other, provides a pattern of personhood as that of individuals in relationship" (*TJM*, 176); the correspondence between belief in the triune God, *imago trinitatis*, and anthroplogy in Moltmann, "Destruction and Liberation of the Earth," in *God for a Secular Society*, 101ff.; Elizabeth Johnson's intriguing synopsis of the image of God and Moltmann's input, in *She Who Is*, 71.

84. Müller-Fahrenholz's commentary on this is full of interesting insights and critiques (*KP*, 160ff.).

85. "He is the image (εἰκὼν) of invisible God, the firstborn of all creation; for in him all things in heaven and on earth were created, things visible and invisible, whether thrones or dominions or rulers or powers—all things have been created by him and for him" (Col 1:15–16). "He is the reflecion of God's glory and the exact imprint (χαρακτὴρ) of God's very being, and he sustains all things by his powerful word" (Heb 1:3).

86. "For those whom he foreknew he also predestined to be conformed to the image

we saw earlier, Maximus employs this archetypal thinking in his *Mystagogy*, where he describes the way redeemed human beings (in the fellowship of the church) function as the image of their divine archetype who work the same effects of God.[87]

Mediated through Christ

Stemming from his analysis of the *imago Dei* in these biblical passages and the Platonic thinking of patristic theology, Moltmann explains that the "*imago Christi* is an *imago Dei* mediated through Christ," so that "the creation of human beings is open for the incarnation," and that "christology is understood as the fulfillment of the anthropology [suggested in Gen 1:26–30], and the anthropology becomes the preparation for the christology."[88] We will look more closely at Moltmann's reflections on *imago Christi* below and consider further how his theological anthropology is structured by his Trinitarian and christological vision.

Royal Theology, Revolutionary Potential

What's more, Moltmann discusses the possible Old Testament background of the *imago Dei* within royal theology,[89] suggesting the revolutionary potential of such an understanding. Consequently, it is not the prince who is the image, deputy, and reflection of God, Moltmann argues, but "the human being—men and women alike in degree, all human beings and every human being." Hence, as "far as the subsequent charge to rule over the earth is concerned, there is no distinction at all between human beings; there is only equality."[90] Maximus also intimates this kind of egalitarian thinking

---

(εἰκόνος) of his Son, in order that he might be the firstborn within a large family" (Rom 8:29).

87. Maximus, *Mystagogia*; CWS, 187.

88. Moltmann, GC, 219.

89. Maximus suggests this kind of royal image thinking found in the Hebrew Bible when he explains the reasons for writing his *Mystagogy*. Accordingly, he says that Christians should study the works of such theologians as Dionysius the Areopagite, in order to learn more about the symbols of the sacred celebration of the holy synaxis, because it "restores the spiritual wage of the divine and very *royal image* which was snatched away from us in the beginning by the evil one through the deception of transgressing the commandment" (CWS, 184, italics mine).

90. Moltmann adds: "Whether or not, historically speaking, we can say that the Priestly Writing already contains a 'democratization' of royal theology, this passage has

The Trinitarian-Christocentric Practice of the Human Calling

(at least in potentiality and thrust), in his understanding of Galatians 3:28. For Maximus, men and women bear the divine image, are restored to the divine likeness, and through baptism transcend the division between male and female to form new humanity in Christ. While Maximus's thinking is embedded in a different historical context, and is expressed in distinct language and concepts, a kindred egalitarian spirit is arguably present.

Likeness to God as Relationship

For Moltmann, moreover, likeness to God is understood as God's relationship to human beings first, and consequently, the human being's relationship to God. He explains, "God puts himself in a particular relationship to human beings—a relationship in which human beings become his image and his glory on earth." Thus, the "nature of human beings springs from their relationship to God." Human beings, accordingly, are called to mirror God's image[91] in three fundamental relationships: as God's *representatives* and in his name, they rule over the earthly creatures;[92] they are God's *counterpart* on earth, those with whom he communicates; and they are the *appearance* of God's splendor and his glory on earth.[93]

Holistic, Communal, Ecological

The image of God, Moltmann posits, is not possession of any particular characteristic, but entails one's whole existence. "The whole person, not

---

certainly had a 'democratizing' effect throughout the whole of Jewish and Christian political history" (*GC*, 219).

91. Maximus, in line with the biblical and patristic tradition, also uses this "mirror" imagery in his theological anthropology, e.g., *Mystagogia*, ch. 7; in *CWS*, 197.

92. Moltmann is careful to define what he means by "rule." He explains that this commission to rule entails stewarding, preserving, nourishing, and helping life continue on the earth. He also proposes that "to subdue the earth" refers to "the nourishment of human beings which, according to [Gen 1:29–30] is evidently supposed to be exclusively vegetarian. The beasts are also to eat only vegetarian food. This means that the right to kill animals is excluded from the lordship of human beings over them. If human beings and animals alike eat vegetarian food, then the 'lordship' of human beings have the function of a 'justice of the peace'" (*GC*, 224).

93. See Stăniloae's reflection on the glory and honor bestowed on human beings as the image of God, how the image implanted in human beings is preserved and developed by means of continuous relationship with God, and how this image is both "gift" and "task" (*Gabe und Aufgabe*), as B. Vyschevslavzev has said (Stăniloae, *Experience of God*, 2:85–86).

merely [one's] soul; the true human community, not only the individual; humanity as it is bound up with nature, not simply human beings in their confrontation with nature—it is these which are the image of God and [God's] glory."[94]

These aspects of the image of God in human beings—the holistic, communal, and ecological—accord with Maximus's teaching on the divine image. As bearers of the image of the triune God, and microcosms of the universe, men and women are called to cooperate with God in the redemption and restoration of humanity and all of creation. As we saw in Maximus, his theological anthropology, soteriology, and spirituality emphasize the restoration of the whole person, as individuals within the larger community, and in light of their organic relationship with nature and all of God's creation.

One final observation worth noting in Moltmann's treatment of the *imago Dei* is his consideration of how God appears on earth in the male-female image (Gen 1:27). Moltmann asserts that male-female likeness to God cannot be lived in isolation, but can be lived only in human community, because we are social beings aligned towards human society.[95] If you recall, it is this notion that leads Moltmann to his perichoretic thinking, in which he employs concepts from Trinitarian and christological reflection to describe humanity in relation to one another, in relation to God, and in relation to all of creation. For Moltmann (and Maximus), thinking about what it means to be human is interwoven with thinking about the triune God and God's self-revelation in Jesus Christ. In other words, their theological anthropology springs out of their Trinitarian and Christological visions. We understand what it means to be authentically human, and consequently, how to realize the human vocation, through sustained contemplation of the triune God as revealed in Christ, creation, Scripture, and tradition.

---

94. Moltmann, *GC*, 220–21. Moltmann also suggests that, according to the biblical traditions, the human face manifests God's relationship to human beings, 221; cf. Balthasar, *Glory of the Lord*, 20, 150, 328–30.

95. Moltmann, *GC*, 222–23. Moltmann adds that thinking of God's image as it appears in men and women is not to be thought of in bisexual terms (as god and goddess at the same time), or transexually (as indifferent towards God's masculine and feminine image), or in solely masculine or neuter terms, but in Trinitarian terms (223). Related to this, McDougall notes the way Moltmann balances individuality with community (*PL*, 161–62).

The Trinitarian-Christocentric Practice of the Human Calling

Commissioned to Rule—Stewardship

Further, it is male and female, as bearers of the *imago Dei*, who are commissioned to rule over the animals and subdue the earth (Gen 1:28-29). To reiterate, this is not license to exploit the earth and its resources, but a graced call to serve as a "justice of the peace," a tenant in God's house, a steward who aids the preservation and continuation of life in God's creation.[96] Thunberg speaks to this, in his consideration of Maximus, the *imago Dei* tradition, and the notion of human beings as God's rational viceroys on earth. He says that "the Christian tradition is often accused of having evaluated humanity's place in creation so highly that it involved an open invitation to use nature's resources to extremes and to destroy nature at will." He argues that this is a false accusation, asserting that Christian anthropology in the patristic period was "concerned primarily with the spirituality of human persons," so that dominion over the earth, part of their share in the divine image, "is understood in terms of spiritual enterprise." Thus, when human beings "become absorbed by the material side of this enterprise, this is regarded as an expression of their sinfulness rather than of their rightful sovereignty."[97] I would add, further, that the human calling as God's viceroys means a right use of creation, a "tilling" of the earth, something that implies protecting, keeping, and responsibly overseeing the natural world and living in harmony with all of God's creatures.[98]

---

96. Moltmann, *GC*, 224–25. This particular area demonstrates how reading Maximus and Moltmann *jointly* on humanity's attitudes and actions towards creation is illuminative, correcting many aberrant ideas and practices in modern societies. See also Sherrard's comments regarding the retrieval and reaffirmation of premodern anthropologies and cosmologies that express the sacredness of existence (*Human Image*, 11ff.).

97. Thunberg, "Human Person," 299–300.

98. Again, Keselopoulos, based on his study of Maximus and Symeon the New Theologian, asserts: The "right use of creation, i.e. the 'tilling,' necessarily implies also a duty of further protecting and conserving creation, the 'keeping.' Right use of creation without at the same time protecting it is not possible" (177–78). It is interesting to find that Keselopoulos, at several points, notes the parallels between Maximus, Symeon, and Moltmann.

Imago Christi

THE MESSIANIC ALIGNMENT OF HUMAN BEINGS

A second facet of Moltmann's exposition on God's human image in creation deals with the *imago Christi*, the messianic alignment of human beings. Moltmann believes that humanity's true likeness to God is found, not at the genesis of God's history with humankind, but at its end. On this note, Moltmann argues, "The idea of the future as a *restitutio in integrum* and a return to the original paradisal condition of creation (*status integritatis*)" cannot "be called biblical nor Christian."[99] This is what Moltmann means by "messianic alignment," as noted earlier. He finds this messianic calling of human beings in Paul's New Testament writings, where Jesus, the raised and transfigured Messiah, is presented as God's true image, the image and glory of the invisible God on earth. Within Christ's fellowship, Moltmann says, "People become what they are intended to be. Their glorification is promised them with their justification and in the process of their sanctification."[100] Though he uses different language, Maximus also clusters related theological concepts in a similar fashion to Moltmann. For example, in *Mystagogy*, Maximus entwines thoughts on justification and deification, bringing out the eschatological orientation of these concepts.[101] Because of his engagement with Orthodox thinkers like Maximus, Moltmann's teaching on these concepts is deepened. The way he joins the ideas of glorification, justification, and sanctification—often the preferred categories of Protestant theologians—with the eschatologically aligned *imago Christi*, enriches his theological anthropology.

---

99. Moltmann, *GC*, 208. Moltmann adds that a "simple comparison between the first chapter of the Bible and the last is enough to refute this traditional doctrine." To counter Bultmann's view on this notion of a return to paradise, Moltmann cites the Orthodox view voiced by Evdokimov: "The kingdom is not simply a return back towards Paradise, but its forward-moving creative fulfillment which takes in the whole of creation" ("Nature," *SJT* 18 (1965) 8, quoted in Moltmann, *GC*, 348n36). Maximus's vision of *theosis*, as I showed above, also reiterates the forward-moving creative realization of humanity and all of creation, rather than a simple return to paradise; cf. Balthasar's reflections on this forward-moving dynamic, *Theological Anthropology*, 109.

100. Moltmann, *GC*, 225; cf. Balthasar's reflections on Maximus, the notion of "becoming what you are" through following the Son, and the progressive realization of the divine image and likeness (in conversation with Newman) (Balthasar, *CL*, 118, 226).

101. Maximus, *Mystagogia*, ch. 24; in *CWS*, 211ff.

CHRIST: GOD'S IMAGE AND GLORY

Moltmann continues his analysis of the *imago Christi* by considering other biblical passages, such as 2 Corinthians 4:4, which speaks of "the glory of Christ," explaining that Christ is "the likeness of God."[102] Moltmann understands Paul to be combining elements of Genesis 1:26 and Psalm 8, so that "the image of God and his glory on earth belong together; they are one and the same. If Christ has been raised and transfigured into the divine glory, he is the true image of God on earth." The gospel of the risen Christ, therefore, "proclaims the appearance of the glory of God in the face of Christ (2 Cor. 4:6),[103] giving this as reason for the sure and certain hope of the beginning of the new creation."[104]

Moltmann also finds this "messianic resurrection theology" in Colossians, which speaks of Christ as "the image of the invisible God, the firstborn of all creation; for in him all things were created" (1:15–16). This archetypal Christology, which Moltmann suggests emerges from Jewish Wisdom literature, asserts that Christ, as the image of the invisible God, is the mediator in creation, the reconciler of the world, and the Lord of the divine rule. In Christ, "God appears in his perfect image, God rules through his image, God reconciles and redeems through his image on earth." And since "it is through Christ that the new, true creation begins, Christ must already be the mystery of creation in the beginning,"[105] an assertion we saw earlier in the christological basis of Maximus's thought on the human calling. There we saw how Maximus speaks in a way that accords with Moltmann's understanding of archetypal Christology, where Christ is understood as the mystery of creation in the beginning, with his incarnation revealing the divine plan for the renewal of humanity and all of creation.

---

102. "In their case [those who are perishing] the god of this world has blinded the minds of the unbelievers, to keep them from seeing the light of the gospel of the glory of Christ, who is the image of God" (2 Cor 4:4).

103. "For it is the God who said, 'Let light shine out of darkness,' who has shone in our hearts to give the light of the knowledge of the glory of God in the face of Jesus Christ" (2 Cor 4:6); cf. Müller-Fahrenholz, *KP*, 180–81.

104. Moltmann, *GC*, 225; cf. Moltmann, "Resurrection of Christ," 82ff.

105. Moltmann, *GC*, 226. Moltmann adds: "The earlier is understood in the light of the later, and the beginning is comprehended in the light of the consummation."

New Creation through Fellowship

Interweaving his Trinitarian and christologically grounded teaching on the image of God, Moltmann explains that the new, true creation in Christ, and restoration of the likeness to God, is realized in the fellowship of believers with Christ, "since he is the messianic *imago Dei*, believers become *imago Christi*, and through this enter upon the path which will make them *gloria Dei* on earth." Through the role of discipleship, believers are integrated into the life of the Trinity, conformed to the image of the Son (Rom 8:29), and grow into the messianic form of Jesus.[106] Moltmann argues, moreover, that this restoration through the fellowship of believers with the triune God and one another, and through Christian discipleship, discloses genuine humanity: "*Being* human means *becoming* human in this process."[107]

Further, the image of God that is restored "is the whole person, the embodied person, the person in [his or her] community with other people, because in the messianic fellowship of Jesus, people become whole, embodied and social human beings," whom "death no longer divides into soul and body, and whom death no longer divides from God and from one another." For, they "already live, here and now, in the process of resurrection."[108]

---

106. In a meditation on Christian discipleship based on vignettes from the Gospels, Maximus links elements of the stories with the threefold approach to the spiritual life. Thus, the follower of Christ advances from being a man of faith (*praktike*) to a disciple (*physike*) to an apostle (*First Century on Theology*, in *Philokalia*, 120–21). In the centuries before and after these, Maximus demonstrates how he entwines teaching on discipleship with *theosis*, growth in Christlikenss, and the restoration of the divine image in human beings.

107. See Maximus's reflections on how Christ's incarnation initiated "a wholly new way of being human," realigning and renewing humanity, and helping to bring about God's original purpose for human being (*Amb.* 7, in Blowers, *CMJC*, 70). See also J. Williams's comments referenced earlier, in which she stresses the connections between believers' participation in the whole person of Christ, their transformation into his likeness by becoming both human and divine, and how this process is structured by Christology and understood by christological thinking ("Pseudo-Dionysius," 194ff.).

108. Moltmann, *GC*, 227. Here is another interesting parallel with Maximus and his notion of the five syntheses accomplished by Christ and his followers. Additionally, "Living in the process of the resurrection" is congruent to Maximus's notion of *theosis*. McIntosh points out in Maximus the deep connections between Christ's resurrection and the grace of human deification, which is a sharing in Christ's dying and rising (*MT*, 58).

The Trinitarian-Christocentric Practice of the Human Calling

INVITED TO RULE WITH CHRIST

Consequently, in light of the messianic gospel and the messianic calling of human beings, men and women are invited to rule with Christ who, as the true and visible image of the invisible God on earth, has received all authority in heaven and on earth (Matt 28:18).[109] Christ's liberating and healing rule, Moltmann argues, "embraces the fulfillment of the *dominium terrae*—the promise given to human beings at creation," a notion that resonates with Maximus. As Keselopoulos asserted, for Maximus, humanity's vocation in the world—"the churching of creation"—involves women and men in Christ making humanity and the environment part of the kingdom of God. This perspective aligns with what Moltmann means by the authority that Christ bestows on his disciples to rule the earth and bring the reign of the triune God to light in the world. Moltmann adds, under "the conditions of history and in the circumstances of sin and death, the sovereignty of the crucified and risen Messiah Jesus is the only true *dominium terrae*." For it "it is to the Lamb that rule over the world belongs."[110] And, as those who follow the crucified, conquering Lamb, bearers of Christ's image are emissaries of God's healing and life-giving kingdom.

Gloria Dei

THE ESCHATOLOGICAL GLORIFICATION OF HUMAN BEINGS

This brings us to the third aspect of Moltmann's analysis of the image of God, *gloria Dei*, the eschatological glorification of human beings. Once again, Moltmann's theology evinces that the human calling in creation is rooted in Trinitarian and christological ground. For example, in eschatological tones, he explains that as creation is creation for the Sabbath, so human beings are created as the image of God for the divine glory. He references Irenaeus, who describes human beings as *Gloria Dei est homo*, God's glory in the world.[111] Human beings, as the image of God, are called

---

109. "And Jesus came and said to them, 'All authority in heaven and on earth has been given to me'" (Matt 28:18).

110. Moltmann, *GC*, 227.

111. Irenaeus, *Adversus Haereses*, IV, 20:7, in *Ante-Nicene Fathers*, 490, "For the glory of God is a living man; and the life of man consists in beholding God." The second part of this well-known quote is often overlooked, that contemplating God is the essence of human life.

to fulfill what they are intended to be from the beginning: creations and reflectors of divine glory on earth. In Maximus's perspective, as we saw earlier, the royal image is restored to human beings in Christ, so that they are enabled to reflect the divine glory in creation, as God intended from the beginning.[112]

Priestly by Nature

Moltmann, relying further on his interpretation of the biblical traditions, believes that the eschatological glorification of God in human beings suggests that they are priestly by nature. They are to stand before God on behalf of the earth, and before the earth on behalf of God.[113] Moreover, they "are not merely commissioned by God; they are also the mode of his appearance in his creation." The messianic calling of human beings, to be conformed to the true image who is Jesus the Messiah, brings humanity into the eschatological flow of history that courses through the present. What is only seen in veiled fashion now, will be seen fully then, when Christ appears and all God's children are made like him (1 Cor 13:12; 1 John 3:2).[114]

Destined for Beatific Vision

As messianically aligned creatures, human beings are destined for this beatific vision. Moltmann explains: "The eschatological becoming-one-with-God of human beings (*theosis*) is inherent in the concept of 'seeing,' for the seeing face to face and the seeing [God] as [God] is transforms the seer into the One seen and allows [him or her] to participate in the divine life and beauty." Hence, "Participation in the divine nature and conformity to God,

---

112. See Thunberg's synopsis of Maximus's ideas on how the divine attributes are seen in human virtues, so that there are reflections of the Trinity in the ongoing incarnation of the Logos in human beings (*MM*, 425–26).

113. See Lossky's discussion of humanity's priestly calling according to Maximus (*OT*, 74ff.); cf. Stăniloae's profound exposition on the creation and vocation of human beings, which draws significantly from Maximus ("Creation of Man," in *Experience of God*, 65–112).

114. "For now we see in a mirror, dimly, but then we will see face to face. Now I know only in part; then I will know fully, even as I have been fully known" (1 Cor 13:12). "Beloved, we are God's children now; what we will be has not yet been revealed. What we do know is this: when he is revealed, we will be like him, for we will see him as he is" (1 John 3:2).

flowering into perfect resemblance, are the marks of the promised glorification of human beings."[115]

A Messianic Fellowship of Service for the Kingdom of God

God's human image in creation, as we are recognizing, is restored and realized in redemptive relationship with God and in what Moltmann calls "a messianic fellowship of service for the kingdom of God."[116] In this section, I demonstrate the Trinitarian-christocentric structure which gives rise to Moltmann's understanding of how human beings cooperate with God in the restoration of all things. Before doing this, I want to point out one particular text that is emblematic of Moltmann's overarching perspective on humanity's graced involvement in the divine drama of making all things new, then move into the Trinitarian-christocentric practices involved in this calling.

As those created in the image of God, who are called and baptized into the community of Christ, and made alive in the Spirit, Christians "are given a part in the renewal of the earth." The Spirit "gives 'to each of his or her own,' and involves men and women together in joint work for the kingdom of God, the new creation of all things."[117] As Keselopoulos said regarding Maximus—that Christians are called and graced to make humanity and creation part of the kingdom of God—so it is with Moltmann. The astounding invitation extended to humanity, the offer to experience new life in Christ and serve as agents of renewal, is a recurring theme in Moltmann's communally aligned theological anthropology.

---

115. Moltmann, *GC*, 228–29; cf. Stăniloae, *Experience of God*, 83ff. Moltmann, additionally, discusses the notion that human beings are at once God's image and a sinner. He considers the various interpretations of the consequences of human sin for the image of God: is the *imago Dei* lost, perverted, or clouded? Regarding Moltmann's hamartiology, see McDougall's constructive critique, *PL*, 163. While McDougall's critique is insightful, it could, perhaps, be strengthened by more detailed consideration of Moltmann's reflections on sin in *CG*, 192ff., in *SL*, 124ff., and in the section in *GC* I noted, 229ff.

116. Moltmann, *CPS*, 289; cf. Müller-Fahrenholz, *KP*, 94–100, for critical commentary on this notion of the messianic fellowship of service for the kingdom of God.

117. Moltmann, *ET*, 284–88. Moltmann explains that the kingdom of God can be *experienced* and *practiced* by believers. In the community of Jesus, "humans become 'co-workers of the kingdom of God'" (in "Jesus and the Kingdom," 12–13). It is this kind of thinking and action that seems to be the response Sherrard is looking for, as mentioned above in the proposal he sets forth in *Human Image*, 1–10.

Worshippers of the Triune God (Doxology)

This community, the messianic fellowship, is recognized, firstly, as *worshippers of the triune God*, answering the call to be a *doxological* people.[118] The filament of doxology runs through most of Moltmann's work, underscoring the primacy of the call to be worshipping creatures. McDougall has indicated this in her study of Moltmann. She underscores several things about doxology in Moltmann's theology. First, she points out how Moltmann argues fervently for a "doxological theology," a worshipful contemplation of the triune God that includes meditation, adoration, and praise. She notes that Moltmann's doxological theology seeks to correct the pragmatism of modernity, with its overemphasis on measuring the truth of Christian doctrines solely in terms of what they achieve. As McDougall explains,

> Such a notion of the "practical," Moltmann argues, can only impoverish the life of faith: "Christian love is not merely a motivation, and Christian faith is more than the point from which action takes its bearings. Being a Christian is also characterized by gratitude, joy, praise and adoration. Faith lives in meditation and prayer as well as in practice."[119]

McDougall also notes how Moltmann anchors his doxological theology in soteriology. Thus, this doxological perspective is understood as a joyful response to the revelation of God in Christ in the economy of salvation. However, doxological theology "moves beyond thanksgiving over God's works to sheer wonder and glorification of God that is born out of love and even participation in the divine life,"[120] says McDougall. According to Moltmann, "Here we know only in so far as we love. Here we know in order to participate. Then to know God means to participate in the fullness of the divine life."[121]

Moreover, Moltmann suggests that the church's worship is determined by the history of God: "The assembled community perceives anew the complete history of Christ, his giving himself up to death for the salvation of

---

118. Cf. Moltmann's comments on "trinitarian doxology" in "Trinitarian Personhood," 309ff.

119. McDougall, *PL*, 19; Moltmann, *TK*, 7.

120. McDougall, *PL*, 19.

121. Moltmann, *TK*, 152. See my further reflections on the links between knowledge, love, and participation (in contrast to modern forms of knowledge as mastering or dominating) in ch. 6.

creation, and his glorification in the life of God for creation's future."[122] He explains, further, that human beings are called to participate in the messianic feast of worship, a feast in which the assembled community proclaims the gospel, responds to the liberation offered in Christ, baptizes in the name of the triune God, and celebrates the Lord's Supper. The church's regular celebration of Christ's life, death, and resurrection anticipates the fellowship of God's kingdom, and transforms the whole of life. It is "a feast of freedom in the presence of the triune God."[123] Therefore, while Moltmann communicates this doxological aspect of the human vocation in different terms than Maximus, it is profoundly structured by his Trinitarian and christological vision.

What's more, this feast of the kingdom of God, celebrating salvation in Christ, in the joy of the Spirit, propels God's people into the heart of a broken world. Moltmann insists that worship and the celebration of the Lord's Supper demonstrate fellowship with Christ's mission to the poor, the imprisoned, the sick, and the despised.[124] Worship, moreover, is to encompass the Christian's whole life, so that her everyday life becomes a reasonable service or spiritual worship of love.[125]

DISCIPLES OF THE CRUCIFIED CHRIST

Intrinsically linked to the call to be worshippers of the triune God, as seen in Moltmann, is the call to be *disciples of the crucified Christ*. Once more, the Trinitarian and christological structure of Moltmann's theology on the call to discipleship is evident. Discipleship means, first, baptism in the name of the triune God (Matt 28:19), an act that draws one into the Trinitarian history of God with the world, including its creation, redemption, and glorification. Baptism, followed by a life in the Spirit and the discipleship of

---

122. Moltmann, *CPS*, 261.

123. Moltmann, *CPS*, 261. The aim of the church's liturgy, Moltmann says, is to reflect the cosmic liturgy of creation and to correspond to the divine liturgy of life (*CPS*, 303). The way that Moltmann demonstrates the interconnection between church's Trinitarian and christologically grounded liturgy with the cosmic liturgy concurs with Maximus; cf. Moltmann's comments regarding the adoration of God on a cosmic level and in all things ("Scope of Renewal," 15ff.).

124. Moltmann, *CPS*, 258; cf. Müller-Fahrenholz's comments on how Moltmann conceives the church's role in serving the marginalized, the downtrodden, and the handicapped (*KP*, 105–36).

125. Moltmann, *CPS*, 272; cf. Rom 12:1–2.

Christ, symbolizes "the praxis of the doctrine of the Trinity,"[126] demonstrating that the doctrine of the Trinity shapes not only the church's worshipful speculation, contemplation, and searching, but also the church's communal practices. This recalls Bruce Marshall's insight that I pointed out earlier, that Christian communities are called to make clear to their members "*how to be trinitarian*" people. Like Moltmann, Marshall argues that the doctrine of the Trinity, a most basic and foundational Christian teaching, informs our identification of God *and* our everyday spiritual life. As he says, the "doctrine of the Trinity ought to shape everyday Christian practice and belief in deep and discernible ways."[127] A careful reading of Moltmann's work reinforces this conviction. For Moltmann, the notion of "being a trinitarian people" fires and forges his entire project, especially his understanding of the church as a community of Christian discipleship.

Second, faith in Christ and baptism in the name of the Trinity, launch one into a life of friendship with Jesus, fellowship with Jesus's friends, and the spreading of friendliness in the fellowship of Jesus.[128] Interestingly, Moltmann references the richness of Catholic tradition and the missional life promoted by Ignatius Loyola and his followers, who saw themselves as the friends of Jesus. Moltmann says that Ignatian spirituality, with its balancing of the inner life of devotion to Jesus and prayer with active service in the world, is exemplary.[129] For Moltmann, friendship with the crucified Jesus and with his followers leads one into friendship with the poor and suffering. Genuine friends of Jesus give themselves to a life of meditation on his passion and contemplation of the presence of his Spirit, so that "turning to Christ and turning to the men and women for whom he died are part of a single movement."[130] Likewise, we find the entwining of similar themes in

---

126. Moltmann, *ET*, 312. Moltmann also says that for Christians, the call entails belief in the triune God, and one's entire (ecclesial and political) life to be determined by the discipleship of the crucified Christ and life in the Spirit of God (*ET*, 304).

127. Marshall, "Trinity," 192–93; cf. Ware's reflections on how Christian life begins with the Trinity in baptism and ends in union with the Trinity; and how the Trinity structures Christian worship, prayer, community, and discipleship ("Human Person," 7ff.).

128. Moltmann, *CPS*, 316; cf. Tollefsen, "Ethical Consequences," 399ff.

129. Moltmann, *CPS*, 276. The equilibrium between prayer and action is important to Moltmann: "Just as meditation cannot be a flight from action, so, conversely, action cannot be a flight from meditation" (285). Moltmann also evinces an appreciative view of particular ascetics and hermits who sought to live out the life of Christ depicted in the Gospels, including such figures as St. Antony and Pachomius (322).

130. Moltmann, *CPS*, 285; Müller-Fahrenholz, *KP*, 116ff., explores this twofold action of turning to Christ and to others.

Maximus. For example, Maximus speaks of the friends of Christ, disciples who share in his suffering, who bring their prayers to fulfillment through their actions, and demonstrate love for God and neighbor through words and actions, prayer, fasting, and almsgiving.[131]

Moltmann, thirdly, asserts that Christian discipleship involves rigorous reflection on Christ *and* implementation of this ever-increasing knowledge in the praxis of love and justice. While similar to the previous point (which highlighted the connection between the inner and outer life), the emphasis is different here. What I am underscoring here is the vital relationship between what Moltmann calls *christopraxis* and *Christology*. Within Moltmann's discussions on Christology and christopraxis, and the organic relationship between dogmatics and ethics, is a strong rebuke of those modern christologies which present a superficial portrait of Christ and what it means to follow him. He blasts "modern Jesuology" with its watering down and reshaping of Christ crucified, its relegation of salvation to the inward realm of the heart, and its individualization of Christian faith.[132]

For Moltmann, theologizing about Christ includes living out the ethics of Jesus. "Faith in Christ," he says, "has its own praxis: the discipleship of Christ crucified." "Who is the criterion of this praxis of justice? It is *Christ*, who is present, hidden, in the poor, the sick and the children (Mt. 25)."[133] Thus, in Moltmann's estimation, shallow discussion about Jesus as an upstanding human being (and nothing more), without considering the serious call to practice Christ's way of life, is inadequate and short-sided.

Spirit-Empowered Servants of the Kingdom of God

In addition to Moltmann's portrayal of the call to Trinitarian doxology and Christian discipleship, is the call to be *Spirit-empowered servants of the kingdom of God*. These three confluent streams of worship, discipleship, and mission flow directly out of Moltmann's Trinitarian and christological vision. As we have seen above in several instances, Moltmann speaks of the Trinity as open for the world. Likewise, humanity in Christ, the church, is

---

131. Maximus, *Philokalia*, 113, 304, 61.

132. Moltmann, *WJC*, 61–63. Some of the modern theologians that Moltmann critiques are Kant and the ethical theology that followed him, Schleiermacher and his emphasis on the inner-consciousness of Jesus, and Rahner's Christology which is set in the framework of anthropology (58–59, 62).

133. Moltmann, *ET*, 295; cf. Moltmann, "Justice for Victims and Perpetrators," 2–12.

to be open for the world.[134] Maximus expresses the church's openness to the world, as we saw in his *Mystagogy*, in its calling to embrace and unify the different peoples of the world, without confusing their distinctive characteristics. It is this openness to the world, as both Maximus and Moltmann assert, that illustrates the notion of the church as the image, the reflection of the Trinity in God's creation.

Moltmann explains further, that the apostolate of Christ is carried on through the church's ministry. Again, it is Moltmann's Trinitarian and christologically-grounded thinking that structures his conception of how Christ's apostolate is extended through his people. The perichoretic relationship between the Father, Son, and Holy Spirit embraces the church and the world into which the church is sent. In the following, notice the Trinitarian pattern and rhythm of Moltmann's thought, how each person of the Trinity propels God's people forward into service. Accordingly, the "community of believers lives in the apostolate of Christ: 'He who hears you hears me' (Lk. 10:16); 'As the Father has sent me, even so I send you' (Jn. 20:21)." In these sayings, Moltmann states, the risen Christ "promises his real presence in the apostolate of the community of his people, who follow his messianic mission to the world; so we proclaim the invitation to be reconciled with God 'in Christ's stead' (2 Cor. 5:20)."

Christ's real presence within the community "fills the proclamation, the sacraments, the fellowship and the *diakonia* of his congregation with authority."[135] We encountered a similar notion of God's infilling of the church in Maximus's *Mystagogy*, where the Holy Trinity makes the divine presence and power known through the doxology, liturgy, sacraments, Scripture readings, and proclamation of the Word.[136]

In pneumatological terms, which demonstrate both Moltmann's Trinitarian structured thinking and his passion to see the doctrine of the Spirit given more attention in contemporary theology and anthropology,

---

134. Moltmann, *CPS*, 318; cf. Moltmann's thoughts on John Paul II's encyclical *Evangelium Vitae*, the correspondence between the *missio Dei* and the church's mission, and mission as inviting people to "hope for the future of God and the new creation of all things" ("Pentecostal Theology of Life," 10–13).

135. Moltmann, *ET*, 266; cf. Moltmann, "Jesus and the Kingdom of God," 13ff., where Moltmann states that as "co-workers of the kingdom of God," Christians "do the same messianic works as Jesus himself." Moltmann says elsewhere, "The power and the command of apostolic succession belongs 'to the church as a whole and with it to every individual member for the ministry in which [he or she] is placed through the gift of the Spirit'" (*CPS*, 312).

136. Maximus, *Mystagogia*, chs. 21, 22; in *CWS*, 203, 204.

The Trinitarian-Christocentric Practice of the Human Calling

Moltmann asserts that the life-giving Spirit carries on the ministry of Jesus among his people.[137] The Spirit of Christ heals the sick and gives renewed health in body and soul. The Spirit forgives sins and lifts the burden of guilt from those who need forgiveness. And the Spirit, through the church that is sent by the Father and Son, frees oppressed and exploited people from unjust structures and human brutality.[138]

Moreover, stemming from his christological reflection on the three roles of Christ, Moltmann says that the whole church (and its every member) is called and empowered by the Spirit to be the *prophetic* people, the *priestly* people, and the *kingly* people.[139] Once again, Moltmann shows how his theologizing about Christ gives rise to theologizing about Christ's church, that community of women and men devoted to fulfilling their calling in the world. That is, for Moltmann, thinking about Christ is deeply connected to thinking about how his followers are called to imitate and follow him in every way possible. As Christ's prophetic people, the church bears witness in word and life to the promise of God's kingdom, its liberation, and its future. As Christ's priestly people, the church intercedes for others and testifies to the gift of new life through the redemptive lordship

---

137. Moltmann, *ET*, 147. Moltmann adds: "... so Jesus continues to act in the Spirit and in the community of his people gathers the 'foolish,' 'weak,' 'low and despised' and those who are of no account in the eyes of the world, in order to put to shame the violent, the people of noble birth, and the wise of the world (1 Cor. 1:26–29)" (147–48). The title of Moltmann's main work on ecclesiology, *CPS*, which we have touched on at key points, reinforces the importance of the role of the Spirit in carrying on the ministry of Jesus through his church.

138. It would be interesting to juxtapose Maximus and Moltmann's pneumatology and its relation to the human vocation. Surprisingly, in all my research into Maximus, I have seen very little written explicitly on the role of the Spirit in his theology. Even a casual reading of Maximus reveals the pervasive presence and influence of the Spirit in the life of the church. For example, just in the material included in the *Philokalia*, Maximus speaks of the Spirit numerous times: the Spirit's ubiquitous presence (180–81); indwelling presence (123, 304); activity as water and fire (152); the law of the Spirit (189); the pledge of the Spirit (110); the Spirit's fruits and gifts (186–87, 217–19); in the Christian life (176, 239); rebirth through the Spirit (256, 284, 287); the Spirit and God's kingdom (290–92). Thunberg, however, does note a work that looks at *pneuma* in Loosen, *Logos und Pneuma*, esp. 87–126. Thunberg suggests that the role of *pneuma* in Maximus's teaching on spiritual development is not original, nor interesting when compared to his doctrine on the Logos and the *logoi* (*MM*, 20).

139. As noted earlier, Ware's reflections on this have informed Moltmann's. See Ware's treatment of humanity's calling to cooperate with God (1 Cor 3:9), as priests of creation who give thanks and offer creation back to God, as kings who mold, fashion, connect, and diversify creation, transfiguring and hallowing it to the glory of God (*Orthodox Way*, 54).

of Christ. As Christ's kingly people, the church participates in the divine rule (Rev 1:5; 5:10; 20:6), which involves manifesting the coming of the kingdom and the new creation now underway.[140]

Love at the Center of the Human Calling

For both Maximus and Moltmann, *love* is at the center of the human calling. Love for God and neighbor, according to both theologians, is the foundation and goal of this calling. This is also the case in Moltmann's teaching on being Spirit-empowered servants of the kingdom of God. For Moltmann, the church participates in Christ's messianic mission, the liberation and uniting of humanity in Christ, and the restoration of all creation in the fellowship of love.[141] In addition, Moltmann's Trinitarian vision leads him to say that God's nature is not almighty power, but love, and this Trinitarian love does not rule through division and separation, but through healing and uniting what has been separated. Thus, redeemed human beings created in the image of the triune God, Moltmann argues, joined in Christian community,[142] are called to embody love of all things, and to fulfill Christ's command to love God and neighbor.[143] Recalling Maximus's teaching, par-

---

140. Moltmann, *CPS*, 300–302. Moltmann adds that the church is also the messianic people, and is no longer subject to special prophets, priests, and kings, because it has found itself and its destiny through the mission and activity of the resurrected Christ. In light of this, the church cannot live as a dumb, muted, passive crowd ruled by a few (302). As those who bear the divine image and participate in the life of the Trinity through faith in Christ, women and men are called to actively serve in the leadership of the church.

141. Moltmann, *CPS*, 64–65. In fact, McDougall proposes that the interconnected themes of Trinity and love serve as a major leitmotif in Moltmann's theology (*PL*, 4ff.). See Tracy, "Trinitarian Speculation," 285ff. Tracy discusses the notion of Christians as agents of God's love, representing the loving face of God in Jesus Christ; cf. Moltmann, "Liberate Yourselves," 106ff.

142. Moltmann, *ET*, 292; cf. Moltmann, "Destruction and Liberation," in *God for a Secular Society*, 101ff. See McIntosh's reflections, where he says that the mystical dimension of theology, which I have pointed out in Maximus and Moltmann, "suggests that Christian anthropology finds its roots in a consideration of trinitarian life," resurrection and which has irreversibly begun in the resurrection and ascension of Jesus Christ" (*MT*, 239).

143. Moltmann, *SL*, 86; *ET* 185, 197. Moltmann, in *CPS*, 284, quotes Bonhoeffer (*Dein Reich komme*, Hamburg 1958, 6, 11): "Only the man who loves the earth and God as a single unity can believe in the kingdom of God." Further, Moltmann demonstrates the practical nature of the *Shema* in his discussion of various crimes against life, slavery, and the polarization between the rich and the poor (*ET*, 185–86). See also Ware's reflections in *Orthodox Way* (a text that influenced Moltmann), 39: "'The most perfect rule

ticularly in the *Mystagogy*, we find many of these accordant themes. As the image of God in creation, the church works the effects of God, including unifying diverse people, while preserving their differences, bringing together male and female in Christ, bringing creatures to rest in the embrace of the Holy Trinity, all within the spirit of love and friendship with God and others.[144]

---

of Christianity, its exact definition, its highest summit, is this: to seek what is for the benefit of all,' states St John Chrysostom. '. . . I cannot believe that it is possible for a man to be saved if he does not labour for the salvation of his neighbor.' Such are the practical implications of the dogma of the Trinity. That is what it means to *live the Trinity*."

144. Maximus, *Mystagogia*; in CWS, 187, 192, 194, 207, 211, 213. See Ware's comments regarding ways that various social units (families, the parish, the workplace, schools, the church universal) can be made an icon of the Trinity: "Because we know that God is three in one, each of us is committed to living sacrificially in and for one another; each is committed irrevocably to a life of practical service, of active compassion." For, our "faith in the Trinity puts us under an obligation to struggle at every level, from the strictly personal to the highly organized, against all forms of oppression, injustice and exploitation. In our combat for social righteousness and 'human rights,' we are acting specifically *in the name of the Holy Trinity*" (*Orthodox Way*, 39).

6

Conclusion

The Human Calling in Creation—Rooted in God

THIS STUDY EXPLORED THE THEOLOGICAL ANTHROPLOGIES OF MAXIMUS the Confessor and Jürgen Moltmann, in order to demonstrate how their conception of the human vocation springs out of their Trinitarian-christocentric visions. Motivated by ecumenical, historical, and practical factors, I sought to engage in constructive dialogue across traditions, showing the importance of a proper understanding of the human vocation, and illustrating how reading Maximus and Moltmann together sheds more light on the human calling in creation.

Throughout the study, I sought to demonstrate how the theological anthropologies of Maximus and Moltmann begin in a different manner than our usual contemporary order. Where modern theologies tend to devise an account of human being first, and then attempt to find ways in which Christ and the Trinity are somehow relevant to this human being, or perhaps account for elements of our human existence that we think we already know about, Maximus and Moltmann have started by trying to meditate upon and to understand Christ and the Trinity. From this starting point, they have seen how the human being comes to exist and is called forth into ever-fuller life in God.

Implications for Contemporary Theology

This insight—starting from contemplation of the Trinity and Christ, then developing a vision of what it means to be human—has a number of important implications for theology today. As Lewis Ayres has argued, re-emphasizing contemplation of the Trinity will have significant consequences

Conclusion

for theological thinking and practice as a whole.[1] We live in an era in which the turn to the subject has influenced our thinking, so that many scholars assume that if we can know anything at all, it is ourselves and our human existence. According to this kind of thinking, theological reflection properly begins from anthropology, then considers how the doctrines of the Trinity and Christ may have something to say about human being. This study proposes that the opposite might be the case. As the theological visions of Maximus and Moltmann suggest, the richest and deepest understanding of human existence and human calling emerges out of reflection on the Trinity and Christ, as opposed to beginning with ourselves. Furthermore, the doctrine of the Trinity and its development in relation to the mystery of Christ, turns out to be far more intrinsic and basic to theological reflection, and more fruitful for theological construction, than some tendencies in modern theology might suggest.

An Illuminating Contrast

To illustrate this tendency in modern theology, as a contrast to the Trinitarian and christologically based approach of Maximus and Moltmann, I point to Immanuel Kant (1724–1804) and Friedrich Schleiermacher (1768–1843). The work of these two major figures in modern theology is voluminous and complex, so I will focus on one aspect of their theology as a way to demonstrate the difference between their approaches and those of Maximus and Moltmann.

The aspect to which I refer is the way that both Kant and Schleiermacher, as theologians emphasizing the turn to the subject, neglect the doctrine of the Trinity.[2] While scholars continue to debate the issue regarding the treatment of the doctrine of the Trinity in modern theology,[3]

---

1. Ayres, *Nicaea and Its Legacy*, 386n6.

2. Regarding Schleiermacher, it is true that there is a christocentric dimension in *The Christian Faith*, but this attention to the centrality of Christ is not matched by careful consideration of the doctrine of the Trinity.

3. See Marshall, "Trinity." His essay on Schleiermacher, characteristics of recent Trinitarian theology, and the alleged Trinitarian renewal in the twentieth century is an outstanding and provocative analysis. Cf. Moltmann, *Trinity and the Kingdom*, 6ff. Whether one agrees with the notion that a Trinitarian renewal has taken place in the twentieth century, it is worth considering the arguments in favor of this position. Moreover, it is also intriguing to note how some Orthodox scholars discern a "rediscovery of the Greek patristic tradition" over the last century, as Sherrard says in his chapter, "Revival of Hesychast Spirituality," 417. Of course, such a rediscovery includes the rich Trinitarian

many agree that the doctrine was neglected and relegated by these two influential theologians.[4] Put briefly, Kant asserted that the doctrine of the Trinity has "no practical relevance at all, even if we think we understand it," we do not, since "it transcends all our concepts."[5] Furthermore, Schleiermacher contributes to the neglect and marginalization of the doctrine of the Trinity. His *Glaubenslehre* (*The Christian Faith*), a nearly eight-hundred page work that has influenced modern Protestantism for generations, addresses the doctrine of the Trinity in the final thirteen pages, under the rubric "Conclusion."[6] In this conclusion, Schleiermacher explains that the orthodox formulation of the doctrine of the Trinity is not "an immediate or even necessary combination of utterances concerning the Christian self-consciousness." While Schleiermacher is adamant in his assertion that Christianity is a monotheistic mode of belief,[7] he offers only a few pages to

---

matrix of Maximus's theology.

4. LaCugna, in *God for Us*, underlines the appendix-like treatment of the Trinity in Schleiermacher. Along with other scholars, LaCugna holds that a renaissance of Trinitarian thought among Catholic, Orthodox, and Protestant theology has occurred in the twentieth century. See Marshall, who raises doubts that speaking about a "renewal" in Trinitarian theology is entirely accurate ("Trinity," 190ff.).

5. Kant, *Conflict of the Faculties*, 65. See Moltmann's comments on Kant's assertion: "Whether we have to worship three or ten persons in the deity is unimportant, Kant claimed, because 'it is impossible to extract from this difference any different rules for practical living.' For theoretical reason God is unknowable, because he exceeds the limits of any possible experience; so it is only in the postulates of practical reason that Kant brings God to the fore, together with 'liberty' and 'immortality.' Here the transcendental definition 'God' is sufficient; for moral monotheism is enough to provide the foundation for free and responsible conduct" (*TK*, 6).

6. Schleiermacher, *Christian Faith*, 738–51. Some theologians, like Claude Welch, posit that Schleiermacher, "the Father of Modern Theology," saw the Trinity as nothing more than an "unnecessary and unwarranted addition to the faith" (Welch, *In This Name*, 5). Other theologians have more recently suggested that Schleiermacher made a more substantial contribution to Trinitarian doctrine than has been recognized previously. I do not find this altogether convincing, considering the minimal amount of space he gives to the doctrine in his chief dogmatic work. Still, it is worth considering the recent reevaluation of Schleiermacher, something Veli-Matti Kärkkäinen points out in *Trinity*, 55.

7. Schleiermacher, *Christian Faith*, 740; cf. Shults and Hollingsworth, *Holy Spirit*, 62ff., where they discuss Schleiermacher and Kant's treatment of pneumatology and Trinitarian doctrine. Christianity, Schleiermacher asserts, "takes it place as the purest form of monotheism which has appeared in history" (*Christian Faith*, 37–38, 52). See Moltmann's appraisal of Schleiermacher's relegation of Trinitarian doctrine, in *TK*, 3. While I do have issues with Schleiermacher's diminutive treatment of the Trinity, he does raise some interesting points in the thirteen pages, especially his conviction that the doctrine should receive "fresh treatment" based on an exploration that goes back to its very beginnings (*Christian Faith*, 747).

Conclusion

explain how the doctrine of the Trinity factors into and informs the Christian faith.[8]

Conversely, this study suggests that Maximus and Moltmann, by rooting their understanding of the human vocation in their Trinitarian and christological reflection, demonstrate the fertility and value of Trinitarian thinking. Through analyzing the Trinitarian matrix, christological basis, redemptive goal, and Trinitarian-christocentric praxis of the human calling in Maximus and Moltmann, this study proffers that the doctrines of Christ and the Trinity provide a heuristic framework for contemplating the mystery of God and ourselves in relation to God and all creation, a comprehensive model for making sense of human being and the human vocation.

Humanity Reenvisioned

A second implication of this study is that the theology of Maximus and Moltmann provides alternatives to the anthropocentricism of modernity. In response to modernity's overemphasis on the turn to the human subject, Maximus and Moltmann offer fresh, constructive ways of envisioning humanity in relation to God and creation. Maximus's teaching on humanity as a microcosm corrects a human-centered, individualistic view of the relationship between humanity and creation. As Pelikan argues, Maximus's understanding of humanity as a microcosm, "the cosmic dimension of his spirituality," underscores the salvation or transformation of the human person along with the world, "that God may be all in all" (1 Cor 15:28). While this corrects an anthropocentric view of humanity's relation to the world, an "individualism" that separates humanity from creation, Pelikan adds that Maximus's teaching also steers clear of a "cosmism" in which "the individual is obliterated and 'salvation' becomes the annihilation of the self rather than the transformation of the self." The primary way that Maximus achieves this balanced view of humanity in relation to the world is by

---

8. See Moltmann's pointed discussion on Schleiermacher, his Trinitarian theology, his Christology that absorbed Arian elements, and how his doctrine of God displays Sabellian features (Schleiermacher, "Über den Gegenstaz," *Theol. Zeitschrift*, 1882, now in *Friedrich Schleiermacher und die Trinitätslehre* 11, ed. Tetz, Gütersloh, 1969; cited in Moltmann, *TK*, 137). Moltmann concludes that the concept of the one God, at the expense of Trinitarian reflection, is what prevails in Schleiermacher: "subordinationism in his christology and modalism in his trinitarian doctrine are the results" (*TK*, 137).

rooting it in his Trinitarian and christological teaching, as we have seen throughout this study.[9]

Moltmann reiterates this point in his own ecological doctrine of creation and humanity. He explains that in "an anthropocentric world view," the world was created for human beings, and that the human being is the crown of creation. Moltmann argues that this is unbiblical, since the biblical traditions teach that God created the world for God's glory, out of love, and that the crown of creation is the Sabbath. While it is true that human beings, as those created in the image of God, have a special place in creation, they stand "together with all other earthly and heavenly beings in the same hymn of praise of God's glory, and in the enjoyment of God's sabbath pleasure over creation, as [God] saw that it was good." For even "without human beings, the heavens declare the glory of God." This "theocentric world view" gives the human being, in light of her special position in the cosmos, the opportunity to understand herself "as a member of the community of creation." Therefore, Moltmann asserts, if Christian theology wants to find the wisdom to interact with creation in generative ways, it must free itself "from the modern anthropocentric view of the world."[10] As with Maximus, this healthy view of humanity springs out of Moltmann's Trinitarian and christological reflection. His teaching on perichoresis provides the structure for his understanding of humanity's relationship to God, to one another, and to the broader creation. The Trinitarian perichoresis, according to Moltmann, is "the wellspring of everything that lives." The God of Christianity, with the reciprocal indwelling and mutual interpenetration of the Trinitarian perichoresis, is the life-giving source of all that exists.[11]

Ancient Sources, Contemporary Existence

A third implication of this study is that wisdom drawn from ancient sources can help us reenvision our understanding of humanity and creation. As Elizabeth Johnson says, we will discover new ways of perceiving ourselves in relation to one another, to God, and to creation, "by a creative combination of hermeneutical retrieval of ancient texts and appropriation of

---

9. Maximus Confessor, *CWS*, 10.
10. Moltmann, *GC*, 31.
11. Moltmann, *GC*, 16–17.

contemporary experience."[12] Moltmann asserts that it is the "earliest traditions of Christian theology" which often provide the most fertile ideas for the "revolution in our attitude" toward creation that is critically important today.[13] As we have seen throughout this study, Moltmann illustrates this kind of critical retrieval and appropriation. Drawing from Origen, Athanasius, Gregory of Nyssa, Gregory of Nazianzus, and Maximus, Moltmann offers fresh readings of these classical theologians, elucidating constructive ways of applying their ideas and practices in our postmodern context.

Contemplative, Participatory Knowledge

A fourth implication of this study concerns an approach to knowledge that is different from tendencies in modern theology. Both Maximus and Moltmann exhibit contemplative epistemologies. In his discussion of knowledge of nature as God's creation, Moltmann makes several important points.[14] First, Moltmann argues that if we are to develop an understanding of creation and ourselves that is faithful to the biblical traditions and relevant to our contemporary milieu, we must move beyond analytical thinking that divides subject and object, and seek to learn a communicative, integrative way of thinking. Re-visiting the pre-modern concept of reason as the organ of perception and participation (μέθεξις), Moltmann suggests, will help this pursuit. Second, Moltmann offers a vigorous critique of modern thinking, saying that it has developed by means of objectifying, analytical, particularizing, and reductionalistic approaches. The goal is to reduce an object or idea to its smallest, indivisible parts, then to reconstruct it. The aim of this kind of thinking is to dominate objects and facts, to *divide et impera* (divide and rule), an ancient Roman principle, one that has informed modern intentions to master nature. Third, Moltmann points out that modern thinking, including nuclear physics, biology, and other sciences, falls short in its description of reality and its advancement of knowledge. Moltmann argues that objects are known and understood more fully when viewed in their constellation of relationships, their environments, and their totality, rather than isolating and segmenting them. If life means existing in relationship, "communication in communion," then death means isolation and lack of relationship. Therefore, to understand reality and that

12. Johnson, *She Who Is*, 19.
13. Moltmann, *GC*, xv.
14. Moltmann, *GC*, 2–4.

which is alive, we must seek to know it in its relationships, community, and surroundings. Fourth, this approach to knowledge transforms the incentive behind cognition. Moltmann asserts, "We no longer desire to know in order to dominate, or analyze and reduce in order to reconstruct. Our purpose is now to participate, and to enter into the mutual relationships of the living thing." This integrative approach to knowledge fosters community between human beings and nature, and between creatures and Creator. To know is to acknowledge our deep connections to one another, to nature, to God, to the broader community of all creation.

If you recall, we considered Moltmann's reflection on the doctrine of the two books in Maximus's theology. Moltmann references this to illustrate what he means by revisiting pre-modern ways of knowing. According to Maximus, the cosmos is like a book and Scripture is like a cosmos. The book of nature, made up of particular letters, syllables, and words that together convey the glory of God, reflects the interconnectedness of the created universe. Likewise, the book of Scripture, itself a cosmos constituted of heaven and earth and things in between, expresses the majesty of the Creator.[15] Therefore, the right way to "read" both books is not to analyze, dissect, and break down the various words, but to approach them contemplatively. For both Maximus and Moltmann, this is a respectful endeavor, one that knows through loving, through participating in, as opposed to objectifying and seeking to dominate.[16] As Maximus explains, the way to true knowledge of God, of creation, and of ourselves, involves deep spiritual engagement, prayerful ascetic practices, and the purification of mind and heart through the love of God in Christ.

---

15. *Ambiguum* 10, *PG* 91. 1128–29a; cf. Louth, *MC*, 108–12.

16. Moltmann's quote, considered previously, is worth repeating: "Here we know only in so far as we love. Here we know in order to participate. Then to know God means to participate in the fullness of the divine life" (*TK*, 152).

Bibliography

Aland, Barbara, et al., eds. *The Greek New Testament*. 4th rev. ed. Stuttgart: Deutsche Bibelgesellschaft, 2005.
Aquinas, Thomas. *Summa Theologica*. Translated by Fathers of the English Dominican Province. 5 vols. New York: Christian Classics, 1981.
Argárate, Pablo. "El hombre como microsmos en el pensamiento de San Máximo el Confessor." *Recherches de théologie ancienne et médiévale* 63 (1996) 177–98.
———. "La unidad dinamica del Cósmos en San Máximo el Confesor." *Teologia* 33 (1996) 35–51.
———. "Maximus the Confessor's Criticism of Origenism: The Role of Movement within Ontology." *Bibliotheca Ephemeridum Theologicarum Lovaniensium* 164 (2003) 1037–41.
Athanasius. *On the Incarnation of the Word*. In *Christology of the Later Fathers*, edited by Edward R. Hardy, 55–110. Louisville: Westminster John Knox, 1977.
Augustine. *Confessions*. Garden City: Image, 1960.
———. *Teaching Christianity* [De doctrina Christiana]. Translated by Edmund Hill. Edited by John E. Rotelle. Hyde Park, NY: New City, 1996.
———. *The Trinity* [De Trinitate]. Translated by Edmund Hill. Edited by John E. Rotelle. New York: New City, 1990.
Ayres, Lewis. "Deification and the Dynamics of Nicene Theology: The Contribution of Gregory of Nyssa." *St. Vladimir's Theological Quarterly* 49 (2005) 375–94.
———. *Nicaea and Its Legacy: An Approach to Fourth-Century Trinitarian Theology*. New York: Oxford University Press, 2004.
Balthasar, Hans Urs von. *Cosmic Liturgy: The Universe according to Maximus the Confessor*. Translated by Brian Daley. San Francisco: Ignatius, 2003.
———. *The Glory of the Lord: A Theological Aesthetics*. Vol. 1, *Seeing the Form*. San Francisco: Ignatius, 1982.
———. *A Theological Anthropology*. New York: Sheed & Ward, 1967.
Barnes, Michel R. "De Régnon Reconsidered." *Augustinian Studies* 26 (1995) 51–79.
Barth, Karl. *Church Dogmatics*. 4 vols. Edinburgh: T. & T. Clark, 1936–69.
Basil, Bishop of Sergievo. "Towards the Millenium: The Transfiguration of the World and Humanity in Christ." *Sourozh* 72 (1998) 28–39.
Bauckham, Richard, ed. *God Will Be All in All: The Eschatology of Jürgen Moltmann*. Edinburgh: T & T Clark, 1999.
———. "Jürgen Moltmann." In *The Modern Theologians: An Introduction to Christian Theology in the Twentieth Century*. edited by David F. Ford, 1:293–310. Oxford: Blackwell, 1989.

Bibliography

———. *Moltmann: Messianic Theology in the Making*. Basingstoke, UK: Marshall Pickering, 1987.

———. "Moltmanns Eschatologie des Kreuzes." In *Diskussion über Jürgen Moltmanns Buch "Der gekreuzigte Gott,"* edited by Michael Welker, 43–53. Munich: Kaiser, 1979.

———. *The Theology of Jürgen Moltmann*. Edinburgh: T. & T. Clark, 1995.

Berthold, G. C. "The Cappadocian Roots of Maximus the Confessor." In *Maximus Confessor: Actes du Symposium sur Maxime le Confesseur*, edited by Felix Heinzer and Christoph von Schönborn, 51–59. Fribourg: Editions universitaires, 1982.

———. "Did Maximus the Confessor Know Augustine?" *Studia Patristica* 17 (1982) 14–17.

Bingaman, Brock. "Karl Rahner and Maximus the Confessor: Consonant Themes and Ecumenical Dialogue." *Heythrop Journal* 55 (2014) 353–63.

———. "Orthodox Spirituality and Contemporary Ecology: John Cassian, Maximus the Confessor, and Jürgen Moltmann in Conversation." In *Spirit and Nature*. edited by Timothy Hessel-Robinson and Ray Maria McNamara, 98–124. Eugene, OR: Pickwick, 2011.

Bingaman, Brock, and Bradley Nassif, eds. *The* Philokalia: *A Classic Text of Orthodox Spirituality*. New York: Oxford University Press, 2012.

Blowers, Paul M. *Exegesis and Spiritual Pedagogy in Maximus the Confessor: An Investigation of the* Quaestiones ad Thalassium. Notre Dame: University of Notre Dame Press, 1991.

———. "Gentiles of the Soul: Maximus the Confessor on the Substructure and Transformation of the Human Passions." *Journal of Early Christian Studies* 6 (1996) 57–85.

———. "Maximus the Confessor, Gregory of Nyssa, and the Concept of Perpetual Progress." *Vigiliae Christianae* 46 (1992) 151–71.

———. *On the Cosmic Mystery of Jesus Christ: Selected Writings of St. Maximus the Confessor*. Crestwood, NY: St. Vladimir's Seminary Press, 2003.

———. "Theology as Integrative, Visionary, Pastoral: The Legacy of Maximus the Confessor." *Pro Ecclesia* 2 (1993) 216–30.

Bonaventure. *Breviloquium*. Translated by José de Vinck. Patterson: St. Anthony Guild, 1963.

Bonhoeffer, Dietrich. *Creation and Fall: A Theological Interpretation of Genesis 1–3*. Translated by John C. Fletcher. London: SCM, 1959.

———. *Letters and Papers from Prison*. Enl. edition. London: SCM, 1971.

Bornet, R. "Explication de la liturgie et interprétation de l'Écriture chez Maxime le Confesseur." *Studia Patristica* 10 (1970) 323–27.

Brown, Raymond E. *The Gospel according to John I–XII*. Anchor Bible 29. New York: Doubleday, 1966.

Burns, J. Patout, trans., ed. *Theological Anthropology*. Philadelphia: Fortress, 1981.

Carter, J. Kameron. *Race: A Theological Account*. New York: Oxford University Press, 2008

Chopp, Rebecca S. "Praxis." In *The New Dictionary of Catholic Spirituality*, edited by Michael Downey, 756–64. Collegeville: Liturgical, 1993.

———. *The Praxis of Suffering: An Interpretation of Liberation and Political Theologies*. Maryknoll: Orbis, 1986.

Clayton, Philip. "God and World." In *The Cambridge Companion to Postmodern Theology*, edited by Kevin Vanhoozer, 203–18. Cambridge: Cambridge University Press, 2003.

Bibliography

Constas, Nicholas. "Eschatology and Christology: Moltmann and the Greek Fathers." In *God's Life in Trinity*, edited by Miroslav Volf and Michael Welker, 191–99. Minneapolis: Fortress, 2006.
Cooper, Adam. *The Body in St. Maximus the Confessor: Holy Flesh Wholly Deified*. Oxford: Oxford University Press, 2005.
———. "Maximus the Confessor on the Structural Dynamics of Revelation." *Vigilae Christianne* 55 (2001) 161–86.
Corrigan, Kevin. *Evagrius and Gregory: Mind, Soul and Body in the 4th Century*. Farnham, UK: Ashgate, 2009.
Cunningham, David S. *These Three Are One: The Practice of Trinitarian Theology*. Oxford: Blackwell, 1998.
Daley, Brian E. "*Apokatastasis* and Apocalyptic: Eastern Eschatology after Chalcedon." In *The Hope of the Early Church*, 201–2. Peabody, MA: Hendrickson, 2003.
Dalmais, I.-H. "S. Maxime le Confesseur, Docteur de la Charité." *Vie Spirituelle* 2 (1948) 296–303.
Dalmais, Irénée-Henri. "La doctrine ascétique de saint Maxime le Confesseur d'apres le *Liber asceticus*." *Irénikon* 26 (153) 17–39.
———. "La fonction unificatrice du Verbe incarné dans les oeuvres spirituelles de saint Maxime le Confesseur." *Sciences Ecclésiastiques* 14 (1962) 445–49.
———. "La théorie des *logoi* des creatures chez saint Maxime le Confesseur." *Revue des Sciences Philosophiques et Théologiques* 36 (1952) 244–49.
———. "L'Anthropologie spirituelle de saint Maxime le Confesseur." *Recherches et Débats* 36 (1961) 202–11.
———. "L'oeuvre spirituelle de saint Maxime le Confesseur." *Supplément de la Vie Spirituelle* 21 (1952) 216–26.
———. "Saint Maxime le Confesseur et la crise de l'origénisme monastique." *Théologie de la Vie Monastique* 49 (1961) 411–21.
———. "Un traité de théologie contemplative: Le commentaire du *Pater noster de* saint Maxime le Confesseur." *Revue d'Ascétique et de Mystique* 29 (1953) 123–59.
Dragas, George Dion. "The Church in St. Maximus' *Mystagogy*: The Problem and the Orthodox Perspective." *Theology* 56 (1985) 385–403.
Dupré, Louis, and Don E. Saliers, eds. *Christian Spirituality: Post-Reformation and Modern*. New York: Crossroad, 1989.
Feenstra, Ronald J., and Cornelius Plantinga Jr., eds. *Trinity, Incarnation, and Atonement: Philosophical and Theological Essays*. Notre Dame: University of Notre Dame Press, 1989.
Fiddes, Paul S. *The Creative Suffering of God*. Oxford: Clarendon, 1988.
Finlan, Stephen, and Vladimir Kharlamov, eds. *Theosis: Deification in Christian Theology*. Eugene, OR: Pickwick, 2006.
Fiorenza, Francis Schüssler. Introduction to *Faith and the Future: Essays on Theology, Solidarity, and Modernity*, edited by Johann-Baptist Metz and Jürgen Moltmann, xi–xvii. Maryknoll: Orbis, 1995.
Florovsky, Georges. *The Byzantine Fathers of the Sixth to Eighth Century*. Vol. 9. Translated by Raymond Miller et al. Vaduz: Büchervertriebsanstalt, 1987.
Ford, David. *The Modern Theologians*. Oxford: Blackwell, 2005.
Gavrilyuk, Paul L. *The Suffering of the Impassible God*. New York: Oxford University Press, 2004.
Greer, Rowan A. *Origen*. London: SPCK, 1979.

Bibliography

Gregory of Nyssa. *The Catechetical Oration of St. Gregory of Nyssa.* Translated by James Herbert Srawley. Cambridge: Cambridge University Press, 2009.

Gunton, Colin E. *The One, the Three and the Many: God, Creation and the Culture of Modernity.* Bampton Lectures 1992. Cambridge: Cambridge University Press, 1993.

Harvie, Timothy. *Jürgen Moltmann's Ethics of Hope: Eschatological Possibilities for Moral Action.* Alderhsot & Burlington: Ashgate, 2009.

Heine, Ronald E. *Origen: Scholarship in Service of the Church.* New York: Oxford University Press, 2010.

Heschel, Abraham. *The Sabbath: Its Meaning for Modern Man.* New York: Farrar, Straus, and Giroux, 1975.

Hodgson, Leonard. *The Doctrine of the Trinity.* Croall Lectures, 1942–1943. New York: Scribner, 1944.

Holder, Arthur G., ed. *The Blackwell Companion to Christian Spirituality.* Oxford: Blackwell, 2005.

Hunsinger, George. "The Crucified God and the Political Theology of Violence." *Heythrop Journal* 14 (1973) 266–79.

Irenaeus. *Adversus Haereses* [Against heresies]. In *Ante-Nicene Fathers.* 4th ed. Vol. 1. Edited by Alexander Roberts and James Donaldson. Peabody, MA: Hendrickson, 2004.

Johnson, Elizabeth A. *She Who Is: The Mystery of God in Feminist Theological Discourse.* New York: Crossroad, 1992.

———. "To Let the Symbol Sing Again." *Theology Today* 53 (1997) 299–311.

Jones, L. Gregory. *Embodying Forgiveness: A Theological Analysis.* Grand Rapids: Eerdmans, 1995.

———. *Transformed Judgment: Toward a Trinitarian Account of the Moral Life.* Notre Dame: University of Notre Dame Press, 1990.

Kant, Immanuel. *The Conflict of the Faculties.* Translated by May J. Grefor. New York: Abaris, 1979.

Kärkkäinen, Veli-Matti. *The Trinity: Global Perspectives.* Louisville: Westminster John Knox, 2007.

Karras, Valerie. "Patristic Views on the Ontology of Gender." In *Personhood: Orthodox Christianity and the Connection between Body, Mind, and Soul,* edited by John Chirban, 113–19. Santa Barbara, CA: Bergin & Garvey, 1996.

———. "A Re-evaluation of Marriage, Celibacy, and Irony in Gregory of Nyssa's *On Virginity.*" *Journal of Early Christian Studies* 13 (2005) 111–21.

———. "Sex/Gender in Gregory of Nyssa's Eschatology: Irrelevant or Non-Existent." *Studia Patristica* 41 (2006) 363–68.

Kelley, J. N. D. *Early Christian Doctrines.* 2nd ed. Peabody, MA: Prince, 2004.

Keselopoulos, Anestis. *Man and the Environment.* Crestwood, NY: St. Vladimir's Seminary Press, 2001.

Kharlamov, Vladimir. "Emergence of the Deification Theme in the Apostolic Fathers." In *Theosis: Deification in Christian Theology,* edited by Stephen Finlan and Vladimir Kharlamov, 51–66. Eugene, OR: Pickwick, 2006.

Kilby, Karen. "Perichoresis and Projection: Problems with the Social Doctrines of the Trinity." *New Blackfriars* 81 (2000) 432–45.

Konmarianos, Pavlos. "Symbol and Reality in the Divine Liturgy." *Synaxi* 71 (1999) 27–37.

Konstantinovsky, Julia. *Evagrius Ponticus.* Farnham, UK: Ashgate, 2008.

LaCugna, Catherine Mowry. *God for Us: The Trinity and the Christian Life*. New York: HarperCollins, 1991.

———. "Re-conceiving the Trinity as the Mystery of Salvation." *Scottish Journal of Theology* 38 (1985) 1–23.

LaCugna, Catherine Mowry, and Killian McDonnell. "Returning from 'The Far Country': Theses for a Contemporary Trinitarian Theology." *Scottish Journal of Theology* 41 (1988) 191–215.

Ladner, Gerhart B. *The Idea of Reform: Its Impact on Christian Thought and Action in the Age of the Fathers*. New York: Harper & Row, 1967.

Lash, Nicholas. "Considering the Trinity." *Modern Theology* 2 (1986) 183–96.

Lonergan, Bernard. *Method in Theology*. Toronto: University of Toronto Press, 2003.

Loosen, Josef. *Logos und Pneuma im begnadeten Menschen bei Maximus Confessor*. Münster: Aschendorffsche, 1941.

Lossky, Vladimir. *The Mystical Theology of the Eastern Church*. Crestwood, NY: St. Vladimir's Seminary Press, 1976.

———. *Orthodox Theology: An Introduction*. Crestwood, NY: St. Vladimir's Seminary Press, 2001.

———. *The Vision of God*. Crestwood, NY: St. Vladimir's Seminary Press, 1997.

Lot-Borrodine, M. *La Deification de l'homme selon la doctrine des pères grecs*. Paris: éditions du Cerf, 1970.

Louth, Andrew. "Apophatic Theology and the Liturgy in St. Maximus the Confessor." *Criterion* 36 (1997) 112–22.

———. "Beauty Will Save the World: The Formation of Byzantine Spirituality." *Theology Today* 61 (2004) 67–77.

———. *Denys the Areopagite*. London: Continuum, 2001.

———. "Dogma and Spirituality in St. Maximus the Confessor." In *Prayer and Spirituality in the Early Church*, edited by Pauline Allen et al., 197–208. Brisbane: Australian Catholic University, 1998.

———. *Maximus the Confessor*. New York: Routledge, 1999.

———. *The Origins of the Christian Mystical Tradition: From Plato to Denys*. Oxford: Clarendon, 1981.

———. "Recent Research on St. Maximus the Confessor: A Survey." *St. Vladimir's Theological Quarterly* 42 (1998) 76–84.

———. "St. Denys the Areopagite and St. Maximus the Confessor: A Question of Influence." In *Studia Patristica*, edited by Elizabeth A. Livingstone, 27:166–74. Leuven: Peeters, 1993.

Mackey, James. "Are There Christian Alternatives to Trinitarian Thinking?" In *The Christian Understanding of God Today*, edited by James M. Byrne, 66–75. Theological Colloquium on the Occasion of the 400th Anniversary of the Foundation of Trinity College, Dublin. Dublin: Columbia, 1993.

Malcolm, Lois. "An Interview with David Tracy." *Christian Century*, February 13–20, 2002, 24–30.

Marshall, Bruce D. "Trinity." In *The Blackwell Companion to Modern Theology*, edited by Gareth Jones, 193–203. Oxford: Blackwell, 2004.

Maurer, Ernstpeter. "Tendenzen neurer Trinitätslehre." *Verkündigung und Forschung* 39 (1994) 3–24.

Bibliography

Maximus the Confessor. *Ambigua ad Thomam*. In *Maximi Confessoris Ambigua ad Thomam una cum Epistula secunda ad eundem*, edited by Bart Janssens, 3–34. Turnhout, Belgium: Brepols, 2002.

———. *Capita de caritate*. In *Massimo Confessore, Capitoli sulla carita*, edited by Aldo Ceresa-Gastaldo, 48–238. Rome: Editrice Studium, 1963.

———. *Epistula secunda ad Thomam*. In *Maximi Confessoris Ambigua ad Thomam una cum Epistula secunda ad eundem*, edited by Bart Janssens, 37–49. Turnhout, Belgium: Brepols, 2002.

———. *Expositio in Psalmum LIX*. In *Maximi Confessoris opuscula exegetica duo*, edited by Peter van Deun, 3–22. Turnhout, Belgium: Brepols, 1991.

———. *Expositio orationis dominicae*. In *Maximi confessoris opuscula exegetica duo*, edited by Peter van Deun, 27–73. Turnhout, Belgium: Brepols, 1991.

———. *Hymni*. In *S. Massimo Confessore: La mistagogia ed altri scritti*, edited by Raff Cantarella, 236–52. Florence: Testi Cristiani, 1931.

———. *Liber asceticus*. In *S. Massimo Confessore: La mistagogia ed altri scritti*, edited by Raff Cantarella, 30–98. Florence: Testi Cristiani, 1931.

———. *Maximus Confessor: Selected Writings*. Translated by George C. Berthold. Classics of Western Spirituality. Mahwah, NJ: Paulist, 1985.

———. *Mystagogia*. In *S. Massimo Confessore: La mistagogia ed altri scritti*, edited by Raff Cantarella, 122–214. Florence: Testi Cristiani, 1931.

———. *On the Cosmic Mystery of Jesus Christ: Selected Writings from St. Maximus the Confessor*. Translated by Paul M. Blowers and Robert Louis Wilken. Crestwood, NY: St. Vladimir's Seminary Press, 2003.

———. *Opusculum de anima*. In *S. Massimo Confessore: La mistagogia ed altri scritti*, edited by Raff Cantarella, 220–32. Florence: Testi Cristiani, 1931.

———. *Quaestiones ad Thalassium*. In *Maximi Confessoris quaestiones ad Thalassium*, edited by Carl Laga and Carlos Steel, 1:3–539, 2:3–325. Turnhout, Belgium: Brepols, 1980–1990.

———. *Quaestiones et Dubia*. In *Maximi Confessoris quaestiones et dubia*, edited by J. H. Declerck, 3–170. Turnhout, Belgium: Brepols, 1982.

———. *Scholia in Ecclesiasten (in catenis: catena trium patrum)*. In *Anonymus in Ecclesiasten commentarius qui dicitur Catena trium partum*, edited by Santo Lucà, 3–87. Turnhout, Belgium: Brepols, 1983.

———. *St. Maximus the Confessor: The Ascetic Life; The Four Centuries on Charity*. Translated by Polycarp Sherwood. Ancient Christian Writers 21. Mahwah, NJ: Paulist, 1955.

McDermott, Brian O. *Word Become Flesh: Dimensions of Christology*. Collegeville: Liturgical, 1993.

McDougall, Joy Ann. *Pilgrimage of Love: Moltmann on the Trinity and Christian Life*. New York: Oxford University Press, 2005.

———. "A Room of One's Own? Trinitarian Perichoresis as Analogy for the God-Human Relationship." In *Wo ist Gott? Gottesräume—Lebensräume*, edited by Jürgen Moltmann and Carmen Rivuzumwami, 133–41. Neukirchen-Vluyn: Neukirchener, 2002.

McFague, Sallie. "Is God in Charge?" In *Essentials of Christian Theology*, edited by William C. Placher, 101–16. Louisville: Westminster John Knox, 2003.

———. *Metaphorical Theology: Models of God in Religious Language*. Philadelphia: Fortress, 1982.

―――. *Models of God: Theology for an Ecological, Nuclear Age*. Philadelphia: Fortress, 1987.

McFarland, Ian A. "Developing an Apophatic Christocentrism: Lessons from St. Maximus the Confessor." *Theology Today* 60 (2003) 200–214.

―――. "Fleshing Out Christ: Maximus the Confessor's Christology in Anthropological Perspective." *St. Vladimir's Theological Quarterly* 49 (2005) 417–36.

McGinn, Bernard, et al., eds. *Christian Spirituality: Origins to the Twelfth Century*. New York: Crossroad, 1985.

―――. *The Essential Writings of Christian Mysticism*. New York: Modern Library, 2006.

―――. *The Foundations of Mysticism: Origins to the Fifth Century*. New York: Crossroad, 2003.

McGuckin, John A. *The Westminster Handbook to Patristic Theology*. Louisville: Westminster John Knox, 2004.

McIntosh, Mark A. *Christology from Within: Spirituality and the Incarnation in Hans Urs von Balthasar*. Notre Dame: Notre Dame University Press, 2000.

―――. *Discernment and Truth: The Spirituality and Theology of Knowledge*. New York: Crossroad, 2004.

―――. *Divine Teaching: An Introduction to Christian Theology*. Oxford: Blackwell, 2008.

―――. "The Maker's Meaning: Divine Ideas and Salvation." *Modern Theology* 28 (2012) 365–84.

―――. *Mystical Theology: The Integrity of Spirituality and Theology*. Oxford: Blackwell, 1998.

Meeks, M. Douglas. Foreword to *The Experiment Hope*, by Jürgen Moltmann, edited and translated by Meeks, ix–xvii. Philadelphia: Fortress, 1975.

―――. "Jürgen Moltmann's *Systematic Contributions to Theology*." *Religious Studies Review* 22 (1966) 95–102.

―――. *Origins of the Theology of Hope*. Philadelphia: Fortress, 1974.

Meyendorff, John. *Byzantine Theology: Historical Trends and Doctrinal Themes*. New York: Fordham University Press, 1974.

―――. *Christ in Eastern Christian Thought*. Crestwood, NY: St. Vladimir's Seminary Press, 1987.

―――. *St. Gregory Palamas and Orthodox Spirituality*. Crestwood, NY: St. Vladimir's Seminary Press, 1974.

Milbank, John. "The Second Difference: For a Trinitarianism without Reserve." *Modern Theology* 2 (1986) 213–34.

Miskotte, Hermannus Heiko. "Das Leiden ist in Gott. Über Jürgen Moltmanns trinitarische Kreuzestheologie." In *Diskussion über Jürgen Moltmanns Buch "Der gekreuzigte Gott,"* edited by Michael Welker, 74–93. Munich: Kaiser, 1979.

Molnar, Paul D. *Incarnation and Resurrection: Toward a Contemporary Understanding*. Grand Rapids: Eerdmans, 2007.

Moltmann, Jürgen. "The Adventure of Theological Ideas." *Religious Studies Review* 22 (1996) 102–5.

―――. "Antwort auf Kritik an 'Der gekreuzigte Gott.'" In *Diskussion über Jürgen Moltmanns Buch "Der gekreuzigte Gott,"* edited by Michael Welker, 165–90. Munich: Kaiser, 1979.

―――. "Antwort auf die Kritik der Theologie der Hoffnung." In *Diskussion über die "Theologie der Hoffnung" von Jürgen Moltmann*, edited by Wolf Deiter Marsch, 201–38. Munich: Kaiser, 1967.

Bibliography

———. *Bibliographie Jürgen Moltmann*. Compiled by Dieter Ising et al. Munich: Kaiser, 1987.

———. *A Broad Place: An Autobiography*. Minneapolis: Fortress, 2008.

———. *The Church in the Power of the Spirit: A Contribution to Messianic Ecclesiology*. Translated by Margaret Kohl. Minneapolis: Fortress, 1993.

———. *The Coming of God: A Christian Eschatology*. Minneapolis: Fortress, 1996.

———. "The Cosmic Community: A New Ecological Concept of Reality in Science and Religion." *Ching Feng* 29 (1986) 93–105.

———. *Creating a Just Future: The Politics of Peace and the Ethic of Creation in a Threatened World*. London: SCM, 1989.

———. "Creation as an Open System." In *The Future of Creation: Collected Essays*, translated by Margaret Kohl, 115–30. Philadelphia: Fortress, 1979.

———. *The Crucified God: The Cross of Christ as the Foundation and Criticism of Christian Theology*. Translated by R. A. Wilson and John Bowden. New York: HarperCollins, 1991.

———. "The Ecological Crisis: Peace with Nature?" *Culture and Religion* 9 (1988) 5–18.

———. *Experiences in Theology: Ways and Forms of Christian Theology*. Minneapolis: Fortress, 2000.

———. "The Fellowship of the Holy Spirit: On Trinitarian Pneumatology." In *History and the Triune God: Contributions to Trinitarian Theology*, translated by John Bowden, 57–69. New York: Crossroad, 1992.

———. "The Future as a New Paradigm of Transcendence." *Concurrence* 1 (1969) 334–45.

———. *God for a Secular Society: The Public Relevance of Theology*. Translated by Margaret Kohl. Minneapolis: Fortress, 1999.

———. *God in Creation: A New Theology of Creation and the Spirit of God*. Minneapolis: Fortress, 1985.

———. "Homecoming for Abraham's and Sarah's Children and Augustine's Lonely Soul." *Dialog* 35 (1998) 277–81.

———. "Hope and History." In *Religion, Revolution, and the Future*, translated by M. Douglas Meeks, 200–220. New York: Scribner, 1969.

———. *How I Have Changed: Reflections on Thirty Years of Theology*. Edited by Jürgen Moltmann. Translated by John Bowden. Harrisburg, PA: Trinity Press International, 1997.

———. "'I Believe in Jesus Christ, the Only-Begotten Son of God': Brotherly Talk of Christ." In *History and the Triune God: Contributions to Trinitarian Theology*, translated by John Bowden, 31–43. New York: Crossroad, 1992.

———. "The Inviting Unity of the Triune God." In *History and the Triune God: Contributions to Trinitarian Theology*, translated by John Bowden, 80–89. New York: Crossroad, 1992.

———. "Justice for Victims and Perpetrators." In *History and the Triune God: Contributions to Trinitarian Theology*, translated by John Bowden, 80–89. New York: Crossroad, 1992.

———. "Justification and the New Creation." In *The Future of Creation: Collected Essays*, translated by Margaret Kohl, 149–71. Minneapolis: Fortress, 2007.

———. "Jesus and the Kingdom of God." *Asbury Theological Journal* 48 (1993) 5–17.

———. "Jesus between Jews and Christians." *ARC* 24 (1996) 61–76.

———. "Liberate Yourselves by Accepting One Another." In *Human Disability and the Service of God: Reassessing Religious Practice*, edited by Nancy Eiesland and Don Sallers, 105–22. Nashville: Abingdon, 1998.

———. *Mensch: Christliche Anthropologie in den Konflikten der Gegenwart*. Edited by H. J. Schultz. Stuttgart: Kreuz, 1971.

———. "My Theological Career." In *History and the Triune God: Contributions to Trinitarian Theology*, translated by John Bowden, 165–82. New York: Crossroad, 1992.

———. "Open Friendship: Aristotelian and Christian Concepts of Friendship." In *The Changing Face of Friendship*, edited by Leroy S. Rouner, 29–42. Notre Dame: University of Notre Dame Press, 1994.

———. "A Pentecostal Theology of Life." *Journal of Pentecostal Theology* 9 (1996) 3–15.

———. "Political Theology." *Theology Today* 28 (1971) 6–23.

———. "Reconciliation with Nature." *Pacifica* 5 (1992) 301–13.

———. "A Response to My Dialogue Partners." *Journal of Pentecostal Theology* 4 (1994) 59–70.

———. "The Resurrection of Christ: Hope for the World." In *Resurrection Reconsidered*, edited by Gavin D'Costa, 73–86. Oxford: OneWorld, 1996.

———. "The Scope of Renewal in the Spirit." *Perspectives* 6 (1991) 14–17.

———. "Some Questions about the Doctrine of the Trinity Today." Introduction to *History and the Triune God: Contributions to Trinitarian Theology*, translated by John Bowden, xi–xix. New York: Crossroad, 1992.

———. *The Source of Life: The Holy Spirit and the Theology of Life*. Translated by Margaret Kohl. London: SCM, 1997.

———. *The Spirit of Life: A Universal Affirmation*. Minneapolis: Fortress, 2001.

———. "Talk Back Session with Dr. Jürgen Moltmann." *Asbury Theological Journal* 48 (1993) 39–47.

———. *Theology and Joy*. Translated by Reinhard Ulrich. London: SCM, 1973.

———. "Theology as Eschatology." In *The Future of Hope: Theology as Eschatology*, edited by Frederick Hertzog, 1–50. New York: Herder & Herder, 1970.

———. *Theology of Hope: On the Ground and Implications of a Christian Eschatology*. Minneapolis: Fortress, 1993.

———. "The Theology of Mystical Experience: Contemplation in a World of Action." In *Experiences of God*, translated by Margaret Kohl, 55–80. Philadelphia: Fortress, 1980.

———. "Toward a Political Hermeneutic of the Gospel." In *Religion, Revolution, and the Future*, translated by M. Douglas Meeks, 83–107. New York: Scribner, 1969.

———. *The Trinitarian History of God*. New York: Crossroad, 1992.

———. "The Trinitarian Personhood of the Holy Spirit." In *Advents of the Spirit: An Introduction to the Current Study of Pneumatology*, edited by D. Lyle Dabney and Bradford E. Hinze, 300–312. Milwaukee: Marquette University Press, 2001.

———. *The Trinity and the Kingdom of God: The Doctrine of God*. Minneapolis: Fortress, 1981.

———. "The Triune God: Rich in Relationships." *Living Pulpit* 5 (1999) 4–5.

———. *Umkehr zur Zukunft*. Munich: Siebenstern Taschenbuch, 1970.

———. *The Way of Jesus Christ: Christology in Messianic Dimensions*. Minneapolis: Fortress, 1990.

———. "What Is a Theologian?" Lecture given at Princeton Seminary, 1999.

Bibliography

———. "Where There Is Hope, There Is Religion." In *The Experiment Hope*, edited and translated by M. Douglas Meeks, 15-29. Philadelphia: Fortress, 1972.

———. "Why Am I a Christian?" In *Experiences of God*, translated by Margaret Kohl, 1-18. Philadelphia: Fortress, 1980.

Moltmann-Wendel, Elisabeth. "Is There a Feminist Theology of the Cross?" In *The Scandal of a Crucified World: Perspectives on the Cross and Suffering*, edited by Yacob Tesfai, 87-98. Maryknoll: Orbis, 1994.

Morse, Christopher. *The Logic of Promise in Moltmann's Theology*. Philadelphia: Fortress, 1979.

Müller-Fahrenholz, Geiko. *The Kingdom and the Power: The Theology of Jürgen Moltmann*. Translated by John Bowden. London: SCM, 2000.

Nellas, Panayiotis. *Deification in Christ: The Nature of the Human Person*. Translated by Norman Russell. Crestwood, NY: St. Vladimir's Seminary Press, 1987.

Nicholls, David. *Deity and Domination: Images of God and the State in the Nineteenth and Twentieth Centuries*. London: Routledge, 1989.

Nichols, Aidan. *Byzantine Gospel: Maximus the Confessor in Modern Scholarship*. Edinburgh: T. & T. Clark, 1993.

Norris, Richard A. *The Christological Controversy*. Philadelphia: Fortress, 1980.

Norris, Russell Bradner, Jr. "Logos Christology as Cosmological Paradigm." *Pro Ecclesia* 5 (1996) 183-201.

Oakes, Edward T. *Pattern of Redemption: The Theology of Hans Urs von Balthasar*. New York: Continuum, 2005.

O'Collins, Gerald. *Christology: A Biblical, Historical, and Systematic Study of Jesus Christ*. New York: Oxford University Press, 1995.

Oden, Thomas C. *Hebrews*. Ancient Christian Commentary on Scripture, New Testament 10. Grand Rapids: InterVarsity, 2005.

———. *Systematic Theology*. Vol. 1, *The Living God*. Peabody, MA: Hendrickson, 2006.

———. *Systematic Theology*. Vol. 2, *The Word of Life*. Peabody, MA: Hendrickson, 2006.

O'Donnell, John J. *Trinity and Temporality: The Christian Doctrine of God in the Light of Process Theology and the Theology of Hope*. Oxford: Oxford University Press, 1983.

———. "The Trinity as Divine Community: A Critical Reflection upon Recent Theological Developments." *Gregorianum* 69 (1988) 5-34.

Olson, Roger E., and Christopher A. Hall. *The Trinity*. Grand Rapids: Eerdmans, 2002.

O'Regan, Cyril. "Von Balthasar and Thick Retrieval: Post-Chalcedonian Symphonic Theology." *Gregorianum* 77 (1996) 227-60.

Origen. *On First Principles*. Translated by G. W. Butterworth. Gloucester, MA: Smith, 1973.

Paeth, Scott R. *Exodus Church and Civil Society: Public Theology and Social Theory in the Work of Jürgen Moltmann*. Alderhsot, UK: Ashgate, 2008.

Palmer, G. E. H., et al., eds. *The Philokalia: The Complete Text*. Compiled by St. Nikidimos of the Holy Mountain and St. Makarios of Corinth. Translated by Palmer et al. Vol. 2. London: Faber, 1981.

Pannenberg, Wolfhart. *Systematic Theology*. Translated by Geoffrey Bromiley. 3 Vols. Grand Rapids: Eerdmans, 1991-1998.

Papanikolau, Aristotle. *Being with God: Trinity, Apophaticism, and Divine-Human Communion*. Notre Dame: University of Notre Dame Press, 2006.

———. "Liberating Eros: Confession and Desire." *Journal of the Society of Christian Ethics* 26 (2006) 115-36.

———. *The Mystical as Political: Democracy and Non-Radical Orthodoxy*. Notre Dame: University of Notre Dame Press, 2012.
Pauw, Amy Platinga. "Attending to the Gaps between Beliefs and Practices." In *Practicing Theology: Beliefs and Practices in Christian Life*, edited by Miroslav Volf and Dorothy C. Bass, 33–48. Grand Rapids: Eerdmans, 2002.
Pelikan, Jaroslav. *The Christian Tradition: A History of the Development of Doctrine*. Vol. 2, *The Spirit of Eastern Christendom (600–1700)*. Chicago: University of Chicago Press, 1974.
Pitstick, Alyssa Lyra. *Light in Darkness: Hans Urs von Balthasar and the Catholic Doctrine of Christ's Descent into Hell*. Grand Rapids: Eerdmans, 2007.
Prooijen, Ton van. *Limping but Blessed: Jürgen Moltmann's Search for a Liberating Anthropology*. Amsterdam: Rodopi, 2004.
Pseudo-Dionysius. *Pseudo-Dionysius: The Complete Works*. Translated by Colm Luibhéid. Mahwah, NJ: Paulist, 1987.
Radde-Gallwitz, Andrew. "Pseudo-Dionysius, the *Parmenides*, and the Problem of Contradiction." In *Plato's* Parmenides *and Its Heritage*, edited by John D. Turner and Kevin Corrigan, 2:243–54. Atlanta: SBL, 2011.
Rahner, Karl. *Grundkurs des Glaubens*. Freiburg, Germany: Herder, 1976.
———. "Remarks on the Dogmatic Treatise 'De Trinitate.'" In *More Recent Writings*, vol. 4 of *Theological Investigations*, translated by Kevin Smith, 77–102. London: Darton, Longman & Todd, 1966.
———. "The 'Spiritual Senses' according to Origen." In *Theological Investigations* 16, translated by David Morland, 81–103. New York: Seabury, 1979.
———. *The Trinity*. Translated by Joseph Donceel. New York: Herder & Herder, 1970.
Ratzinger, Joseph. "Liebe." In *Lexikon für Theologie und Kirche*, edited by Michael Buchberger et al., 6:1031–36. 2nd ed. Freiburg: Herder, 1957.
Reed, Esther. "Redemption." In *The Blackwell Companion to Modern Theology*, edited by Gareth Jones, 227–42. Oxford: Blackwell, 2004.
Riou, Alain. *Le monde et l'église selon Maxime le Confessor*. Paris: Éditions Beauchesne, 1972.
Rosenwig, Franz. *Der Stern der Erlösung*. Heidelberg: Schneider, 1954.
Rusch, William G. *The Trinitarian Controversy*. Philadelphia: Fortress, 1980.
Russell, Norman. *The Doctrine of Deification in the Greek Patristic Tradition*. New York: Oxford University Press, 2006.
Schleiermacher, Friedrich. *The Christian Faith*. London: T. & T. Clark, 2005.
Schmaus, Michael. *Die psychologische Trinitätslehre des Heiligen Augustinus*. Münster: Aschendorff, 1927.
Schwöbel, Christoph. "Imago Libertatis: Human and Divine Freedom." In *God and Freedom: Essays in Historical and Systematic Theology*, edited by Colin E. Gunton, 57–81. Edinburgh: T. & T. Clark, 1995.
Sherrard, Philip. *Human Image: World Image*. Ipswich, MA: Golgonooza, 1992.
———. "The Revival of Hesychast Spirituality." In *Christian Spirituality: Post-Reformation and Modern*, edited by Louis Dupré and Don E. Saliers, 417–31. New York: Crossroad, 1989.
Sherwood, Polycarp. *An Annotated Date-List of the Works of Maximus the Confessor*. Rome: Herder, 1955.
———. *The Earlier Ambigua of St. Maximus the Confessor*. Rome: Herder, 1955.

Bibliography

———. "Survey of Recent Work on St. Maximus the Confessor." *Traditio* 20 (1964) 428–37.

Shults, F. LeRon, and Andrea Hollingsworth. *The Holy Spirit*. Grand Rapids: Eerdmans, 2008.

Stăniloae, Dumitru. "The Christology of St. Maximus the Confessor." *Sourozh* 52 (1993) 10–16.

———. *The Experience of God*. Vol. 1, *Revelation and Knowledge of the Triune God*. Brookline, MA: Holy Cross Orthodox, 1998.

———. *The Experience of God*. Vol. 2, *The World: Creation and Deification*. Brookline, MA: Holy Cross Orthodox, 2000.

Stapakis, Basileios, comp. *The Philokalia: Master Reference Guide*. Translated and edited by G. E. H. Palmer et al. Minneapolis: Light & Life, 2004.

Tanner, Kathryn. *God and Creation in Christian Theology: Tyranny or Empowerment?* Oxford: Blackwell, 1988.

———. "Theological Reflection and Christian Practices." In *Practicing Theology: Beliefs and Practices in Christian Life*. edited Miroslav Volf and Dorothy C. Bass, 228–42. Grand Rapids: Eerdmans, 2002.

Tanner, Norman P., ed. *Decrees of the Ecumenical Councils*. 2 vols. London: Sheed & Ward, 1990.

Thunberg, Lars. "The Human Person as Image of God: Eastern Christianity." In *Christian Spirituality: Origins to the Twelfth Century*, 291–312. New York: Crossroad, 1985.

———. *Man and the Cosmos: The Vision of St. Maximus the Confessor*. Crestwood, NY: St. Vladimir's Seminary Press, 1997.

———. *Microcosm and Mediator: The Theological Anthropology of Maximus the Confessor*. Chicago: Open Court, 1995.

Tollefsen, Torstein. "The Ethical Consequences of the Christian Conception of Nature as Created by God." *St. Vladimir's Theological Quarterly* 45 (2001) 395–408.

Torrance, Alan J. *Persons in Communion: An Essay on Trinitarian Description and Human Participation*. Edinburgh: T. & T. Clark, 1996.

Tracy, David. "The Hermeneutics of Naming God." *Irish Theological Quarterly* 57 (1991) 253–64.

———. "Trinitarian Speculation and the Forms of Divine Disclosure." In *The Trinity: An Interdisciplinary Symposium on the Trinity*, edited by Stephen T. Davis et al., 273–93. New York: Oxford University Press, 2004.

Traherne, Thomas. *Thomas Traherne: Centuries, Poems, and Thanksgivings*. Vol. 1. Edited by H. M. Margoliouth. Oxford: Clarendon, 1960. Reprint, Oxford: Mowbray, 1985.

Tsirpanlis, Constantine N. "The Dyothelitic Christology of St. Maximus the Confessor." *Patristic and Byzantine Review* 20 (2002) 10–17.

———. *Introduction to Eastern Christian Thought and Orthodox Theology*. Minnesota: Liturgical, 1991.

Tugwell, Simon. "Evagrius and Macarius." In *The Study of Spirituality*, edited by Cheslyn Jones et al., 168–74. New York: Oxford, 1986.

Vanhoozer, Kevin J., ed. *The Cambridge Companion to Postmodern Theology*. Cambridge: Cambridge University Press, 2003.

Vishnevskaya, Elena. "Divinization and Spiritual Progress in Maximus the Confessor." In *Theōsis: Deification in Christian Theology*, edited by Stephen Finlan and Vladimir Kharlamov, 134–45. Eugene, OR: Pickwick, 2006.

Bibliography

Volf, Miroslav. "After Moltmann: Reflections on the Future of Eschatology." In *God Will Be All in All: The Eschatology of Jürgen Moltmann*, edited by Richard Bauckham, 233–57. Minneapolis: Fortress, 2001.

———. *After Our Likeness: The Church as the Image of the Trinity*. Grand Rapids: Eerdmans, 1998.

———. "The Trinity Is Our Social Program? The Doctrine of the Trinity and the Shape of Social Engagement." *Modern Theology* 14 (1998) 403–23.

Völker, Walther. *Kontemplation and Ekstase bei Pseudo-Dionysius Areopagita*. Wiesbaden, Germany: Steiner, 1958.

———. *Maximus Confessor als Meister des geistlichen Lebens*. Wiesbaden, Germany: Steiner, 1965.

Ware, Timothy (Kallistos). "The Human Person as an Icon of the Trinity." *Sobornost* 8 (1986) 6–23.

———. "La théologie orthodoxe au vingt-et-unième siècle [Orthodox theology in the twenty-first century]." *Irénikon* 77 (2004) 219–38.

———. *The Orthodox Church*. London: Penguin, 1997.

———. *The Orthodox Way*. Crestwood, NY: St. Vladimir's Seminary Press, 1995.

Weber, Otto. *Grundlagen der Dogmatik*. 2 vols. Neukirchen: Buchhandlung des Erziehungsvereins, 1955–1962.

Welch, Claude. *In This Name: The Doctrine of the Trinity in Contemporary Theology*. New York: Scribner, 1952.

Welker, Michael, ed. *Diskussion über Jürgen Moltmanns Buch "Der gekreuzigt Gott."* Munich: Kaiser, 1979.

Williams, Daniel Day. *The Spirit and the Forms of Love*. New York: Harper & Row, 1968.

Williams, Janet P. "Pseudo-Dionysius and Maximus the Confessor." In *The First Christian Theologians*, edited by G. R. Evans, 186–200. Oxford: Blackwell, 2005.

Williams, Rowan. *On Christian Theology*. Oxford: Blackwell, 2000.

———. "*Sapientia* and the Trinity: Reflections of the *De Trinitate*." In *Collectanea augustiniana: Mélanges T. J. van Bavel*, edited by Bruning et al., 317–32. Leuven: University Press, 1990.

Yeago, David S. "Jesus of Nazareth and Cosmic Redemption: The Relevance of St. Maximus the Confessor." *Modern Theology* 12 (1996) 163–93.

Index

abandonment, forms of, 36n18
active suffering, 28
Ambigua (Maximus), 17, 32–33, 40, 41, 74, 103, 133, 135, 136
anthropology, christologically grounded, 57
antidosis idiomaton, 39
apatheia, 27–28, 124
apophatic theology, 17
apotheosis, 67
Aquinas, Thomas, 105
archetype, 146–47
Aristotle, 120, 133
ascension, 139
asceticism, 87–90, 113
asugkutos, 41
Athanasius, 48, 49, 58, 60, 67–69
Augustine, 105, 121
Ayres, Lewis, 11, 166–67

Balthasar, Hans Urs von, 7–8, 10–11n20, 16n9, 94, 100, 105, 121
   on Christ as supreme synthesis, 33n11
   on Christians being in the Trinity, 18–19
   on Maximus's contribution to theology, 43–44
   on Maximus's theology, 17, 58–59n89
   on Maximus's use of christological terminology, 30–31
   on *perichoresis* and salvation, 27n46
   on syzygy, 33n11
baptism, 81–82, 88, 137, 159–60
Barth, Karl, 56, 105
Basil of Caesarea, 58, 60, 68, 120, 121

Bauckham, Richard, 45, 53n74, 54, 62
being, 133
being–well-being–ever-being, 102
blessed conversion, 34, 36
Blowers, Paul, 31, 38, 31
body, preoccupation with, 122
Bonaventure, 95, 105
Bonhoeffer, Dietrich, 60
Byzantine Theology (Meyendorff), 9

Calvinist theology, 50
Cappadocians, 15
cataphatic theology, 17
Centuries on Love (Maximus), 110
chastity, 136
Christ. *See also* Jesus
   centrality of, 30–44
   communion with, 137
   demonstrating how to fulfill human vocation, 34
   doctrine of, 4
   effecting mediation between God and creation, 141–43
   energies of, 41
   five-fold mediation work of, 135
   formation of, 126–27
   as foundation and goal of creation, 52
   hypostatic union in, 73–74
   imitation of, 138, 139–40, 141n66
   as incarnate mediator, 32
   incarnated in his followers, 98
   incarnated in the virtues, 126–29
   incarnations of, 31n6
   as mediator, 117
   as model for followers, 136
   mystery of, 30–31, 33–34

Index

Christ. *See also* Jesus (*continued*)
  portrayed as moving in God's eschatological history, 62
  ruling with, 155
  self-emptying of, 88, 89, 92, 125
  synthesis of, 33–34, 38
  two natures of, 69
  unity of, 37–38
Christian ethics, 29
Christology
  anthropological, 51–52
  cosmological, 46–47, 49, 50–51
  shifting, from Christ's cross and resurrection to incarnation and birth, 60
  transitional, 61–62
christopraxis, 55, 161
Christus prolongatus, 55n80
church
  as agent of deification, 76–80
  attendance at, 79–80, 86
  context and role of, 62
  engaging in same activity as God, 20
  as God's icon in the world, 79
  grace and, 79–80
  life of, and human vocation, 143
  liturgy of, 83–86
  made in the Trinity's image, 21
  similarity of, to human beings, 80
  worship by, determined by God's history, 158–59
Church's Mystagogy, The. See Mystagogy
civil religion, 52
Clement of Alexandria, 67, 121, 124, 130, 133, 136
Coming of God, The (Moltmann), 48, 49
Commentary on the Our Father (Maximus), 92
communicatio idiomatum, 39
concupiscence, 123
contemplation, 90–93, 113, 132, 136
  of Scripture, 95–98
  of the self, 98–101
  of the world, 93–95

contemplative life, 2n6
cosmos
  cross-centered perspective on, 35
  five syntheses in, 134–43
Council of Chalcedon, 5, 37–39, 145
creation
  adumbrations of the Trinity in, 19, 29
  churching of, 143–44
  completion of, 105, 107
  contingency of, 24
  divine purpose for, 34
  divine revelation of, 107
  divine structure of, 17
  doctrine of, 105
  expressing God's will, 25
  God's purpose for, 71
  goodness of, 16, 122
  Holy Trinity as source and goal of, 15
  human calling in, xi, 2
  integration of, 58
  intelligible and sensitive, synthesis of, 140
  logoi of, 16
  manifesting God's love, 24
  perichoresis within, 23–25
  redemptive goal of, 5
  restoration of, 5
  Sabbath and, 104, 106, 113
  spiritualizing of, 12
  Trinitarian understanding of, 115–16
cross, the, 59
  at center of Trinitarian community of seeking love, 27
  Trinitarian theology of, 28–29
Crucified God, The (Moltmann), 27, 35
crucifixion, 132–33, 138
  interconnected with incarnation and resurrection, 34–35
  spiritual, 36–37
Cyril of Alexandria, 69

Dante, 24
degree Christology, 54

deification, 44, 47, 49, 50, 67, 69.
    See also *theosis*
  as divine purpose for human beings, 70
  incarnation and, 128
  means of, 75–89
  process of, 93
  theology of, 39
Democritus, 120
Denys the Areopagite, 15, 16, 32, 40, 65n3, 69–70, 90, 121, 122n11, 133, 134
Descartes, Rene, 56
detachment, 124–25, 127, 136
Diadochus of Photike, 90
Dionysius the Areopagite. See Denys the Areopagite
divine Eros, 3, 26
divine-human exchange, 34
divine ideas, tradition of, 16–17, 29
divine unknowing, 32
divinization. See deification; *theosis*
doctrine, spirituality and, 119
double commandment, 123
double penetration, 41
doxological theology, 158
dualism, 56

earth, life on, crisis of, 59
Ecclesiastical Hierarchy (Dionysius the Areopagite), 76
ekdemia, 32
ekstasis, 32
embodiment, 57
enoptice, 130
Epistle 2 (Maximus), 129
eros. *See* divine Eros
ethicum, 130
Eucharist, 21, 83–86, 144
Evagrius, 15, 16, 90–92, 121, 124, 126, 127–28, 130, 131, 136, 145
ever-being, 133–34
exchange of properties, 39

fall, the, 120–21, 122, 136
fellowship of believers, 154
Fourth Century on Love (Maximus), 63, 101

fruitfulness, 13n1

Glaubenslehre (*The Christian Faith*; Schleiermacher), 168
gloria Dei, 155–57
gnosis, 130
God
  celebrating creation, 24
  centering on, 16–17
  creatures' reversion to, 111
  essence and energies of, 72–73
  finding, in the world, Scripture, and self, 92–93
  glory of, 153
  human image of, 5–6
  ignorance about, 32
  image of, 3, 25, 102, 153
  love of, 24, 25–26
  male-female likeness to, 150
  mystical union with, 136
  presence of, bringing peace to creation, 117
  in relationship with humans, 149
  rest from and rest in, 107, 109, 111–12
  separation from, 123
  suffering of, 27–28
  synthesis of, with creation, 141–43
  transcendence and immanence of, 107–8, 115
  union with, 141n66
God in Creation (Moltmann), xii, 23–24, 105, 146
grace, 76, 81, 96, 99, 134n42
  church and, 79–80
  divine, 71–72
Gregory of Nazianzus, 19, 31, 40, 41, 60, 68, 74, 120, 121, 136
Gregory of Nyssa, 60, 68, 94, 120, 124, 127, 130–31, 136

heaven/earth synthesis, 139–40
historical Jesus, 51
Holy Trinity
  adumbrations of, 17–20, 29, 101–4
  church and, 20–21

Holy Trinity (*continued*)
   circulatory character of, 22
   contemplation of, 166–67
   creation of, xii
   doctrine of, 4, 13–14, 160
   embracing the church and the world, 162–64
   humans called to union with, 20, 25, 29
   human vocation rooted in, 3
   love flowing from, 28
   openness of, 25–26
   perichoresis within, 22–23
   as source and goal of creation, 14–15
hope, 65
human beings
   becoming children of God, 67
   calling of. *See* human beings, vocation of
   church's similarity to, 80
   deification of, 34, 128
   desire of, 122–23nn11–12
   destined for beatific vision, 156–57
   disintegration of, 121
   divine purpose of, 34, 70
   egalitarian relations among, 79
   eschatological glorification of, 155–57
   God's image in, 25
   holistic understanding of, 56
   interconnected with wider creation, 100
   as mediators, 130–34, 139, 143
   as microcosms, 120–23, 169
   messianic alignment of, 152
   nature of, 2n5
   participating in life of the Trinity, 18
   priestly by nature, 156
   realizing their calling, 2
   realizing their potential, 42
   redemptive goal of, 104, 115
   reintegration of, 123, 124, 125
   in relationship with God, 149
   rest for, 109–10
   restoration of, 104
   self-love and, 121–23, 126
   soul of, 103
   as Spirit-empowered servants of God's kingdom, 161
   Trinitarian adumbrations in, 17–20, 101–4
   Trinitarian structure of, 102
   vocation of, 3, 6, 11, 20–21, 25, 31, 35, 38, 53, 63, 64
Human Image (Sherrard), 59n90
humility, 123–24
hypostatic union, 73–74

Ignatian spirituality, 160
imago Christi, 148, 152–55
imago Dei, 146, 147–52
incarnation, 47, 69, 92, 98, 138
   deification and, 128
   divine-human exchange in, 34
   interconnected with crucifixion and resurrection, 34–35
   linked with creation, 115
   soteriological effects of, 32–33
incarnation Christology, 54
Irenaeus, 39, 58, 60, 67, 155
iron in the fire, analogy of, 42, 43

Jesuology, 51, 52
Jesus. *See also* Christ
   earthly life and ministry of, 54–55
   friendship with, 160–61
   Sabbath and, 114
John Chrysostom, 60
John of Damascus (John Damascene), 3, 22–23, 40
Johnson, Elizabeth, 170–71

Kant, Immanuel, 167–68
kenosis, 88, 89
Keselopoulos, Anestis, 7, 143, 155, 157
Kilby, Karen, 23n
knowledge, approaches to, 171–72

Ladner, Gerhart B., 68
Letter 2: On Love (Maximus), 123–24
liturgy, 145
logoi, in creation, 94

Index

Logos Christology, 31
logos spermatikos, 16
Logos theology, 16-17
Lonergan, Bernard, 9n14
Lord's Prayer (Maximus), 72n28
Lossky, Vladimir, 42-43, 74, 138, 139
Louth, Andrew, 38, 90, 91
love
  at center of human calling, 164-65
  detachment and, 124
  double commandment of, 123
  erotic community of, 26
  joining God and creation, 142
  primacy of, 6
Lutherans, doctrine of world annihilation, 50

Macarian Homilies, 90
Malcolm, Lois, 9n14
male/female synthesis, 136-37
Man and the Cosmos (Thunberg), 64
Man and the Environment (Keselopoulos), 143-44
Marshall, Bruce, 160
Maximus the Confessor, 60, 64
  on adumbrations of the Trinity, 101-4
  appropriating from Neoplatonic thought, 102
  on asceticism, 87-90
  on baptism, 81-82, 88
  Chalcedonian perspective of, 37-44
  on Christ tabernacling among humans, 116
  Christology of, 30-37
  on contemplation, 93-101
  criticism of, 11-12
  cross-centered perspective of, 35-37
  on detachment, 124-25
  divine ideas tradition and, 16-17, 29
  on the divine image, 150
  ecclesiology of, 83
  on the Eucharist, 83-86
  Evagrius's influence on, 90-92
  on 1 Kings 19, 108-9
  on humility, 123-24
  on the human vocation, 3, 145-46
  on integration of creation, 58
  on love as culmination of virtues, 125-26
  on means of deification, 75-93
  on mediation, five-fold work of, 135-43
  mystical theology of, 118, 124
  on penance, 83
  on *perichoresis*, 39-43
  pneumatology of, 163n138
  on prayer and contemplation, 90-101
  on renewal in Christ, 56
  on Sabbath rest, 110-13
  on the sacraments, 81-82
  on self-love, 121-23, 126
  on spiritual development, 133-34
  on spiritual life, stages of, 130-33, 154n106
  on *theosis*, 64-65, 70-75
  theological anthropology of, xi, 2, 4, 6-7, 112
  theology of, xiii n2, 8, 111, 118, 124
  Trinitarian-christocentric praxis in, 120-46
  on Trinity as source and goal of creation, 14-15
  understanding humanity as body and soul, 140
McDougall, Joy Ann, 7, 26, 158
McGuckin, John, 67, 69
McIntosh, Mark, 2n4, 9n16, 27n44-45, 77, 78-79, 118-19, 124
mediation, five-fold work of, 135-43
messianic alignment, 152
messianic fellowship, 157-64
messianic resurrection theology, 153
metaphorical language, 9n13
Meyendorff, John, 9, 17n11
mind-reason-spirit, 103

191

Index

modernity, anthropocentrism of, 7, 169
modern theology, starting with human person, 3–4
Molnar, Paul D., 54n77
Moltmann, Jürgen, 64
  on adumbrations of God, 101n115
  on *apatheia*, 27–28
  on the call to discipleship, 159–60
  calling for new christological paradigm, 45–46, 52–53
  Christology of, 45–62, 59–62, 107
  on Christology and christopraxis, 161
  on creation's groaning and redemption, 95
  criticism of, 11
  cross-centered theology of, 35–36
  developing a Trinitarian theology of the cross, 28–29
  doxological theology of, 158
  on 1 Kings 19, 108–9
  on God seeking love, 25–27
  on God's history with the world, 14–15
  on God's human image in creation, 146–65
  on God's transcendence and immanence, 107–8
  holistic Christology of, 55–59
  on the human vocation, 3, 21–25
  on Jesus's earthly life and ministry, 54–55
  on Kant, 168n5
  missional feature in theology of, 25–29
  on the monastic triad, 90n88
  on Old Testament messianic hope, 53–54
  on perichoresis, 22–25, 170
  on physical creation, 51
  on prayer and action, 160n129
  proposing retrieval of biblical and patristic anthropology, 57
  on the Sabbath, 105–10, 113
  on the Spirit carrying on Jesus's ministry, 163
  theocentric worldview of, 170
  theological anthropology of, xi, xii, 2, 4, 6–7, 109, 137
  theology of, xiii n2, 8
  on theosis, 47–50
  Trinitarian doctrine of, 107
  Trinitarian linkages in, 116
  Trinitarian-christocentric praxis in, 146–65
  on the Trinity's community of love, 79
Monothelite controversy, 37, 38n23
mortification, 89. *See also* asceticism
Moses, life of, 131
Müller-Fahrenholz, Geiko, 55n81
Mystagogy (Maximus), 5, 6, 20–21, 40, 58, 76, 77, 83, 84, 92–93, 96, 131, 143–44, 145, 148, 152, 162, 165
mysterium magnum, 33, 70
mystical resurrection, 112
mystical theology, 65

negative theology, 17
Neoplatonism, 133
Newman, John Henry, 118–19
Nichols, Aidan, 126, 129

Oetinger, Friedrich, 57
oikos theology, 115
Old Testament, messianic hope in, 53–54
opposites, penetration of, 41
Origen, 15, 16, 39, 58, 60, 67, 94, 124, 126–27, 130

paradise/earth synthesis, 138
Passion, identification with, 28
patristic period, cosmological Christology of, 46–47
patristics, 10n18
Paul, Trinitarian theology of, 15
peace, 117
Pelikan, Jaroslav, 119, 169
penance, 83
perichoresis, 3, 22–25, 39, 40–43
Philo of Alexandria, 120, 121
physicum, 130

physike, 80, 90, 91, 94, 131, 136, 140
Plato, 120, 121
praktike, 80, 90, 91, 131, 136, 140
prayer, 90–93
Proclus, 133
Pseudo-Dionysius. *See* Denys the Areopagite

Questions to Thalassius 22 (Maximus), 127

Rahner, Karl, 54n77
reciprocity, 67, 129
reconciliation, 57
redemption, 49, 51, 57
  as goal of human calling, 64, 115
  Sabbath as feast of, 114
reintegration, 123, 125
religion, privatization of, 52
repentance, 83
resurrection, 59, 132, 138
  of the body, 57–58n87
  interconnected with incarnation and crucifixion, 34–35
  mystical, 112
Rosenzweig, Franz, 106–7
royal theology, 148–49

Sabbath, 115
  creation and, 106, 113
  divine revelation of, 107
  as feast of redemption, 106, 114
  Jesus Christ and, 114
  linked to spiritual life, 110
  metaphor of, 104
  mystery of, 107–8
  peace of, 117
  rest in, 105, 109–13
sacraments, 81–82
Schleiermacher, Friedrich, 52, 167–69
Scripture
  contemplation of, 95–98
  as a cosmos, 172
  embodied view of, 96
Second Century on Theology (Maximus), 72–73
self, contemplation of, 98–101

self-love, 3, 121–23, 126
Sermons (Gregory of Nazianzus), 31, 74
sexual purity, 136
Shekinah, 115–16
Sherrard, Philip, 2n6, 59n90
Sherwood, Polycarp, 19, 21n26
sin, consequences of, 120–21
soul, primacy of, 56
Spirit Christology, 54
Spirit of Life, The (Moltmann), 48
spiritual development, threefold pattern of, 133–34
spiritual healing, 80
spirituality, doctrine and, 119
spiritual life
  pattern of, 91
  stages of, 130–33
spiritual perfection, 39, 124
spiritual rebirth, 137
Stăniloae, Dumitru, 12n26, 48
stewardship, 151
Stoic philosophy, 120
suffering, 27–28
synaxis, 83, 85, 86
synthesis, 33–34, 36, 134

tantum-quantum formula, 67, 74–75
Thalassius, 121
theologia, 80, 90, 91, 111, 131, 136, 140
theology, 132
  Maximus's contribution to, 43–44
  Trinitarian source of, 88
Theology of Hope (Moltmann), 8, 64
theosis, 5, 17, 43, 47–50, 63, 115. *See also deification*
  Cappadocians' view of, 68–69
  effecting mystical union between God and creation, 75
  as gift of divine grace, 71–72
  patristic tradition of, 66–70
  scriptural texts on, 65–66
Thunberg, Lars, 7
  on Augustine and Maximus, 121
  on deification, 67, 69, 70, 73
  on detachment, 124–25

193

Index

Thunberg, Lars (*continued*)
   on Gregory of Nyssa, 68
   on *imago Dei* tradition, 151
   on Maximus, 39, 41, 42, 43, 64, 73, 75, 84, 86, 98, 102–3, 128–29, 135n44, 137
   on mediation of God and God's creation, 142
   on *perichoresis*, 40, 41
   on self-love, 123
Tillich, Paul, 106
Timaeus (Plato), 120
Tome of Leo (Leo I), 39
Tracy, David, 9
transfiguration, 97
transformation, Calvinist theory of, 50
Trinity. See Holy Trinity
Trinity and the Kingdom, The (Moltmann), 21, 47
tritheism, 22

two natures, Christology of, 46–47

unity, Trinitarian based, 20

virtues, Christ's ongoing incarnation in, 126–29
Volf, Miroslav, 2–3n7

Ware, Kallistos, 20n2, 165n144
Way of Jesus Christ, The (Moltmann), 45, 49, 53n74, 62, 105
well-being, 133
Williams, Janet, 49–50n64
Williams, Rowan, 9n13, 13–14
world
   contemplation of, 93–95
   structures of, overturning, 79
worship, 85, 158–59

Year of Jubilee, 114

www.ingramcontent.com/pod-product-compliance
Lightning Source LLC
Chambersburg PA
CBHW070327230426
43663CB00011B/2239